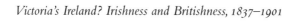

Victoria's Ireland? Irishness and Britishness, 1837–1901

The first two volumes in this series are published by Irish Academic Press.

Victoria's Ireland?

Irishness and Britishness, 1837–1901

Peter Gray

EDITOR

FOUR COURTS PRESS

Set in 10.5 on 12 point Bembo for
FOUR COURTS PRESS
7 Malpas Street, Dublin 8, Ireland
e-mail: info@four-courts-press.ie
http://www.four-courts-press.ie
and in North America by
FOUR COURTS PRESS
c/o ISBS, 920 N.E. 58th Avenue, Suite 300, Portland, OR 97213.

© Four Courts Press and the various authors 2004

A catalogue record for this title
is available from the British Library.

ISBN 1–85182–758–7

Printed in Great Britain by
MPG Books, Bodmin, Cornwall.

Contents

Preface

The essays in this volume represent a selection of the papers delivered at the conference 'Victoria's Ireland?: Irishness and Britishness 1837–1901', held at the University of Southampton in April 2001, under the auspices of the Society for the Study of Nineteenth-Century Ireland. I would like to thank the Society's officers, in particular James Murphy, Larry Geary, Margaret Kelleher and Leon Litvack, for their support in the production of this volume.

I am grateful for financial support provided by the Faculty of Arts, University of Southampton. I would also like to thank the staff of Osborne House, Isle of Wight, for their assistance in making one of Queen Victoria's favourite residences available to us as a venue for part of the conference. I also acknowledge the gracious permission of Her Majesty Queen Elizabeth II for permission to reproduce material from the Royal Archives in James H. Murphy's chapter.

I am indebted to Michael Adams, Martin Fanning, and the staff of Four Courts Press for their patience and helpful advice given in the course of editing this volume.

In memory of Fr Donal A. Kerr (1927–2001)

Introduction: Victoria's Ireland?
Irishness and Britishness, 1837–1901

PETER GRAY

The reign of Queen Victoria (1837–1901) accounted for more than half of the lifespan of the Union of Great Britain and Ireland. Coming in the wake of upheavals associated with the aftermath of rebellion, the polarisation of the Catholic emancipation and 'second reformation' campaigns, and the initiation of the Repeal movement, Victoria's accession coincided with a period of political quiet and initially appeared to presage a new beginning in the British-Irish relationship. Her reign witnessed a series of attempts to 'complete' the project of the 1801 Union, widely regarded by its defenders and critics alike as unfinished; these in turn provoked counter-reactions among both defenders of Irish difference, and others rejecting the desirability or possibility of British (or English) integration or accommodation with an 'inferior' people. In a variety of realms – state policy, political and economic discourses, literary and cultural production – British state- and nation-building agendas were promoted, challenged or synthesised over the course of the Victorian era.

This collection of interdisciplinary essays focuses on the articulation and interplay of 'Irish' and 'British' identities during the Victorian period in Ireland, Great Britain and beyond. To some commentators inherently antagonistic, to others potentially complementary, 'Irishness' and 'Britishness' were described and contested with increasing intensity throughout the long period of Victoria's reign. These essays use a range of approaches to throw light on the complexities of that relationship, including the Victorian monarchy's attitude towards Ireland and Irish reactions to it, debates about Irish difference and integration, and varied constructions of Ireland's place in the imperial world order. Particular attention is given to the Great Famine as a rupturing force in Victorian Irish–British relations and to attempts made to contain or even to reconcile the resulting cleavage through literature, economic theory and public policy. A further theme running through some of these essays is the significance of the 1860s–70s as second, pivotal, period of transformation in the British–Irish relationship.

James H. Murphy's essay sets the tone for the volume through an assessment of Victoria's engagement with Ireland and the changing attitudes towards monarchy in Ireland during the course of her reign. His thesis is that the failure of the monarchical 'golden link' between Ireland and Britain was contingent and was evident only from the 1870s. Prior to that decade conditional monarchism was part of a mainstream nationalist repertoire inherited from Daniel

O'Connell. Paradoxically it was the conscious attempts by the British political establishment to deploy the 'reconciling magic of monarchy' in opposition to Irish nationalism that made simultaneous allegiance increasingly untenable and paved the way for the success of the 1890s caricature of Victoria as the 'Famine Queen'. Despite the residual appeal of the glamour of monarchy and the persistent fantasy of Victoria's private sympathy for Ireland (still evident during her final visit in 1900), public monarchism had been largely 'squeezed out' in Catholic and nationalist Ireland by the time of her death.

Victoria's personal ambivalence towards the Irish – alternating between a matronly enthusiasm for their participation in royal visits and British wars and an increasingly personalised antagonism towards any manifestation of Irish nationalism – was shared by many of her British subjects. In his essay, Gary Peatling subjects the historian and political commentator Goldwin Smith to close scrutiny. Rejecting any reductionist 'imperialist' reading of Smith's writings on Ireland, Peatling traces the contradictions therein, and suggests that the essentialist racism that Smith manifested towards the Irish conflicted with his advocacy of local self-government within the empire and the necessity of 'training the Celt' to political responsibility.

If Goldwin Smith never resolved the dilemma of how the Irish could be simultaneously part of and alien to British society, more practical questions of accommodation and resistance to the British body politic faced Irish nationalist MPs serving at Westminster. James McConnel argues that the domestic realities of politics have been unduly neglected, and sets out to rectify this oversight for the rank and file of the Irish Parliamentary Party between 1885 and 1914. He concludes that the early hostility demmonstrated towards nationalist MPs, and the strains imposed on this largely middle-class cohort by London life, encouraged strong internal bonding, but that this tended to diminish over time with growing 'fraternalisation' and integration into the domestic (and indeed, sporting) life of Parliament.

The second section, 'Literature, Leisure and Identity', begins with Cora Kaplan's study of racial discourses of 'Irishness' as manifested in the writings of Charles Kingsley and Thomas Carlyle. After a discussion of the racial theories of Robert Knox, whose essentialist reductionism and emphasis on Anglo-Saxon racial superiority to all other white 'races' marked the outer limit of Victorian racial logic, Kaplan describes Kingsley and Carlyle as representatives of a more ethically troubled and confused centre, whose representations of the Irish and of Irishness veered uneasily between racial differentiation and the pull of a pan-European discourse of whiteness. Without shying from the numerous deployments of racialised language – from Kingsley's depiction of 'human chimpanzees' on his 1860 fishing trip to Sligo, to Carlyle's observation of Irish immigrants 'sunk from decent manhood to squalid apehood' – this nuanced analysis concludes that both used these discourses inconsistently and instrumentally, in contrast to their more essentialist representations of non-white subjects.

Patrick Maume draws our attention the very different representation of Irishness offered in the popular entertainments of Robert Martin, Unionist political activist, brother of Violet Martin (of the 'Somerville and Ross' partnership) and creator of the comic persona 'Ballyhooly'. Martin's life and art were self-consciously modelled on the Leveresque tradition of Tory hedonism, featuring fantasies of escape from social constraints and the restoration of a depoliticised feudal relationship between landlord and tenant (as well as between the imperial matriarch, Victoria, and her Irish subjects). Martin's legacy lay more in the virulent reaction he provoked from nationalist critics than in the Unionist music-hall tradition he played a leading role in promoting.

The theme of Victoria's place in Irish society is taken up by Tom Hayes in his essay on sport and dining in Limerick. Like James Murphy, he identifies the 1870s as a transitional decade, in which the previously uncontroversial toasting of the Queen on sporting occasions gave way to a more politically polarised and non-deferential sporting environment in which renditions of 'God Save Ireland' acquired greater prominence. The nationalisation of Irish sport predated the emergence of the GAA, and was manifest in such unlikely venues as the Shannon rowing regattas, archery meets and cricket matches.

The three papers in the section on 'Ireland and the Victorian World Order' consider contrasting ways in which Irish agents and commentators responded to the challenges and opportunities presented by the British Empire. Jennifer Ridden discusses the attempts undertaken by members of the Irish liberal Protestant elite to define and mould a liberal and pluralistic empire as an entity in which Irishness could coexist rather than conflict with an imperial Britishness, and in which the Irish could take full advantage of the opportunities offered by Britain's global expansion. Two case studies drawn from the Limerick-Clare liberal Protestant circle illuminate the argument: as governor of New South Wales in the years immediately preceding Victoria's accession, Sir Richard Bourke faced down considerable local opposition in his drive to render the colony a neutral environment acceptable to Irish Catholic settlers. Perhaps more surprisingly, William Smith O'Brien also harboured hopes for an empire open to Irish migration and thus playing a positive role in the amelioration of Irish poverty – hopes not entirely dispelled by his turn to radical nationalism and experience of transportation to Van Diemen's Land. The legacy of these Irish liberal imperialists – in helping shape the reception of Irish migrants in the Australian colonies, and opening the possibility of moderate nationalist engagement with a 'pluralist' self-governing colonial system – was significant.

Looking beyond to another empire, Pandeleimon Hionidis investigates both Irish responses to the Cretan revolt of 1866–9, and contemporary parallels drawn between Cretan rebels and Irish Fenians. In general, Irish reactions mirrored attitudes towards the Irish 'national question', with the Protestant press denouncing the insurgents, the moderate nationalist press sympathising with the ends but not the means of revolt, and the 'advanced nationalists' coming closest to endorsement of the revolt as a just struggle against imperial oppression.

Later in the century this 'advanced' association with other 'struggling nation-alities' and anti-colonial struggles found its most articulate and committed spokesman in Michael Davitt. Carla King finds a consistency in Davitt's stance throughout his career, founded in a critique of British imperialism as essentially exploitative and self-interested. Davitt's interests and activities were wide-rang-ing, but it was the Boer War that triggered his most intense anti-imperialism. His enthusiastic support for the Boers gave rise to certain contradictions (his deployment of antisemitic language against the Uitlanders flew in the face of his public support for Jewish refugees from Tsarist pogroms, for example), but contributed to the growing polarisation in turn of the century Ireland over the country's participation in the imperial project.

The catastrophe of the Great Famine, perhaps more than any other develop-ment, problematises the concept of 'Victorian Ireland'. Cora Kaplan describes how a combination of guilt and denial prompted both Kingsley and Carlyle into 'genocidal fantasies' during and in the wake of the Famine. The final four essays in this volume further examine several dimensions of the disaster, its representa-tion, and its legacy for post-Famine Ireland. Melissa Fegan and Yvonne Siddle discuss how two novelists – the Irishman William Carleton and the Irish-resi-dent Englishman Anthony Trollope, respectively – experienced the catastrophe and sought to render it meaningful to themselves and their audiences. Fegan introduces Carleton as the pre-eminent shaper of literary images of Ireland in the early-Victorian period. His famine novel *The Black Prophet* (1846–7) helped mould the concept of the Great Famine as it unfolded, but interpreted it through tropes and assumptions drawn from the past that failed to encompass the sheer scale of the disaster. Overwhelmed by what he witnessed, Carleton's later fiction tended to regress from the social engagement and humanitarianism of his best writing. In contrast, Anthony Trollope's literary career blossomed in the aftermath of the Famine. Yvonne Siddle stresses the significance of his Irish sojourn in Trollope's personal development, and interprets his providentialist denial of British responsibility for mass mortality in this light. Trollope's *Castle Richmond* (1859–60) was written with the benefit of hindsight, but was marred as a novel by his continuing preoccupation with justifying the policy adopted in 1846–50 and the economic ideologies which underpinned it.

Those ideologies, and the retrospective defence of Famine policy in Irish liberal economic discourse, are the subjects of my own essay. I argue that the public activities of the 'Dublin School' of political economists in the later 1840s and 1850s amounted to a concerted effort to rationalise and justify the Famine as an emancipatory moment of socio-economic modernisation. Eighteen forty-nine – the year of Trollope's epistolary defence of Trevelyanism, of the Encumbered Estates Act, and of Queen Victoria's first visit to Ireland – was thus regarded as a year zero of Irish regeneration. This self-deluding optimism was not, however, to survive the economic downturn of 1859–63 and the ideological shifts of the 1860s, and the political-economic 'memory' of the Famine tended thereafter to diverge between pessimistic Malthusianism and a historicist economics supportive of state intervention acknowledging Ireland's separate path of social development.

Finally, Virginia Crossman's essay explores how policy-makers' fears of a replication of the Great Famine gave rise to a tension between orthodoxy and pragmatism in 1879–84. Faced with a crisis in the west provoked by economic depression and the potato failure of 1879, poor law officials proved reluctant to abandon an institutional 'memory' of the 1840s that stressed the necessity of caution and relief tests, but found themselves outflanked after 1880 by a Gladstone administration that eased the terms and conditions of relief – much to the frustration of the still-living Charles Trevelyan. The growing politicisation of poor relief after 1880 gave rise to further tensions and marked a growing deviation in social policy between Ireland and Great Britain.

Taken together, these essays indicate a series of unresolved tensions and conflicts between the concepts of 'Irishness' and 'Britishness' during Victoria's reign. Hopes that equalised access to imperial opportunities (with or without Home Rule) would reconcile the Irish to a neutral imperial Britishness proved elusive (despite a degree of success in integrating the Australian and Canadian Irish). Despite a degree of domestication of IPP members at Westminster after 1885, constitutional nationalists (in sport, as in politics) became ever more vociferous in their rejection of the 'British' symbolism associated with crown and empire. The enthusiastic and rambunctious celebration of both in the Unionist entertainments of Robert Martin, and the attempted political utilisation of royal visits by the British political establishment, merely tended to increase this polarisation.

For a number of Victorian public intellectuals, such as Smith, Kingsley and Carlyle, reconciling the political logic of the Act of Union with the racialised constructions of Britishness (and/or Englishness) increasingly in vogue in the nineteenth century proved problematic. Environmentalism offered an alternative, developmental, interpretation of Irish 'difference', but frustration with the reluctance or inability of the Irish to 'become British' in the early, reformist, years of Victoria's reign prompted many liberal integrationists to welcome the Famine as a *deus ex machina*, a beneficent providential intervention to break the log-jam impeding Ireland's progress towards an anglicised modernity. The reluctance of both Trevelyan and Trollope to abandon this illusion may reflect a reluctance to give up a belief in the project of 'making Ireland British'. If nationalists were always antagonistic, it was no doubt reassuring to the British integrationists to have the public support of a small but influential cadre of Irish liberal political economists. However, the latter's loss of confidence in the narrative of progress and *volte face* towards historicism in the 1860s undermined the integrationist position and left a choice between a bleak Malthusian (and racialised) pessimism, and a historicist reformism that, whether in its

Gladstonian Liberal or 'Constructive Unionist' manifestations, pointed again towards Irish difference and un-Britishness. Despite the personal popularity or curiosity exhibited on Victoria's infrequent visits, 'Victoria's Ireland' proves something of a misnomer. Any hopes that the reign of the 'girl Queen' would heal the wounds of the past and see the Union completed in letter and spirit were dashed well before 1901.

Fashioning the famine queen

JAMES H. MURPHY

Throughout the nineteenth century the monarchy was often spoken of as the 'golden link' or 'golden bridge' between Britain and Ireland. Yet it meant different things on either side of the Irish Sea. With the decline in the actual powers of the monarchy, self-appointed constitutional experts such as Walter Bagehot, whose *The English Constitution* was published in 1867, backed the view that the role of the monarchy was to provide an emotional focus to mitigate divisions in society.[1]

For British politicians, therefore, the golden bridge of the monarchy was a means whereby the Irish might become reconciled to their position within the United Kingdom. For Irish nationalist politicians, meanwhile, the golden bridge could provide a continuing symbolic link with Britain, which might, to an extent, disguise the high degree of autonomy they hoped to gain through Repeal or Home Rule.

Most Irish nationalists were monarchists, therefore, of either the enthusiastic or the grudging but realistic varieties. This ought not to come as a surprise. In the nineteenth century the vast majority of countries were monarchies of one form or another. International relations were predominantly relations between monarchs, a fact which gave Queen Victoria a greater political influence than her domestic constitutional position warranted. In the age of nationalism, subjecthood was still as viable a form of political identity for the individual as membership of a nation, and the two were by no means incompatible in principle. Monarchy seemed the natural form of government and had the blessing of the Catholic Church, a fact of great significance in Ireland where the overwhelming majority of nationalists were Catholics.[2]

Though in theory accepting of the monarchy, many nationalists became in practice increasingly anti-monarchical in temperament. In the case of a few, such as the republican Maud Gonne, this was for ideological reasons. In the case of the many, however, it was a logical political response to the anti-nationalist function which the monarchy was seen to be playing, albeit a response which in time became ingrained and visceral.

Temperamental anti-monarchism ought not to be necessarily equated with espoused republicanism. Some of the most virulent anti-monarchists of the

---

1 For a full account of the relationship between the British monarchy and Irish nationalism see James H. Murphy, *Abject Loyalty: Nationalism and Monarchy in Ireland during the Reign of Queen Victoria* (Cork, 2001). 2 See Tom Garvin, *1922: The Birth of Irish Democracy* (Dublin, 1996), p. 11.

1880s, for example, were the young Turks of the Irish Parliamentary Party, William O'Brien, Tim Healy and the Redmond brothers, who officially supported the continuance of the monarchy in Ireland. The views on the monarchy of the ageing Fenian, and official republican, John O'Leary, seemed benign by contrast. For him Queen Victoria was 'a highly respectable foreign lady' who 'symbolized that British rule which was hateful to my soul' but who could not help being 'the English Queen of Ireland'.[3]

Republicanism was the preference of only a minority in Ireland and stood not so much for a particular vision of society as for a particular version of Ireland's relationship with Britain: total separation. It was a relationship in which the last link, golden or otherwise, had been broken and as such it was not accounted by the majority as a very realistic option. For the sake of the coherence of its empire, Britain would never allow this. In any event Britain was the dominant world power. As its nearest neighbour Ireland could never hope to live in isolation from it.[4]

II

It is not possible to gauge scientifically what ordinary people in nineteenth-century nationalist Ireland thought of the monarchy. But it may be possible to construe their views to an extent from the public discourse of their political leaders.[5] However, the connection between the culture of official political discourse and the opinions of ordinary people is a complex one. To a degree each reflects the other. What politicians can say in public is determined both by a sensitivity to their constituency in the broad sense and by the constraints of what it is allowable to say in public at any given time. Politicians who offended against the views of those they sought to represent were often subject to an immediate rebuke in an age of public meetings and processions, before the era of the television studio and the need for opinion polls. Thus in July 1883, when nationalist politicians co-operated with Liberals and Tories in a trade exhibition in Cork which opened with the singing of 'God Save the Queen,' there was a significant public boycott of the event.[6]

Until the 1870s the political culture which constrained Irish politicians worked in favour of monarchy, thereafter it worked against it. In April 1869 Daniel O'Sullivan, the mayor of Cork, made semi-private remarks insulting to the royal family which were subsequently reported in the newspapers. Enmeshed as they were in the general political culture of the United Kingdom

3 John O'Leary, *Recollections of a Fenian and Fenianism* (2 vols, London, 1898), vol. 2, 131. 4 See Alan O'Day, *Irish Home Rule, 1867–1921* (Manchester, 1998), p. 6. 5 See Richard Williams, *The Contentious Crown: Public Discussion of the British Monarchy in the Reign of Queen Victoria* (Brookfield, VT, 1997), p. 2. 6 *FJ [Freeman's Journal]*, 4 July 1883.

at the time, Irish politicians found themselves supporting the British outrage at his remarks. Yet by the early 1880s the self-assertiveness of nationalist politicians had grown to such an extent that insults about the royal family were almost *de rigeur* for those who wanted to advance their political careers in Ireland.

As for the views of ordinary people, they not only influenced politicians but were also influenced by them.[7] This was especially so concerning enthusiasm for monarchy. The nationalist political class came to deride popular support for monarchy as the result either of a sense of colonial inferiority, which they termed 'flunkeyism', or as the phoney result of direct pressure from the landlord and higher commercial classes, which were Protestant and pro-Union, on the lower ranks of society. And once nationalism had decisively set its face against monarchy in the early decades of the twentieth century, individuals could express support for monarchy only at the cost of having their Irishness questioned. Yet interest in monarchy continued and continues to exist, as evidenced in recent decades by the large number of Irish television viewers of royal weddings and funerals. It remains an unresolved issue.

III

For most of the nineteenth-century elections of members of parliament in Ireland, as in Britain, were rather imperfect affairs from the point of view of modern democracy. Until 1872 electors voted in public and were subject to pressure and bribery. The Catholic Relief Act of 1829 allowed Catholics to sit as MPs but reduced the number of electors in the process. Gradual parliamentary reform occurred by means of legislation in 1832, 1850, 1868, 1884 and 1885, which redrew constituency boundaries and progressively reduced property qualifications for voting, though universal male and partial female voting rights were not conceded until 1918.

In such circumstances public meetings, banquets and processions were of enormous importance. Such meetings could have a number of ostensible purposes: to listen to speeches, to agree on resolutions, to draw up memorials, to make pledges, to greet returned heroes or bid farewell to departing ones, to bury the recently deceased or memorialise the venerable dead. But their real purposes included gauging public support, assuring allegiance, pressurising authority and securing a mandate for action.

There were five major forces in nineteenth-century nationalist Ireland which were capable to attracting significant support from different sectors of the public, as evidenced by attendance at mass gatherings: physical-force activism, religion, land agitation, constitutional politics and monarchy. There were of course other minor movements which attracted mass support but they tended

---

7 Williams, *Contentious Crown*, p. 2.

to fall within the ambit of one of the five major forces. Thus Father Mathew's Temperance Movement of the 1840s came to an extent under Daniel O'Connell's spell and many of the cultural, language and sporting movements that sprang up towards the end of the century were infiltrated by the Irish Republican Brotherhood.

Quite obviously, largely constitutional political movements relied heavily on the effects of the mass meeting, from the 'monster' meetings of O'Connell's Repeal Association in the 1840s to the great public meetings, often associated with elections in a more enfranchised age, of the Irish Party in the 1880s. One of the reasons why constitutional political leaders in nationalist Ireland were so nervous of the monarchy was because support for it was demonstrated in essentially similar ways. Royal visits occasioned great gatherings of people along the routes of royal processions, which could be compared with numbers attending nationalist political meetings. And there is no doubt that hundreds of thousands of people did turn out to see royal visitors to Ireland. It is often asserted, for example, and probably not without justification, that one million people saw Queen Victoria during the course of her 1853 visit to Dublin.[8]

Given the large numbers turning out for royal visits, two questions arise. What was the disposition of the crowds, and what was the significance of their disposition? Though nationalist politicians often tried to play down the level of enthusiasm, few seriously disputed that on most royal visits the crowds were enthusiastic. One of those who did was John O'Leary, who nearly fifty years afterwards claimed to recall that on her 1849 visit Queen Victoria 'was received with considerable curiosity, and, as far as one could judge a total absence of all other feelings. She passed down the broadest street in Dublin, or perhaps in Europe, amid a gaping crowd, but, as far as I could see or hear, without a single cheer or other sign of sympathetic interest. And her Majesty did not like her position, if one were to judge by her looks and no wonder either.'[9] O'Leary's account is contradicted by all contemporary accounts of the 1849 visit, which report enormous enthusiasm on the part of the crowds.

Another way of gauging the existence of widespread enthusiasm is through English sources. Referring to Queen Victoria's entry into Dublin on her 1900 visit, her assistant private secretary, Frederick Ponsonby, noting that there was some booing at two points on the route, nonetheless, wrote of it that 'Although I had seen many visits of this kind, nothing had ever approached the enthusiasm and even frenzy displayed by the people of Dublin.'[10]

Such reactions were not the sole province of those who wanted to see the monarchy popular in Ireland and thus might be expected to overstate enthusi-

---

8 The one million figure is claimed in the entry on Queen Victoria in Leslie Stephen and Sir Sidney Lee (eds), *DNB* [*The Dictionary of National Biography*], vol. 22 (Supplement) (London, 1909), p. 1304. **9** O'Leary, *Fenianism*, vol. 2, 61. **10** Frederick Ponsonby, *Recollections of Three Reigns* (London, 1951), p. 63.

asm. Of crucial significance, therefore, is English opinion opposed to royal visits to Ireland, which, by criticising the popular welcome for royalty, acknowledged its reality. Thus for Richard Monckton Milnes the huge welcome which Queen Victoria received in Ireland in 1849 was 'idolatrous and utterly unworthy of a free, not to say ill-used, nation'.[11]

The question of what such enthusiasm signified is a more complex one. A common English, and sometimes Irish, explanation was that the Irish were natural monarchists and, being Celtic and thus supposedly emotional, prone to enthusiasm for the royal family. 'The [Irish] people are more easily moved to loyalty for the Queen and royal family than the English or Scotch', the lord lieutenant, Lord Spencer, told Gladstone in 1885.[12] Four years later an English MP complained to the House of Commons that Irish MPs had not helped English Radicals to oppose increased royal grants. However, he went on, 'I am not surprised at this because chivalric devotion to persons and great respect for hereditary rank have been, and still are, more powerful factors with the Irish race than they are with ourselves.'[13]

Some nationalists claimed conveniently that the crowds which welcomed royal visitors were merely the representatives of a distinct, non-nationalist minority. Thus when Victoria's second son, Prince Alfred, duke of Edinburgh, visited Dublin in 1884 *United Ireland* claimed that he had been greeted by 'the few flunkeys who are always to be found in Dublin', whereas 'the vast bulk of the people' ignored him.[14]

The less settling truth was probably that those who greeted royal visitors were often the same people who supported Home Rule, and even the Fenians. Some may have been interested in mass gatherings of a variety of political complexions as a form of entertainment.[15] Others may simply have been unself-consciously capable of sustaining several sorts of allegiances simultaneously. In April 1868, for example, the viceroy, Lord Abercorn, told Queen Victoria that former Fenians had been seen cheering the prince and princess of Wales on their recent visit.[16]

No doubt the fickleness of the populace was an unsettling thought for nationalist leaders and was the principal cause of their growing hostility towards the monarchy. In truth, however, support for the monarchy was less deeply rooted than support for nationalism, as Queen Victoria herself noted in 1897 in the wake of the enthusiastic reception which the recent visit of the duke and

11 Quoted in *DNB*, vol. 22 (Supplement), p. 1298.   12 Lord Spencer to W.E. Gladstone, 26 January 1885, in Peter Gordon (ed.), *The Red Earl: Papers of the Fifth Earl Spencer, vol. 1 (1835–1885)* (Northampton, 1981), p. 291.   13 E.H. Pickersgill, in *Hansard's Parliamentary Debates*, 3rd Series, vol. 338, col. 1333 (25 July 1889).   14 *United Ireland*, 6 September 1884.   15 R.V. Comerford writes that many people attended the funeral of Terence Bellew MacManus in 1861 'because it was a spectacle and an excuse for ovating', *The Fenians in Context* (Dublin, 1985), p. 79.   16 RA [Royal Archives], D 24/34, Lord Abercorn to Queen Victoria, 25 April 1868.

duchess of York had occasioned: 'It was the same on the occasion of our three visits there, but alas, it did not produce a lasting effect, and the Queen feels that this may still be the case.'[17]

And yet the reception of royal visitors was a key preoccupation for nationalist leaders to the extent that they often felt it necessary to engage in a hermeneutics of royal occasions in order to explain, or explain away, popular enthusiasm. In his *The Last Conquest of Ireland (Perhaps)*, John Mitchel assesses Queen Victoria's 1849 visit which, due to his transportation to Tasmania, he had not personally witnessed.

In the course of only two paragraphs Mitchel offers four explanations for the warmth of her reception. The first is that it was the doing of 'the great army of persons, who, in Ireland, are paid to be loyal, [and] were expected to get up the appearance of rejoicing'. The second is 'the natural courtesy of the people' which prevented them from protesting against the visit. The third is 'the Viceroy's precautions against any show of disaffection'. And the fourth is the people's expectation, false as it turned out, that a lack of protest might bring clemency for those recently convicted and transported on account of the brief 1848 rebellion.[18] The cheering crowds were thus acting in a fashion which showed that they were simultaneously venal, instinctively respectful, cowed by the threat of force, and pursuing a shrewd political calculation.

If nationalist leaders were unwilling easily to accept that royal visitors were popular in Ireland and were perplexed in their own attempts to account for the reception of the population, there are perhaps three further personal factors which help to make royal popularity in Ireland comprehensible. The first was the fame – celebrity in today's terms – of the ruling family of what was in the nineteenth century the world's greatest empire. Secondly, there was the glamour of younger royal visitors. This was still an advantage to the 30-year-old Queen Victoria in 1849 and was certainly an advantage to the princess of Wales in 1868 and to Princess Louise who visited Ireland in 1871.

The final factor had to do with what was perceived as the personal disposition of royal visitors in favour of Ireland. If the crown as an institution was set in favour of the Union, perhaps the wearer of the crown might be better disposed to a change which might favour nationalist Ireland. This was rarely the case, but Irish Catholic nationalists persisted in fantasising otherwise, a practice which was possible only because of the very limited information which the wider public had of what members of the royal family actually thought about Ireland.

All this meant that the popularity of the crown in Ireland was more a matter of the personal popularity of individual members of the royal family than it was in Britain, a fact confirmed by the widely reported story of what an old woman

17 RA, D 43/39, Queen Victoria to Lord Cadogan, 3 September 1897. **18** John Mitchel, *The Last Conquest of Ireland (Perhaps)*, (London, n.d.), pp. 215–16.

in the crowd had shouted to Queen Victoria about her children on her arrival in Kingstown in 1849, 'Ah, Queen, dear, make one of them Prince Patrick and Ireland will die for you!'[19] It was advice which Victoria took, naming her third son Arthur William Patrick Albert.

IV

In the most general sense of the word the politics of nineteenth-century Ireland can be seen in terms of the major forces in Irish life – physical-force activism, religion, land agitation, constitutional politics and monarchy – moving away from conflict and coming into a variety of alignments. In the 1830s and 1840s O'Connell, for whom physical-force activism was always anathema, tried unsuccessfully to recruit monarchy for Irish nationalism and for repeal of the Union. In the 1860s there was a clash between Fenianism and the Catholic Church.

By the 1880s, however, constitutional politics, physical force activism, land agitation and Catholicism had all more or less merged into a nationalist accommodation, if not always a nationalist consensus. The Land League and Irish Parliamentary Party were intimately connected with each other. The 'new departure' initiative of the late 1870s was an attempt to garner support for constitutional politics from at least some sections of the physical force tradition. Finally, in 1884 there was agreement between the Catholic bishops and the Irish Parliamentary Party whereby the latter agreed to press Catholic claims in education.

Monarchy alone remained as a Trojan horse of Unionism within the nationalist polity. It was opposed both because nationalist politicians feared its influence might indeed reconcile Irish people to the Union, and because enthusiasm for monarchy in Ireland was used to feed a British discourse which saw Ireland as a country that could be appeased by concessions short of Home Rule and which did not take nationalist demands seriously. These were the reasons for the often virulent nature of nationalist opposition to monarchy and for the extremes of emotion which it evoked. It was the enemy within which had to be turned into the much more manageable enemy without. It had to be excised from the 'common myths and historic memories' of the Irish nation.[20]

British opinion, too, had to be made to see that Ireland was not a contented part of the United Kingdom; insulting the monarchy was the most public and yet the safest and easiest way to do so. Ironically, though, this was a fact also recognised by British governments who at times almost seemed relieved that nationalists were blowing off steam against the monarchy rather than opposing

---

19 Stanley Weintraub, *Victoria* (London, 1996), p. 205. **20** Anthony D. Smith argues that five factors contribute to the entrenching of national identity: a homeland, common myths and historic memories, common non-public culture, common legal rights and duties, and a common economy with territorial mobility, *National Identity* (London, 1991) p. 5.

the state in more active ways. In 1872 Lord Spencer wrote to Queen Victoria, in a rather insensitive manner given her devotion to the memory of her late husband, that he was at least consoled 'such childish tricks' as the recent attack on the statue of Prince Albert in Dublin indicated that 'no grave acts of rebellion or armed force are contemplated'.[21]

V

The absence of palpable monarchy from Ireland for long periods, for which Queen Victoria was much criticised in Britain, punctuated by moments of its sudden presence, had the effect of bringing latent and sometimes dormant ideological conflicts into a heightened tension and eliciting a reaction. Thus, beginning in the 1860s, a discernible, if not always neatly defined, tendency emerged whereby royal occasions provoked counter assertions of nationalist identity and discontent.[22] This tendency grew in intensity in two phases, the first in the late 1870s and early 1880s, and the second in the late 1890s, accompanying changes in society and generational shifts in nationalist and republican leadership. Sometimes, indeed, reaction against the monarchy had the effect of pushing nationalism forward, as with the galvanising celebrations of the 1798 rebellion in 1898 which were a response to the celebrations of the queen's diamond jubilee in 1897. To an increasing extent nationalism began to find self-definition in what at times came close to being a dialectic of opposition to monarchy.

As O'Connell had generally wanted to claim loyalty to the crown for Irish nationalism, he had been ambivalent about the implications of the sobriquet of 'uncrowned king' and preferred the Enlightenment title of 'Liberator'. It was not so in the 1880s. In time the 'uncrowned king' title was used of Parnell, whom Queen Victoria once tellingly referred to as a 'Pretender'.[23] Queen Victoria was increasingly known to have Conservative political tendencies. But this did not matter as her power was now quite limited. What did matter was that, encouraged both by the Liberals, who wanted a focus for domestic unity to transcend class divisions, and by the Conservatives, who wanted a unifying national ideology to support imperial expansion abroad, the monarchy had become the symbolic focus of British national cohesion.

In 1889 John Morley, one of the most popular Liberal politicians ever to hold office in Ireland, told the Commons that 'the Monarchy has entered into

21 RA, D 27/104, Lord Spencer to Queen Victoria, 10 June 1872.   22 A similar pattern is discernible in other countries and in more recent times. The highly successful tour of South Africa undertaken by King George VI and Queen Elizabeth, after World War I, was quickly followed by the victory of the Afrikaner National Party. Queen Elizabeth II's visit to Australia for its bicentenary in 1988 was followed by the beginnings of the Australian republican movement.   23 Queen Victoria to Lord Granville, 29 January 1881, in George Earle Buckle (ed.), *Letters of Queen Victoria* (2nd series, 3 vols, London, 1928), vol. 3, 186.

the very web of English national life, and is the outward and visible symbol of the historic character of the nation'.[24] The *Dictionary of National Biography* put the matter succinctly:

> The crown after 1880 became the living symbol of imperial unity, and every year events deepened the impression that the queen in her own person typified the common interest and the common sympathy which spread a feeling of brotherhood through the continents that formed the British empire.[25]

This judgment was generally true, except in the case of nationalist Ireland, where Queen Victoria's embodiment of imperial Britain was to the detriment of her popular standing. Nor were nationalist activists slow to draw comparisons between Parnell and Queen Victoria unflattering to the latter, as in the following American journal article, which contrasts the Irish taxation money going to support the queen with Parnell's service *gratis* to Ireland:

> The contrast presented by the character of Queen Victoria and Mr Parnell is not only striking – it is even startling. Nothing can be more noble and generous than the one; nothing more selfish, mean, and vixenish that the other. Mr Parnell donates his talents, his fortune, his life to the Irish. He loves them with all his heart. Victoria deprives them of £8,000, and hates them with all the mean spite and petty malice of her waspish nature. He is the 'uncrowned king of Ireland.' She is regarded as a sceptred impostor. He would exalt the Irish into free men; she would degrade them into slaves and beggars. She gives them 'an alms out of her own bag' and sinks them into involuntary mendicancy, which galls and humiliates their national pride.[26]

VI

In considering Queen Victoria's posthumous reputation in Ireland it is ironic to note that the very success of her 1900 visit ensured a deepening personal hatred of her among many staunch nationalists for whom loyalty to the monarchy was now incompatible with Irish national identity and who were disconcerted by the continuing capacity of monarchy to capture public acclaim in Ireland. Their opposition to her needed a focus and they found it in creating an image of Queen Victoria as the famine queen.

24 *FJ*, 30 July 1889. **25** *DNB*, vol. 22 (Supplement), p. 1366. **26** C.M. O'Keeffe, 'Queen Victoria and Mr Parnell', *Celtic Monthly*, 3 (June 1880), 521. This appeared three years before Parnell received a testimonial of £37,000 from the Irish people.

The Irish association of Queen Victoria with blame for the Famine, though it may have had earlier roots, began to become widespread at the time of her 1887 golden jubilee, when in England she became the symbol for British imperial success. If she could take the credit for Britain's successes she was also liable for Britain's failures, some Irish nationalists argued. The jubilee, for example, was celebrated at the Church of the Holy Innocents, 37th Street, New York, with a requiem mass for those who had died in the Famine, complete with catafalque surrounded by six candles.[27] The famine-queen myth also came to be associated with the allegation that Queen Victoria, as a sign of her supposed indifference to Irish suffering, had given only five pounds for famine relief. In fact £2,000 and then a further £500 were donated on her behalf. It is uncertain when or how the story of the £5 arose but it may be associated with a real incident during the mid-1890s when the queen gave £5 to Mary Donnelly whose family was swallowed up in the Kerry mud slide. *United Ireland* drew attention to the incident and used it to criticise the amount of Irish tax payers' money the queen was receiving for her upkeep.[28]

The famine-queen caricature sees Queen Victoria as being somehow directly responsible not only for the Famine but also for the entire canon of nationalist grievances during her reign. The famine queen largely displaced the hostile memory of those British politicians, such as Lord Clarendon, the 'starvation Viceroy',[29] and Lord John Russell, the 'Attorney General of Starvation',[30] who at the time of the Famine had been the real objects of nationalist ire in a way in which the queen had not been. In 1848, for example, the *Freeman's Journal* had commended another paper for drawing 'the line of demarcation between the starvation ministry and the Queen'.[31]

The early twentieth-century antipathy to Queen Victoria was particularly strong among radical nationalist women of English or Anglo-Irish background. It was their efforts in particular which resulted in her lasting vilification in nationalist mythology as the famine queen. Prominent among the promoters of the slogan were Maud Gonne and Anna Parnell. The latter's poem on the death of Queen Victoria is a good example of their efforts:

> Not four more years have passed to-day
> And now the Queen, the Famine Queen,
> Herself has passed away,
> And that dread form will never more be seen,
> In pomp of fancied glory and of pride,
> or humbled, scored, defeated as she died;
> For by God's will she was amongst the first to fall
> Beneath those mills of His that grind so wondrous small.[32]

27 *New York Times*, 22 June 1887. 28 *United Ireland*, 23 January 1897; *FJ*, 16 May 1897. 29 *FJ*, 4 April 1850. 30 Ibid., 29 May 1878. 31 Ibid., 12 July 1848. 32 Anna Parnell, '22nd

Maud Gonne's major attack on Queen Victoria's 1900 visit took the form of her 'Famine Queen' article in Arthur Griffith's *United Irishman*, causing most of the copies of the paper to be seized by the police on publication day.[33] According to Gonne, the queen, whose soul was 'vile and selfish', hated Ireland, a country 'whose inhabitants are the victims of the criminal policy of her reign, the survivors of sixty years of organised famine'. She contrasted the fate of 'poor Irish emigrant girls, whose very innocence makes them an easy prey', with 'this woman, whose bourgeois virtue is so boasted, and in whose name their homes were destroyed'. The article comes to a climax with the queen transformed into a mythic hybrid of a ghoul and witch, confronting a defiant, personified Ireland. The English were afraid of losing the Boer War and:

> In their terror they turn to Victoria, their Queen. She has succeeded in amassing more gold than any of her subjects, she has always been ready to cover with her royal mantle the crimes and turpitudes of her Empire and now, trembling on the brink of the grave, she rises once more to their call ... Taking the Shamrock in her withered hand, she dares to ask Ireland for soldiers – for soldiers to fight for the exterminators of their race. Ireland's reply, 'Queen, return to your own land ... See! Your recruiting agents return alone and unsuccessful from my green hills and plains, because once more hope has revived and it will be in the ranks of your enemies that my children will find employment and honour.'[34]

In fact the visit was so arranged as to wrong-foot such criticism. The queen did not engage in army recruitment and spent most of her public appearances meeting children.

The famine queen passed quickly into the common parlance of nationalist mythology. As late as 1995, for example, the discovery of a statue of the queen at University College, formerly Queen's College, Cork, where it had been buried several decades earlier, enabled the myth to have another outing in the letters columns of Irish newspapers from correspondents hostile to the statue being put on public display.[35]

Nor did Queen Victoria's reputation concerning Ireland fare much better in English discourse. This was for very different reasons, though out of a similar over-estimation of the power of monarchy as that which had caused national-ist antipathy. In England Queen Victoria became the scapegoat for the failure of British policy in Ireland. The tone was set within a few years of her death by Sir Sidney Lee in the *Dictionary of National Biography's* discussion of the success of her 1900 visit:

January 1901', in Jane McL. Côté, *Fanny and Anna Parnell* (Dublin, 1991), p. 262. **33** *FJ,* 7 April 1900. **34** Elizabeth Coxhead, *Daughters of Erin: Five Women of the Irish Renaissance* (London, 1965), p. 45–6. **35** See Luke Gibbons, *Transformations in Irish Culture* (Cork, 1996), pp. 171–2.

But it brought into broad relief the neglect of Ireland that preceded it, and it emphasised the errors of feeling and judgment which made her almost a complete stranger to her Irish subjects in their own land during the rest of her long reign.[36]

In the 1930s Frank Hardie castigated the failure to build on the success of her 1849 visit as 'the greatest mistake of her life' and reported that 'It has been said that Queen Victoria lost Ireland for England.'[37] In the early 1950s, when it was clear that the British Empire was in its twilight years, Algernon Cecil, wrote:

> if Victoria had brought herself to cross the Irish Sea year by year, or even rather less often, she would have won the hearts of her Irish subjects … and, as he [Lord Salisbury] saw, more than Eire hung upon the result. 'If Ireland goes,' he once told his daughter, from whom I had the story, 'India will go fifty years later.' Ireland went, and India, to all intents and purposes, not so much as fifty years later.[38]

The queen's supposed neglect of Ireland had ludicrously now become the cause of the break-up of the entire British empire. This was a line of argument which at once obviously over-estimated the influence of the monarchy and under-estimated Irish nationalism. It was part of the discourse which had sustained the British will to continue to rule in Ireland and enabled members of the political establishment to believe that nationalist grievances were superficial and that Ireland could become a contented part of the United Kingdom, if only it was only given justice or received enough royal attention.

In this view Queen Victoria was responsible for fatally damaging the Union of Britain and Ireland through her neglect of the latter. The monarchy had injured the constitution. But the truth was quite the reverse. It was the monarchy in Ireland which was fatally damaged by its zealous commitment to a very problematic constitution.

---

36 *DNB*, vol. 22 (Supplement), p. 1368. 37 Frank Hardie, *The Political Influence of Queen Victoria, 1861–1901* (Oxford, 1935), pp. 18, 177. 38 Algernon Cecil, *Queen Victoria and her Prime Ministers* (London, 1953), p. 83.

Victorian imperial theorist?
Goldwin Smith and Ireland

G.K. PEATLING

It is increasingly common in Irish cultural and historical studies to find two thematic propositions suggested or assumed: that there is a close correlation between British/English conquest and imperialism in Ireland on the one hand and anti-Irish prejudice on the other, and that these bonded forces have exerted significant influences on British and Irish cultural formations and on Irish history.[1] It may be suggested, however, that even influential work in such fields has based such conclusions on a narrow range of examples, and the typicality of these texts is often assumed rather than proved.[2] Declan Kiberd has suggested that 'Victorian imperial theorists' such as Matthew Arnold established 'a tyranny of books over facts' in representations of contemporary Ireland.[3] If 'postcolonial' scholars are to avoid an equivalent risk of merely reiterating hypotheses about the historical milieu rather than testing them, it is surely desirable that researchers renew their resolve to move beyond the charmed circle of choice quotations and favourite demons. This essay contributes towards such a project by offering a case study of Goldwin Smith, a Victorian cultural commentator whom few would acquit of the charge of expressing hostile prejudice towards the nationalist Irish. Nonetheless, close examination suggests that while commonly accepted hypotheses about anti-Irish prejudice explain some factors in Smith's thought about Irish history and politics, they do not offer the best possible explanations of the most salient relevant facts.

II

In an influential book, Kiberd argues that after the English conquest:

> Ireland was soon patented as not-England, a place whose peoples were, in many important ways, the very antithesis of their new rulers from overseas. These rulers began to control the developing debate; and it was to be their version of things which would enter universal history.[4]

---

1 See for instance Declan Kiberd, *Inventing Ireland: the Literature of the Modern Nation* (London, 1996); David Lloyd, *Anomalous States: Irish Writing and the Post-colonial Moment* (Dublin, 1993), especially pp. 3, 18–19; Edward Said, *Culture and Imperialism* (London, 1993), especially p. 266; Stephen Howe, *Ireland and Empire: Colonial Legacies in Irish History and Culture* (Oxford, 2000). **2** Howe, *Ireland and Empire*, p. 137. **3** Kiberd, *Inventing Ireland*, pp. 30, 31. **4** Ibid., pp. 6, 9.

Among the assumptions that one might unpack here is a notion of imperialism as an attempt at 'cultural programming',[5] involving both a body of cultural representations and administrative and political practice, with each branch exerting potent determining influences over a colonised society. In particular, it is suggested by some writers that British/English imperialism in Ireland had an originating influence over subsequent (particularly regrettable) manifestations in Irish society and culture, especially via British antipathy to, and negative stereotyping of, Irish culture.[6] Luke Gibbons has argued that Irish individuals abroad demonstrating racism were 'identifying with the existing supremacist ideologies, derived mainly from the same legacy of British colonialism from which they were trying to escape'.[7] Outside of the field of Irish cultural studies, the work of Perry Curtis has also affected more overtly historical writers, with Hugh Tulloch suggesting that a 'deep-seated English phobia towards Catholic Ireland – Ulstermen were always honourably exempt – helps explain why, as parliament granted varying degrees of self-determination to dominions within the empire, similar concessions to Ireland were considered unthinkable'.[8]

Some of the writers mentioned have certainly advanced lively interpretations of aspects of Irish literature and culture. Nonetheless, both the foregrounding of cultural formations in definitions of 'imperialism', and the emphasis of the relevance of 'imperialism' to British-Irish history, can be disputed. Many would accept that some aspects of British-Irish relationships have, in certain chronological phases, conformed to a typology of 'imperialism', while other aspects have not and do not.[9] Proponents of (post)colonial models accept this, and, indeed, suggest that it makes their interpretations more valid: 'the experience of Irish people, as both exponents and victims of British imperialism', Kiberd writes, 'makes them so representative of the underlying process'.[10] But there is a tension between the conceptions of Ireland sitting 'between two worlds',[11] and Ireland as postcolonial country. If colonialism and postcolonialism are advocated as models which ubiquitously explain cultural and political formations, even where the fit seems awry, blunted by overuse they will lose any rapier-like heuristic power in the telling particular instance. It will then appear necessary to supplement imperialism with some other model to interpret the manifold distinctions between 'imperialist' thinkers and discourses. The depiction of 'imperialism' as the 'determining political horizon of modern Western

5 This is a key aspect of Kiberd's definition of imperialism, ibid., p. 5.   **6** R. Kearney, *Postnationalist Ireland: Politics, Literature, Philosophy* (London, 1997), p. 50, p. 217, n. 29.   **7** Luke Gibbons, *Transformations in Irish Culture* (Cork, 1996), pp. 6–7, 175.   **8** H. Tulloch, *James Bryce's 'American Commonwealth': the Anglo-American Background* (Woodbridge, 1988), p. 129; L.P. Curtis, Jr., *Anglo-Saxons and Celts: a Study of Anti-Irish Prejudice in Victorian England* (Bridgeport, CT, 1968); L. Perry Curtis, Jr., *Apes and Angels: the Irishman in Victorian Caricature* (rev. edn., Washington, DC, 1996).   **9** Howe, *Ireland and Empire*.   **10** Kiberd, *Inventing Ireland*, p. 5.   **11** Gibbons, *Transformations in Irish Culture*, p. 3; Richard Kearney, *Transitions: Narratives in Modern Irish Culture* (Manchester, 1988), p. 9.

culture',[12] thus might not only undermine the explanatory force of the concept itself, but also prevent a comprehensive interrogation of historical and cultural discourses. It is advisable at the very least to acknowledge other causal factors, and save colonialism and postcolonialism from the appearance of being omnipresent elements of the historical fabric which it is trite to flag.

It is thus desirable to distinguish in the British-Irish context what 'British imperialism in Ireland' can explain, and what it cannot. As a small contribution to this aim, this essay will evaluate, in relation to one historical subject, the strength of two relevant propositions: that the association between justification of conquest, imperialism and prejudice is close, and that 'imperialism' (in the broadest sense) and anti-Irish prejudice have a salient cultural and political determining power.

III

Goldwin Smith was born in 1823 and educated at Eton and Oxford. He was an established and active Oxford liberal by the time that he was appointed to the Regius Professorship of Modern History in 1858. His advocacy of the greater autonomy of the white colonies of the empire from the United Kingdom, and especially of the secession of Canada from the empire and its likely union with the United States, thereafter acquired attention.[13] In 1868 he became Professor of English and Constitutional History at Cornell University. Presently he settled in Canada, where he lived until his death in 1910. He continued to acquire notoriety by propagating views on political and religious questions which were (at least within a British frame of reference) heterodox.

Arguably the last detailed examination of Smith's life and work was Elizabeth Wallace's biography, published in 1957. Wallace can be criticised for making questionable claims for her subject as a pioneer of ideas such as of the Commonwealth of Nations, and understating some of his more noxious prejudices, such as misogyny and anti-semitism.[14] But closer study of Smith's thought about Ireland can be justified on several grounds. While Wallace is keenly aware of Smith's anti-Irish prejudices and errors in interpreting British-Irish history, her reflections on these themes appear undertheorised to any scholar familiar with the more recent work of Perry Curtis and Edward Said.[15] Nonetheless, recent theorists of anti-Irish prejudice and racialisation also instance 'Goldwyn [*sic*]' Smith without close attention to his work and life.[16]

12 E. Said, 'Secular interpretation, the geographical element, and the methodology of imperialism', in Gyan Prakash (ed.), *After Colonialism: Imperial Histories and Postcolonial Displacements* (Princeton, 1995), pp. 21–39, especially p. 37.   13 Goldwin Smith, *Canada and the Canadian Question* (London, 1891); *The Political Destiny of Canada* (Toronto, 1878).   14 E. Wallace, *Goldwin Smith: Victorian Liberal* (Toronto, 1957), pp. v, 183, 184, 209–10, 280, 286–7; Tulloch, *James Bryce's 'American Commonwealth'*, p. 37.   15 Wallace, *Goldwin Smith*, pp. 93, 95–6, 185–6.   16 Gibbons, *Transformations in Irish Culture*, pp. 150–2, p. 203 n.6.

Smith's fifty-year sequence of attention to Ireland was unusually persistent
for a British radical. Although many contemporaries dismissed aspects of Smith's
work,[17] from the 1860s his ideas about Ireland influenced radicals, anti-imperi-
alists, and, especially, later Home Rulers. In 1868, Smith argued that local self-
government could act as 'political training-schools' in Britain and Ireland, and
he never totally disowned the project of 'training the Irish Celt for a full and
active partnership in those free institutions which are the original patrimony of
the Anglo-Saxon'.[18] Though he simultaneously rejected the option of creating
a national assembly in Ireland, within twenty years Home Rule was being justified in Britain with similar language, sometimes with deliberate reference to
Smith.[19] Such arguments were of course hardly less patronising to Irish nationalists than many used by Unionists. The fact that Smith abstained from joining
these admirers in support of Home Rule in the 1880s led to some broken
friendships,[20] and in some cases to equally sudden later reconciliation.[21]

Smith's anti-Irish prejudice was not unusual. His assumptions of 'Celtic' Irish
inconstancy and lack of instinct for rational political order were comforting sup-
ports to those unwilling to consider political compromise with prominent
groups in Ireland.[22] Similar assumptions were probably influential in British
policy-making as late as 1920–1,[23] and more recent manifestations in British culture are now the subject of much reflection. Notwithstanding his reputation as
an anti-imperialist, Smith's support of the supposed necessity of British rule in
India does suggest that he shared aspects of the imperialism of his contemporaries,[24] and indeed, he feared that Irish Home Rule might set a precedent for
such parts of the British empire.[25] Smith's argument that there would have been
no 'settled polity' in Ireland without English interference in the country was

17 C. Harvie, 'Ideology and Home Rule: James Bryce, A.V. Dicey and Ireland, 1880–7',
English Historical Review, 111 (1976), 298–314, especially, p. 300.   **18** Goldwin Smith,
Dismemberment No Remedy (London, 1886), p. 22; *Irish History and the Irish Question* (Toronto,
1905), pp. 6–7: C. Harvie, 'Ireland and the intellectuals, 1848–1922', *New Edinburgh Review*,
38–9 (Summer–Autumn 1977), 35–42, especially p. 37.   **19** J. Morley, 'Some arguments considered' in J. Bryce (ed.), *Handbook of Home Rule* (2nd edn, London, 1887), pp. 246–61, especially p. 259; R. Barry O'Brien, 'The "Unionist" case for Home Rule', in ibid., pp. 154–93,
especially pp. 178–86.   **20** Goldwin Smith, 'Why send more Irish to America', *Nineteenth
Century*, 13 (June 1883), 913–19, especially pp. 918–19; Viscount Bryce of Dechmont (James
Bryce) papers, Bodleian Library, Oxford, MS Bryce 16, fol. 52, Smith to Bryce, 15 July 1884;
Frederic Harrison papers, British Library of Political and Economic Science, London School
of Economics, 1/66, fols. 2–6, Harrison to John Morley, 1886.   **21** Smith to Harrison, 2
March 1900, and note by Harrison, in A. Haultain (ed.), *A Selection from the Correspondence of
Goldwin Smith* (London, 1913), pp. 345–6; Wallace, *Goldwin Smith*, pp. 95–6.   **22** Goldwin
Smith, *The Irish Question: Three Letters to the Editor of the 'Daily News'* (London, 1868), p. 23.
23 Charles Townshend, *The British Campaign in Ireland, 1919–1921: the Development of Political
and Military Policies* (Oxford, 1975), p. 200.   **24** Smith, 'The expansion of England',
Contemporary Review, 45 (January–July 1884), 524–40, especially pp. 527–8; T.J. Dunne, 'La
trahison des clercs: British intellectuals and the first Home Rule crisis', *Irish Historical Studies*,
23 (1982), 134–73, especially pp. 156–7.   **25** Smith, *Dismemberment No Remedy*, p. 30.

close to providing a retrospective justification for such intervention.[26] He further approved the Cromwellian policy in Ireland, which, he suggested, was not to extirpate the Irish people but to 'extirpate Irishry … that is, to root out the lawlessness, turbulence, and thriftlessness which were the faults or rather the misfortunes of the Celt, and to plant English law, order, industry and prosperity in their room'.[27] Although Smith described the policy of exterminating the Irish people in his day as 'untenable' (a strikingly neutral adjective), he was to suggest encouraging them to emigrate to a crown colony such as Jamaica.[28]

It would be a distortion however to dwell upon an assumed connection between 'supremacism' and 'imperialism' in interpreting Smith's thought towards Ireland. Smith not only placed the project of British rule in Ireland at a higher priority than 'imperialism' on a wider scale, but also expressed fear lest the latter jeopardise the former. No 'far-off object of aggrandisement', he wrote in 1905, 'can be half so important as a contented and loyal Ireland'.[29] In any case, Smith's views ultimately evolved in the direction of Home Rule, and his attitude to imperialism was capable of working in a direction contrary to his anti-Irish prejudice. In the 1880s, notwithstanding his renowned anti-imperialism, Smith spoke up for a form of Unionism barely softened by the reforms usually offered to make the policy more palatable. He was thus a liberal more Unionist than most Unionists. In the 1900s, notwithstanding his renowned prejudice against nationalist Ireland, Smith spoke out, albeit sporadically and ambiguously, for an audacious scheme of Home Rule for Ireland, subject only to restrictions on the foreign policy of this 'otherwise independent' nation.[30] He had thus become a Unionist more nationalist than most Home Rulers. Initial examination of Smith's thought thus quickly invites the search for an interpretation of greater relevance than any 'colonial/postcolonial' hypothesis.

IV

As a historian, no less than as an object of historical study, Smith has not stood the test of time. In the former case at least, the verdict of posterity seems fair. His standards of professionalism, at least as demonstrated by a number of aspects of his studies of Irish history, were not high. First, he lacked direct knowledge of Ireland. By his own (naively self-satisfied) admission, one mid-century trip to Ireland exercised a major influence over all his writing on the country.[31] The

26 Smith, *Irish History and the Irish Question*, pp. 50–3.   **27** Goldwin Smith, *The United Kingdom: a Political History* (London, 1899), p. 627.   **28** Goldwin Smith, *Irish History and Irish Character* (Oxford, 1861), p.193; Smith to Lord Farrar, 16 January 1883, in Haultain, *Correspondence of Goldwin Smith*, pp. 143–5; Smith, 'Why send more Irish to America', pp. 915–17.   **29** Smith, *Irish History and the Irish Question*, p. 226.   **30** Smith to Justin McCarthy, 2 April 1903, in Haultain, *Correspondence of Goldwin Smith*, pp. 397–8; Smith, *My Memory of Gladstone* (London, 1904), pp. 68–9, n. 69–70; Wallace, *Goldwin Smith*, p. 93.   **31** Smith, *Irish History and the Irish Question*, p. iii; Goldwin Smith, *Reminiscences*, (ed. A. Haultain, New York, 1910), pp. 304–5.

hosting of this trip by Edward Cardwell, then Irish chief secretary, may have influenced Smith's acceptance of Unionist assumptions. Smith also put relatively little effort into the consultation of historical manuscripts.[32]

Second, Smith's selective consideration of Irish history reinforced established myths. In 1886, when Smith was at his least reliable, he suggested that Irish Catholics under Charles I had 'massacred every Protestant on whom they could lay their hands', while more recent coercion acts were necessary 'to keep the Irishmen from butchering each other'.[33] Smith's cognate hypothesis that the Irish felt 'attachment to the rule of persons', rather than an archetypal English attachment to institutions for their 'practical usefulness', led him into confusion when considering more intricate Anglo-Irish interactions. He argued that Edmund Burke's Irishness was expressed in the passion of his commitment to a particular constitution. Nonetheless, this did not stop Smith from suggesting that Burke's 'feelings' had become those of 'our whole English nation'.[34]

In private correspondence during the Franco-Prussian war of 1870, Smith drew close links between the despotic and Celtic Napoleonic French empire, the Irish, and a Democratic Party in America allegedly implicated in continued sympathy for slavery.[35] Smith's commitment to causes such as abolitionism could not always provide a progressive veneer to such assumptions as race being among the 'important factors in history'.[36] Invoking fashionable ideas of 'natural selection', Smith suggested that the Irish were 'like other Celts … by nature politically weak'.[37] Proposals that Teutons be placed under Celtic rule, whether in Ulster or on the Rhine, horrified him as a subversion of the natural order of things.[38] In 1882 Smith suggested that 'American Irishmen in their third or fourth generation [might be] equal to their fellow-citizens, not only in industry and sobriety but in political intelligence, political self-control, and what many of them so hideously lack here – political gratitude'.[39] But he expressed uncertainty concerning those elements of Irish national character which were 'innate and indelible', and those which were 'historic accident',[40] arguing in 1899 that Home Rule and other political controversies were the consequences of essential differences between an 'English nation' of 'purely Germanic birth' and the 'emotional' Celtic influences which survived on the periphery of this nation.[41] Smith's notion of race was not only crudely essentialist (even by contemporary standards) but inconsistent.[42] Smith was more willing to palliate past British government misdeeds than nation-

32 Wallace, *Goldwin Smith*, p. 17. 33 Smith, *Dismemberment No Remedy*, pp. 7, 9. 34 Smith, *Irish History and Irish Character*, pp. 18–19. 35 Goldwin Smith papers (Bodleian Library, Oxford, microfilm copies), MS Film 971, especially Smith to Max Müller, 8 August 1870, Smith to George Waring, 8 August 1870. 36 Smith, 'The greatness of England', *Contemporary Review*, 34 (December 1878 – March 1879), pp. 1–18, especially p. 9. 37 Ibid., p. 13; Smith, *Dismemberment No Remedy*, pp. 9–10, 19, 20. 38 Smith papers, MS Film 970, Smith to Bryce, 22 July 1866; Smith, 'Why send more Irish to America', pp. 913–15. 39 Smith, 'What science is saying about Ireland', *Pall Mall Gazette*, 25 March 1882, p. 2; 'The greatness of England', p. 9. 40 Smith, *Irish History and the Irish Question*, pp. 221–2. 41 Smith, *The United Kingdom*, pp. 4–5. 42 Compare

alist and protonationalist Irish violence by reference to the moral and cultural context,[43] and less willing to see the former as the responsibility of a contemporary or timeless national or ethnic community, notwithstanding his hyperbolic pride in England's 'glorious history of ten centuries'.[44]

Such errors had established Smith's reputation by the 1880s as a partisan whose policy recommendations rarely deserved serious consideration, but his assailants also merit criticism. Frederic Harrison, for instance, attacked Smith in 1886 for relocating from Britain: Smith was a 'man who tried three countries, and is still not happy ... come to lecture us about nationality and patriotism in his vacation'.[45] Rootedness and hybridity here appear in unexpected orientations. Smith's decision to move to the United States in 1868 can in part be related to his dissatisfaction with the plutocratic nature of British society,[46] and thus he could be seen, although the term sounds strange, as a member of a British diaspora, whose oscillating, unformed identities recall Homi Bhabha's reading of Frantz Fanon.[47] Such connections as Smith established with Canadians of Scots-Irish roots who were Unionist in sympathy provide further evidence for this reading of Smith.[48] Not satisfied by Harrison's English nationalism,[49] Smith believed that the destinies of Britain and Ireland were closely bound together. In 1861 he anticipated Matthew Arnold's more famous elucidation of the complementary qualities of Celt and Saxon, suggesting that a diverse society composed of both might be more satisfying than the rooted and monolithic.[50] This pluralist inflection in Smith's work, of course, declined in the 1880s. Yet if his half-hearted advocacy of blending with the Celtic Irish diminished before the temptation of limiting their movement through coercion or expulsion, it did not entirely vanish.[51]

Contradictory modes of Smith's prejudice evolved in a number of directions. Smith's racial thought left little room for change and moral responsibility. Past British government actions in Ireland were excused on historicist grounds, and even the Irish were at some level pardoned their strange attributes since these were (at least in the short term) ethnically and historically determined; it

for instance Ernst Renan and John Mackinnon Robertson, Ernest Renan, 'What is a nation?', in Homi K. Bhabha (ed.), *Nation and Narration* (London, 1990), pp. 8–22, especially pp. 15–17; G.K. Peatling, 'British secularism, national identity and the Irish question', *Linacre Journal*, 4 (Fall 2000), 5–21. **43** Smith, *Irish History and Irish Character*, p. 44–9; *Irish History and the Irish Question*, pp. 158–60. **44** Smith, 'The fallacy of Irish history', *Nineteenth Century*, 41 (1884), pp. 38, 44; *Irish History and the Irish Question*, pp. 122–3; *Dismemberment No Remedy*, p. 31. **45** F. Harrison, *Mr Gladstone! – or Anarchy!* (London, 1886), p. 12. **46** Wallace, *Goldwin Smith*, pp. 38–40. **47** Homi Bhabha, 'Remembering Fanon: self, psyche and the colonial condition' in Frantz Fanon, *Black Skin, White Masks* (trans. Charles Lam Markmann, London, 1986), pp. vii–xxv. **48** Smith, *Reminiscences*, pp. 409, 444–5. **49** Harrison, 'A word for England', *Positivist Review*, 6:63 (March 1898), 49–53. **50** Smith, *Irish History and Irish Character*, pp. 14, 193; Matthew Arnold, 'On the study of Celtic literature', in R.H. Super (ed.), *The Complete Prose Works of Matthew Arnold, Vol. III: Lectures and Essays on Criticism* (Ann Arbor, 1962), pp. 291–386, especially p. 347. **51** Smith, *Irish History and the Irish Question*, pp. 225–6.

followed that any improvement requiring outside assistance. Smith's fellow liberal John Stuart Mill shared a disparaging attitude to the inhabitants of nationalist Ireland,[52] and a recognition late in life of an irreducible nationalist Irish ethnicity and thus of the need for separate self-government for the country.[53] Such combinations of racialist belief and 'emancipatory' outcome do not support Bhikhu Parekh's criticisms of Millite liberalism,[54] instead suggesting the performative power of naive assumptions of the essentialist indivisibility of national groups and of the relative immutability of 'national character'.

As a common defence against the charge that the Union entailed a mistreatment or prejudicial treatment of the Irish people, Goldwin Smith and other Unionists suggested that Irishmen (Irishwomen were of course hardly discussed in this context) were not only acceptable individually, but had succeeded individually, and were encouraged to succeed individually, within British and imperial contexts. A model of the loyal Irish imperial servant was constructed, and exemplars were venerated; 'Everything in the Empire,' Smith insisted, 'social grade included, is open to Irishmen.'[55] In Smith's case at least, 'phobia towards Catholic Ireland' only very imperfectly explains reluctance to grant the same large degree of 'self-determination' Smith was prepared to countenance for colonies of white settlement. For Smith, it was also the case that the question of separate self-determination was irrelevant, since, for certain delimited purposes, the Irish formed part of 'the people of the British Islands' and of the ruling imperial elite.[56]

For Unionists such as Smith, it was political action by the nationalist Irish as a community which was marred by unacceptable behaviour.[57] But Smith's notion of a Celtic character bore an important resemblance to the nationalist doctrine of a timeless and pre-political Irish nation. Smith attempted to suggest that 'Irish nationality died in its infancy', and even implied that separatist sentiment had been artificially perpetuated since the Union by the survival of the word 'Irish'.[58] Smith professed the intention 'to make patriotism' (by which he meant a pride in the 'greatness of England') 'possible' among the Catholic Irish, but found such a plan to 'cancel' the Irish people's 'past', and thus to 'change their character and habits', impractical.[59] Smith had inadvertently inscribed 'the Irish nation' into his analysis – a group of people with the insistently distinctive characteristics that Smith deplored in the Irish could only with difficulty be

52 E.D. Steele, 'J.S. Mill and the Irish question: reform, and the integrity of the empire, 1865–70', *Historical Journal*, 13:3 (1970), 419–50, especially pp. 426, 430–1, 435–6. **53** B.L. Kinzer and A.P. and J.M. Robson, *A Moralist In and Out of Parliament: John Stuart Mill at Westminster, 1865–1868* (Toronto, 1992), pp. 149–83. **54** Bhikhu Parekh, 'Liberalism and colonialism: a critique of Locke and Mill', in Jan Nederveen Pieterse and Bhikhu Parekh (eds), *The Decolonization of Imagination: Culture, Knowledge and Power* (London, 1995), pp. 81–98. **55** Smith, *Irish History and the Irish Question*, p. 172; *Reminiscences*, p. 308; Smith, 'The administration of Ireland', *Contemporary Review*, 48 (July–December 1885), pp. 1–9, especially p. 5. **56** Smith, *Canada and the Canadian Question*, pp. 260, 258. **57** Smith, *Irish History and Irish Character*, p. 6. **58** Smith, *Irish History and Irish Character*, p.3 9; *Irish History and the Irish Question*, pp. 154, 161. **59** Smith, *The Irish Question*, pp. 8, 11, 23.

defined as other than a race or a nation. There is little evidence that any Unionist suggestions that differences of condition between Britain and Ireland could be ignored were seriously followed through for almost any part of Smith's active life.[60] This want of evidence may suggest doubts about the close connections between culture and administrative and political practice that are increasingly assumed; it may also suggest that the temptation to treat the Irish as a troublesome 'people' proved a terminal obstacle to Britons' political will to accept Irishmen and women as assimilated and equal fellow-citizens. The latter explanation suggests that the enshrining of the category of the nation was a fundamental aspect of the thought of Smith and others.

Nationalist (and, indeed, racist) world-views share the characteristics of gossip. Negative rumours about other groups are reiterated until seeming to express truths too profound for doubt, while negative facts about one's own group are suppressed or rationalised.[61] While such structures of information retrieval and inference can consolidate a prejudiced world-view, distorted positive stereotypes of one's nation and negative images of the 'Other' can nonetheless be vulnerable to unavoidable contrary facts. Smith's inflated view of the 'greatness of England' and its achievements was to be disappointed by the rise in England of perceived vices such as party feeling, socialistic legislation, feminism, and imperialism.[62] Smith's assumptions about the English and Irish nations (or non-nations, depending on his mood) thus reached no point of equilibrium. Conflicting discourses in Smith's poorly thought-out writings on Ireland created at least four possible avenues of advance for the objects of his prejudice. First, there was the eventual tendency towards acceptance of a radical measure of self-government. Second, there was a 'two nations' theory, which, in emphasising Protestant Ulster's differences from nationalist Ireland, tacitly acknowledged the latter to be a nation.[63] Third, Smith suggested that Ireland, even with its unattractive attributes, could make a contribution to a pluralistic United Kingdom, countering hegemonic complacent and conservative attitudes towards 'political, ecclesiastical and social questions'.[64] Fourth, there were suggestions that English/British interference with Ireland was not justified by the assumption that the Irish people were less civilised.[65] If cultural productions such as Smith's were as representative of the cultural and political dynamic of

---

60 K. Theodore Hoppen, 'Nationalist mobilisation and governmental attitudes: geography, politics and nineteenth-century Ireland', in L.W.B. Brockliss and D. Eastwood (eds.), *A Union of Multiple Identities: the British Isles, c.1750–c.1850* (Manchester, 1997), pp. 162–78. **61** Norbert Elias and John L. Scotson, *The Established and the Outsiders: a Sociological Enquiry into Community Problems* (2nd edn, London, 1994), pp. 89–105. **62** Smith, *The United Kingdom*, p. 1; *Dismemberment No Remedy*, p. 31; Smith, 'The moral of the late crisis', *Nineteenth Century*, 20 (July – December 1886), 305–21, especially pp. 306–8; Smith to Rosebery, 20 December 1907, Smith to E.S. Beesly, 12 September 1901, in Haultain (ed.), *Correspondence of Goldwin Smith*, pp. 491–2, 374–5. **63** Smith, *The Irish Question*, p. 17; *Dismemberment No Remedy*, p. 30. **64** Smith, *Irish History and Irish Character*, p. 193; 'The greatness of England', p. 17; *The United Kingdom*, p. 1. **65** Smith, *Irish History and the Irish Question*, pp. vi, 50–3, 67, 93–8.

British supremacism as some commentators would have us believe, it is legitimate to conclude that the same commentators may considerably overestimate
the discursive force of British imperialism and prejudice on Irish history.

V

David Fitzpatrick has provocatively questioned the extent to which anti-Irish
prejudice has been a defining element of Irish migrant experience:

> The evidence of discrimination against Irish settlers is abundant and
> incontrovertible, as also is the prevalence of hostile ethnic stereotypes jus-
> tifying such discrimination. Yet, in many contexts, the practical impact of
> anti-Irish rhetoric and discrimination was negligible … rational action
> triumphed over sentiment in dictating the decisions of employers and
> marriage seekers.[66]

Goldwin Smith deserves little respect today as a historian. His intellectual inade-
quacies and anti-Irish prejudice remain deplorable, but the cognate implications
of his writings were less determined and more contradictory than the consequences usually assumed to emanate from 'imperial theorists'. The existence of
these alternative possibilities cannot be ascribed to 'rational action' – there often
seems to be little, indeed, about Smith that can be ascribed to 'rational action'.
Smith's construction of nations and races, not the 'liberal' invisible hand of individual self-interest, was the source at once of prejudice or racism and (at length)
of a project of emancipation. Such constructions, often participated in by victims
or possible victims of prejudice themselves, are ideological distortions, but are also
deeply ambiguous developments, attempts at precipitate negation of which may
in certain conjunctures actually make matters worse for a victimised group.

   Much recent interpretation of anti-Irish prejudice such as Smith's seems to
have been inspired by the observations that some aspects of Irish history can be
understood as colonial, or more recently, postcolonial, and, more controversially,
that models, observations and assumed patterns from other former colonial societies can be imported. The difficulty arises that many aspects of Ireland's history
cannot easily be interpreted with these models, and much debate arises from the
significance of such institutions and events. One such was the parliamentary
representation of Ireland under the Union. In the 1880s, some Unionists,
including Smith, advocated reducing or removing this representation.[67] His
argument was not accepted by Victorian administrators. Ironically, if this anti-
imperialist had his way at the time, one would now be able to apply the model
of postcolonialism to Irish history with substantially less qualification.

66 D. Fitzpatrick, 'Battle in the books 5: how Irish was the diaspora from Ireland?' *British
Association of Irish Studies Newsletter*, 25 (January 2001), 5–9, especially p. 7.   67 Smith, 'The
administration of Ireland', pp. 6–7: Smith papers, MS Film 970, Smith to Bryce, 26 June 1882.

The Irish Parliamentary Party in Victorian and Edwardian London

JAMES McCONNEL

Writing in 1928 of Lord Morley's biography of his father, Herbert Gladstone observed that while it was 'a comprehensive exposition of his public life' it 'left but little room for the domestic life, which in the matter of time far exceeded the days given by Mr Gladstone to public affairs.'[1] Arguably, the same criticism can be made of many modern political biographies and histories, including those concerning the members of the Irish Parliamentary Party. For, despite the attention historians have given to the party's activities at Westminster and in Ireland, there is little acknowledgement that Irish MPs led lives outside the chamber or beyond the platform. In short, the fact that as well as being Members of Parliament these men also had professional and personal lives is rarely glimpsed.[2] The reasons for this oversight are several. This aspect of the lives of most MPs was by its very nature private and so largely unpublicised. Moreover, the most obvious source of such information, members' private correspondence, largely no longer exists. However, what is probably most important is the assumption that private lives are of little consequence to public actions. Yet the study of Ireland's most distinguished parliamentarian, Charles Stewart Parnell, serves as a useful corrective to this view. Despite the absence of a Parnellite manuscript collection, scholars have considered in some detail not only Parnell's family background in County Wicklow,[3] but his long-standing affair with the wife of one of his party colleagues.

Of course, the private lives of Irish backbench members were never as interesting or historically significant as Parnell's. But on a more modest level their personal lives were seen as having a direct bearing on the performance of their public functions. Separatist and heterodox nationalists criticised Irishmen who attended Westminster not only on political grounds, but also because of the fear that they would become 'anglicised' through association with England.[4] This had been one of the objections of some Fenians (such as John O'Leary) to the

---

1 Herbert Gladstone, *After Thirty Years* (London, 1928), p. xiii.   2 This article considers only Irish nationalist MPs. For Unionist members, see Alvin Jackson, *The Ulster Party: Irish Unionists in the House of Commons, 1884–1911* (Oxford, 1989).   3 R.F. Foster, *Charles Stewart Parnell, The Man and His Family* (Brighton, 1976); *Paddy and Mr Punch* (London, 1993), pp. 40–61.   4 Patrick Maume, *The Long Gestation: Irish Nationalist Life 1891–1918* (Dublin, 1999), pp. 9–10, 50; Patricia Lavelle, *James O'Mara: A Staunch Sinn Feiner, 1873–1948* (Dublin, 1961), p. 72.

new departure.[5] Parnell himself (as Arthur Griffith was later at pains to point out) had expressed similar sentiments.[6] O'Brienites and Irish-American separatists also criticised MPs as 'enervated by association with English Liberals'.[7] The image of the 'poor savage celt' divesting himself of the most obvious indications of his peasant background in order to 'edge ... his way into some Bayswater drawing-room' was one employed in some contemporary novels.[8]

While not without some currency, before 1916 this view co-existed with the idea (central to the party's self-image) that life and work at Westminster imposed unique financial, social and domestic pressures on Irish parliamentarians. The classic description of the embattled condition of the party at Westminster was produced by the veteran nationalist T.P. O'Connor (1880–1929) in 1929. O'Connor's account of everyday life for the average backbench Irish member in London was essentially a story of self-sacrifice, loneliness and extreme stoicism. 'I must drop a reminiscent tear', he wrote, 'as I think of these humble, uncomplaining, penniless men, some of them middle-aged, who gave all those years of silent and uncomplaining servitude to the cause'. According to O'Connor, Victorian Irish MPs lived ascetic lives in London – residing in cheap lodgings close to the House, spending their waking hours in the Palace, separated from family, ostracised by their British colleagues and too poor to afford any of the entertainments the imperial capital offered.[9]

Clearly, O'Connor's description of the party (written when he was in his late seventies) was deeply sentimental, nostalgic and consciously penned as a posthumous defence of his former colleagues. But how accurate was his account as a description of the experiences of Victorian and Edwardian backbench MPs in London?

II

As with all Members of Parliament, the amount of time Nationalist MPs actually spent 'sitting, acting and voting' in the chamber was only a portion of the total time they spent within the precincts of the House of Commons. Accordingly, by the late nineteenth century the Palace of Westminster had developed a range of facilities for its members which earned it the frequently used sobriquet of 'the best club in London'. Although individual Members of Parliament were entitled to nothing more than a peg for their hats and a locker, the nine acre site included a library of five rooms with space for about 90 MPs

5 John O'Beirne Ranelagh, 'The Irish Republican Brotherhood in the revolutionary period, 1879–1923', in D.G. Boyce (ed.), *The Revolution in Ireland, 1879–1923* (London, 1988), p. 137. 6 *FJ [Freeman's Journal]*, 13 October 1910, p. 9.   7 *Cork Accent*, 17 February 1910, p. 1; *G–A [Gaelic-American]*, 1 January 1910, p. 3.   8 George Moore, *Parnell and his Island* (London, 1887), pp. 142–3.   9 T.P. O'Connor, *Memoirs of an Old Parliamentarian* (London, 1929), pp. 61–6.

to work, a newspaper reading room, several smoking rooms, a post office, a terrace (which ran almost the full length of the Palace and which in summer was a 'society resort'), several dining rooms and 'vast kitchens' for the preparation and cooking of meals.

A combination of close attendance, poverty and a prohibition on pairing (at least in the 1880s and after 1900) meant that many Irish nationalist MPs spent considerable time in the precincts of the Palace, and had frequent opportunities to use its facilities. Indeed, as Michael McCarthy, the Unionist pamphleteer and former parliamentary lobbyist, put it, '[they] literally squatted at St Stephen's, coming down early and never leaving until the attendants shouted "Who goes home."'[10] Boredom would have been a constant problem, and Irish MPs discovered different ways to occupy themselves.[11] According to T.P. O'Connor some Irish MPs smoked and played cards in the Irish whips' room.[12] By 1914 William Field (MP 1892–1918) had a 'usual place in the shady corner of the Library' which he habitually occupied.[13] Alfred Webb (1890–95) also spent much of his time in the library and also remembered pleasant afternoons with Irish colleagues on the terrace,[14] as did J.P. Boland (1900–18).[15] Stephen Gwynn (1906–18) fondly recalled conversations with 'Long John' O'Connor (1885–1918) over bottles of House of Commons' claret.[16] Others, by contrast, engaged in more intellectual pursuits. Arthur Lynch (1909–18) read some of the 'extraordinary' books from the library.[17] Tom O'Donnell (1900–18) gave Irish lessons to several of his colleagues,[18] William Lundon (1900–9) discussed Celtic literature with Lloyd George,[19] while Justin McCarthy (1879–1900) recalled conversations with John Dillon (1880–1918) on their mutual passion for Herodotus.[20] In turn, others had fond memories of their conversations with McCarthy. Indeed, for Michael Bodkin (1892–95), his company at dinner time was 'a delightful oasis in the dreary desert of the parliamentary day.'[21]

10 M.J.F. McCarthy, *The Irish Revolution* (London, 1912), p. 460. 11 Michael Bodkin, *Recollections of an Irish Judge: Press, Bar and Parliament* (London, 1914), pp. 194, 203. This seems to have been a particular problem during the passage of the third Home Rule Bill in 1912, see John Dillon's speech reported in *FJ*, 19 May 1913, p. 7. 12 O'Connor, *Memoirs*, p. 63. According to the Liberal MP, Sir Alfred Pease, the Irish members particularly favoured 'a dismal underground smoking-room' – probably a reference to the whips' room, Sir Alfred Pease, *Elections and Reflections* (London, 1932), p. 250. 13 *Hansard's Parliamentary Debates*, 5th series, vol. 61, col. 477 (17 April 1914). 14 Alfred Webb, *The Autobiography of a Quaker Nationalist*, ed. Marie-Louise Legg (Cork, 1999), pp. 56–7. 15 J.P. Boland, *Irishman's Day: A Day in the Life of an Irish MP* (London, 1944), pp. 99–100. 16 Stephen Gwynn, '"Long John"– A Parliamentary Memoir', in *Memories of Enjoyment* (Tralee, 1946), p. 84. 17 Arthur Lynch, *My Life Story* (London, 1924), p. 262. 18 J.A. Gaughan, *A Political Odyssey: Thomas O'Donnell* (Dublin, 1983), p. 32. 19 *FJ*, 19 May 1913, p. 8. 20 Justin McCarthy, *Reminiscences* (2 vols, London, 1899), II, 379. 21 Bodkin, *Recollections*, p. 241.

Bodkin dined in Parliament not only for the stimulating company, but also because poverty forced him to.[22] The practice of Irish MPs taking meals in the House because of their impecuniosity long pre-dated the 1880s.[23] It also continued after Parnell; writing at the beginning of the twentieth century Sir Henry Lucy observed in his diary 'As for tomorrow, the House adjourns at six o'clock, and no one, not even an Irish Member, stays for dinner.'[24] Although such comments were occasionally the cause of tension,[25] in truth (as one parliamentary commentator observed), 'for quality and quantity combined, [the House of Commons' shilling dinner] can hardly, I think, be got for the money anywhere else in this country.'[26]

III

The surviving evidence suggests that the political distinctions of the chamber were reflected elsewhere in the House. Irish nationalist members of all periods, for instance, seem to have habitually sat together during mealtimes.[27] However, Irish MPs were far more 'clubbable' than this might at first suggest. For as William O'Brien (1883–1918) put it:

> Man by man, the House of Commons is full of bonhomie. Its judgements of men are often wrong, but they are never wrong by reason of any undue regard for the length of a man's purse or the number of his quarterings ... [it is only] when the hearty, tolerant (once in a way stupid) Englishmen of the smoking room or terrace flock in at the division-bell ... [that they] speak, as it were, *ex cathedra*, in the name of England, ruler of the waves ...[28]

Beyond the chamber friendships and acquaintances could and did develop between members from different parties, and for many members the smoking room was where the informality of the House was at its most evident. Indeed, one nationalist MP of the 1890s (who neither smoked nor drank while in

22 Bodkin, *Recollections*, p. 188.   **23** Charles Dickens, 'A parliamentary sketch', in Michael Slater (ed.) *Dickens' Journalism* (London, 1994), p. 158. The author is obliged to Mr A.J. Heesom for this reference.   **24** Sir Henry Lucy, *The Balfourian Parliament, 1901–05* (London, 1906), p. 484.   **25** *Hansard*, 4th series, vol. 102, col. 575 (6 February 1902).   **26** Charles King, *The Asquith Parliament* (London, 1910), p. 88. Also see Robert Farquharson, *The House of Commons from Within* (London, 1912), p. 155. This high opinion was not shared by all, see, for instance, the comments of the *Freeman's* parliamentary correspondent, *FJ*, 21 February 1912, p. 7.   **27** Sir Richard Temple, *The House of Commons* (London, 1899), p. 44. This custom was maintained into the new century, as evidenced by the picture of 'The Irish Round Table at the House of Commons', 'in the seats reserved for them by courtesy', *Illustrated London News*, 30 October 1909, p. 615.   **28** William O'Brien, 'London revisited', *Contemporary Review*, 69 (June 1896), 808–9.

Parliament because of his poverty) found what he described as the 'social freemasonry' of the smoking-room extremely congenial.[29]

Of course, such personal friendships and acquaintances were made between individuals and did not necessarily affect the standing of Irish backbenchers *per se*. It is clear, however, that attitudes (barring those of Tory backwoodsmen) towards nationalist members did change between 1885 and 1914. Men who were apparently regarded with curiosity, not to say hostility, in the 1880s, came to be seen (sometimes even affectionately) as part of its political furniture. In part this followed the decline of obstruction and the advent of the Liberal alliance. But within the House of Commons itself, perceptions of Irish members seem to have been principally influenced by their growing reputation for humour.

Historically, Parliament had laughed at, rather than with, Irish members. E.M. Whitty wrote in 1853 that the House was grateful to 'Celtic Gentlemen' for the amusement they provided, '[they] are as silly, as broguey, as useless, as quarrelsome, and as contemptible as ever they were'.[30] Though perhaps less disdainful, later generations of British parliamentarians also had entertainment at the expense of Irish members. In particular 'bulls' (mistakes or unintentionally humorous mixed metaphors) were synonymous with nationalist MPs.[31] According to Shane Leslie, 'There was always a new Irish story passing through the lobbies'.[32] However, in later years Irish members seem also to have won a reputation for their wit and humour.[33] As the former lobby correspondent, Sir Alexander Mackintosh, wrote, '[after 1918] Irish Nationalists were missed by old British colleagues. Life was seldom dull while they were in force at Westminster, with their vivacity and humour. Personally they were not unpopular.'[34]

Michael Bodkin put Parliament's appreciation of humour down to the fact that 'all [other] forms of entertainment are rigorously excluded from the precincts of Westminster.'[35] Chess was the exception to this rule, and, interestingly, was played by several nationalist members to a high standard. Colonel John Nolan (1872–1906), for instance, had a reputation while in Parliament as the best player in the House of Commons; James O'Mara (1900–7) won an inter-parliamentary

29 Bodkin, *Recollections*, pp. 202–3.　**30** E.M. Whitty, *History of the Session 1852–3: a Parliamentary Retrospect* (London, 1853), pp. 127–8.　**31** F.M. Thomas (ed.), *Fifty Years of Fleet Street being the Life and Recollections of Sir John R. Robinson* (London 1904), p. 47. See also Spencer Leigh Hughes, *Press, Platform and Parliament* (London, 1918), p. 161; Sir Henry Lucy, *Lords and Commoners* (London, 1921), p. 90.　**32** Shane Leslie, *The Film of Memory* (London, 1938), p. 369.　**33** See, for instance, the story of Joseph Ronayne in Michael MacDonagh, *Irish Life and Character* (London, 1905), p. 279; *The Pageant of Parliament* (2 vols, London, 1921), vol. 1, 127. This story forms the basis for a similar episode in Arthur Lynch, *O'Rourke the Great: A Novel* (London, 1921), pp. 87–90.　**34** Sir Alexander Mackintosh, *Echoes of Big Ben: a Journalist's Parliamentary Diary (1881–1940)* (London, 1946), p. 85. Others expressed similar sentiments at the disappearance of the Irish Party, see Harry Furniss, *Some Victorian Men* (London, 1924), p. 111; A.S.T. Griffith-Boscawen, *Memories* (London, 1925), p. 263; Lucy, *Lords and Commoners*, p. 113.　**35** Bodkin, *Recollections*, p. 205.

chess tournament as MP for South Kilkenny, and John Howard Parnell (1895–1900) was a member of the Commons' Chess Circle and was on the team that played a match via cable against the American House of Representatives.[36] In 1914 David Sheehy (1885–1918) was numbered among 'a distinguished little band which forgathers in one of the smoking rooms to play chess.[37]

Sportsmen in the House of Commons also fielded a cricket team against sides from English public schools, such as nearby Westminster. Several Irish members followed or enjoyed cricket; indeed, J.P. Boland had captained the Christ Church XI when at Oxford and been invited to play for the University. However, he did not play for Parliament because as a party whip there was 'always the risk of vital divisions before 6.30 p.m. when the match, if played on a parliamentary day, might be expected to end'.[38] Lack of time may also account for why so few nationalist MPs participated in the annual parliamentary golf tournament, although Vincent Kennedy (1904–18) did play in 1907.[39] However, if golf and cricket proved inconvenient, other parliamentary occasions were not so problematic. For instance, in May 1911 the Parliamentary Aerial Defence Committee organised a flying demonstration at Hendon at which numerous Irish MPs attended; among those who flew in the aircraft were two nationalist members.[40]

Anecdotal as this evidence largely is, it nonetheless suggests that the old party refrain 'in Parliament, but not of it',[41] was by 1914 to a considerable extent no longer true (if, indeed, it had ever been quite so absolute). Although formally the party continued to exempt itself from symbolic occasions such as the opening of Parliament,[42] many members of the Edwardian party do not appear to have remained aloof from the domestic life of the House of Commons and, whatever their rhetoric, it seems that working in an alien assembly was not as inhospitable as was sometimes claimed.[43]

IV

As a demonstration of their ideological commitment and in response to the hostility shown by some British MPs, during the 1880s Irish MPs subscribed to a 'self-denying ordinance' which led them to boycott London society.[44] William O'Brien fondly recalled socialising with his colleagues, who were 'as merry as

---

36 *FJ*, 1 February 1912, p. 9; Lavelle, *James O'Mara*, p. 37; *II [Irish Independent]*, 28 November 1910, p. 4; L.A. Atherley-Jones, *Looking Back. Reminiscences of a Political Career* (London, 1925), p. 50. **37** *London Opinion*, 7 March 1914, p. 419. **38** Boland, *Irishman's Day*, p. 24. **39** *The Times*, 7 April 1909, p. 16. **40** *II*, 13 May 1911, p. 4. **41** McCarthy, *Irish Revolution*, p. 460. **42** *FJ*, 15 February 1912, p. 7. **43** This had limits. For instance, in July 1912 many British members attended a garden party hosted by the king at Windsor, for which the Commons allowed itself a half-holiday. None of the Irish party attended, *FJ*, 19 July 1912, p. 6. **44** Stephen Gwynn, *John Redmond's Last Years* (London, 1919), p. 13.

campaigners in their mess tent'.[45] T.P. O'Connor, by contrast, had memories of dreary evenings spent talking about nothing but politics.[46] J.F.X. O'Brien (1885–1905)recalled that Parnell did not approve of 'social intercourse' within the party.[47] After 1900, a better feeling seems to have existed within the party and there were more social occasions organised for Irish MPs.[48]

Beyond the immediate company of their parliamentary colleagues, Irish MPs also associated themselves with the wider London-Irish community through the large number of clubs and societies founded by earlier generations of Irish immigrants.[49] Of course, Irish MPs tended to be most involved in political organisations,[50] but they also actively participated in the meetings of Irish literary and sporting groups. For instance, Irish MPs joined the Southwark Irish Literary Club in the 1880s and the Irish Literary Society in the 1900s.[51] In the 1890s numerous Irish members attended Gaelic games as spectators, while in the new century Boland was a moving force in the annual Aonach of the London Gaelic League.[52] In 1914, 12 Irish members played in a tournament against the London Irish Golfing Society.[53] Seventeen Irish MPs were members of the Irish Club in London; Tom Condon said of it in 1913, 'The institution, to those of them who were merely birds of passage in London, was more than a club – it was a home.'[54]

But while Irish members continued to be involved at various levels with the Irish community in London, in later years many Irish MPs (though by no means all) seem to have accepted the hospitality of politically sympathetic British hosts.[55] In 1893, for example, an open-air production of *The Tempest* at Pope's Villa in Twickenham was hosted by the Radical Henry Labouchere; among the numerous guests were Sir William Harcourt (then chancellor of the exchequer), John Redmond (1881–1918), Dr Kenny (1885–96) and John Dillon (1880–1918).[56] Edwardian Irish members continued to be invited to social gatherings hosted by members from both sides of the House.[57] Gentlemen's clubs were another environment wherein nationalist MPs mixed with their British colleagues, among whom club membership was widespread.[58] With a handful of exceptions, the great majority of Irish MPs who joined a club did so after

45 O'Brien, 'London revisited', p. 810.   **46** O'Connor, *Memoirs*, p. 65.   **47** J.F.X. O'Brien, unpublished autobiography, O'Brien Papers [OBP], National Library of Ireland, Ms 13,429. **48** Boland, *Irishman's Day*, p. 20.   **49** Jonathan Schneer, *London 1900: the Imperial Metropolis* (New Haven and London, 1999), p. 172.   **50** For instance, John O'Connor was president of the Irish Parliamentary Branch of the London UIL. This branch regularly hosted guest lecturers, among them Irish MPs.   **51** M.F. Ryan, *Fenian Memories* (Dublin, 1945), pp. 157–8. **52** Ibid.; Boland, *Irishman's Day*, p. 44.   **53** *II*, 6 May 1914, p. 4.   **54** *FJ*, 18 March 1913, p. 6. **55** Gwynn, *Redmond's Last Years*, p. 13.   **56** W.S. Blunt, *My Diaries: Being a Personal Narrative of Events, 1888–1914* (2 vols, London, 1919), vol. I, 137.   **57** Gaughan, *Odyssey*, p. 32. John O'Connor, for instance, often went to stay at Walmer, the residence of Robert Reid, *Daily Telegraph*, 29 October 1928, p. 15.   **58** Anthon Taddei, *London Clubs in the Late Nineteenth Century* (Oxford, 1999), p. 15.

1886 and were members of the National Liberal Club: 36 in the late 1880s (following the Liberal alliance) and approximately 30 in 1914.[59] Irish MPs were remembered with affection by English clubmen.[60]

Although only a minority (albeit a substantial one) of nationalist MPs joined London clubs or were prominent in London society, this was a source of criticism from disgruntled nationalists at home who saw it as dangerous fraternisation.[61] Members of the party clearly resented such criticism, but though frequently prepared to allude to their hardships they rarely advanced beyond generalities with regard to the strains of living in London.[62] And yet practical difficulties there undoubtedly were. Members had not only to feed, clothe and house themselves while living in London, but provide the same for their families if they were married, run businesses in Ireland *in absentia*, and commute between the two islands.

V

Very little is known about how MPs regarded their adopted city. Stephen Gwynn described himself as 'willingly a Londoner; I am as much at home in these streets where I never even think of meeting an acquaintance, as in Dublin where one constantly stops or is stopped by the way for a little conversation'.[63] Some were appalled by the poverty of the metropolis,[64] while others found the incessant rain and the air pollution intolerable.[65] Moreover, for many Irish members, accustomed to the small, modestly populated towns of provincial Ireland, London must have seemed a 'strange landscape'.[66] George Moore wrote of how, when his fictional MP, James Daly, walked out of Euston station he was 'dazzled, bewildered, and a little cowed'.[67] For some, awe was tempered by feelings of ambivalence or even antipathy. J.F.X. O'Brien, who lived in London for many years and brought his children up there, apparently 'hate[d] living in the enemies country and long[ed] to return to Ireland'.[68] And William O'Brien recalled how 'to me the most delightful prospect in all great London was the Euston railway platform, because it was the way out of it.' Yet, despite this, he also had a sneaking regard for the imperial capital. As he wrote in 1896 'I never saw London in such monstrous health ... No suggestion of a *fin de siècle* here.'[69]

59 Conor Cruise O'Brien, *Parnell and his Party, 1880–1890* (Oxford, 1957), p. 331; *II*, 19 January 1914, p. 4. **60** Robert Steven, *The National Liberal Club* (London, 1925), p. 20. **61** For instance, see *FJ*, 11 January 1910, p. 9; *G-A*, 15 January 1910, p. 3; 24 September 1910, p. 3. **62** For example, see *FJ*, 8 December 1909, p. 8. **63** Stephen Gwynn, *Experiences of a Literary Man* (London, 1926), p. 11. **64** James Hogan, *Australian in London*, pp. 224–5; *Hansard*, 5th series, vol. 41, col. 139 (15 July 1912); *Connacht Tribune*, 11 December 1909, p. 5. **65** *Longford Leader*, 23 November 1912, p. 4. **66** *FJ*, 6 November 1913, p. 8. **67** Moore, *Parnell*, p. 141. **68** J.F.X. O'Brien to Thomas Sexton, undated, OBP, Ms 13,429. **69** O'Brien, 'London revisited', pp. 808–9, 812.

On a more practical level, the finding of suitable accommodation for Irish members was one of their most important requirements. But while house-hunting was possible for some British members,[70] many Irish MPs would have been unfamiliar with London and its housing market and would, therefore, have been dependent on house agents or more experienced colleagues. Michael Meagher (1906–18), for instance, wrote to James O'Mara, shortly after the former had been elected in 1907, 'at your convenience look up suitable quarters for me in a quiet corner of the suburbs of the city and in direct communication by train with the House of Commons. You know I am a green man being never in London.'[71] Although a small number of Irish MPs chose to live permanently in London, most only lived there during the session. They lived in a variety of accommodation; some in 'hotels', others in their clubs, but the majority in 'furnished lodgings … [which they took] by the week, and left them at the termination of the parliamentary session'.[72]

Although Michael Bodkin held that 'comfortable lodgings can be had at a reasonable cost within measurable distance of the House',[73] the weight of anecdotal evidence would seem to contradict this statement. T.P. O'Connor, for example, referred to backbench members as having lived in pairs in cramped lodgings in the 'cheap district of Pimlico'. C.J. O'Donnell, himself an MP between 1906 and 1910, remembered that '[m]ost of them lived in squalor across the river in Lambeth'.[74] George Moore also depicted his fictional Irish member living in Lambeth,[75] while in his fictionalised account of the life of an Irish MP, *O'Rourke the Great*, Arthur Lynch wrote of O'Rourke living in 'digs' consisting of 'one bedroom, second floor back, in a dingy lodging-house, of which, however, the grimy entrance was cleaner than his little den.'[76] But while quite plausible (given their modest incomes), each of these authors may have had an interest in depicting Irish members as poor and miserably domiciled, and more recent research suggests that Irish MPs of all eras lived in different types and conditions of accommodation in various parts of London.[77]

For those MPs who were married, living in London usually entailed protracted separation from their wives and families. However, marriage itself was not the norm within the party. As John Redmond told his colleagues in 1912, 'One of the reproaches that still attaches, I am sorry to say, to our Party, is that the number of bachelors amongst us is too great'.[78] The reasons for this were several. For those elected in the 1880s, involvement in agrarian radicalism often meant that they led disrupted personal lives. For instance, William O'Brien's

70 For instance, see A.T. Bassett, *The Life of the Rt. Hon John Edward Ellis, MP* (London, 1914), p. 61. **71** Michael Meagher to James O'Mara, 17 February 1906, O'Mara Papers, National Library of Ireland, Ms 21,545 [3]. **72** *FJ*, 9 January 1913, p. 7; 11 July 1914, p. 7. **73** Bodkin, *Recollections*, p. 188. **74** C.J. O'Donnell, *Outraged Ulster* (London, 1932), p. 26. **75** Moore, *Parnell*, p. 142. **76** Lynch, *O'Rourke*, p. 95. **77** See James McConnel, 'The View from the Backbench: Irish Nationalist MPs and their Work, 1910–1914' (unpublished PhD thesis, University of Durham, 2002), p. 262. **78** *FJ*, 9 May 1912, p. 7.

'myriad public activities ... his incessant speechmaking, his dodging of the police, his frequent jail terms, all coupled with his duties as editor and Member of Parliament – were not conducive to regulated living',[79] nor to meeting potential wives (though this lifestyle seems not so much to have prevented marriage, as delayed it).

Although in later decades imprisonment and evasion of the police were no longer so commonplace, marriage for those Irish MPs who entered Parliament as bachelors may still have remained difficult because their dual lives at Westminster and in Ireland, their relative poverty and the anti-social hours they worked may not have made them particularly eligible as husbands. Nonetheless, there was a certain social cachet attached to being an MP,[80] and some Irish members did successfully court their future wives on the terrace or at dinner in the House.[81] However, such opportunities were not confined to single men. Even for those who were married, the social milieu of the terrace, combined with extended absences from home, could lead to what T.P. O'Connor described as 'temporary scrapes'.[82] Ironically, O'Connor himself may have had several such 'scrapes'.[83] His wife, a socially ambitious American divorcee, did not provide the domestic security O'Connor craved, though in fairness O'Connor was not an attentive husband and she suffered considerably from his long absences. By 1907, she was threatening to divorce O'Connor unless her maintenance was paid. The consequent scandal would, as the leadership knew, have been disastrous and so she was paid for her silence.[84] This was not the only backbench marital scandal which had to be discretely managed between 1880 and 1918.[85]

VI

Because of prevailing middle class morality, Catholic doctrine and (after 1891) the legacy of the Parnell scandal, divorce was obviously difficult for an Irish nationalist representative. However, marital complications were not the only means by which MPs could embarrass the party. Equally problematical was the attraction (particularly to often impecunious Irish members) of non-executive directorships offered by companies wishing to exploit the status or contacts of

79 Joseph V. O'Brien, *William O'Brien and the Course of Irish Politics, 1881–1918* (Berkeley, 1976), p. ix. **80** Bodkin, *Recollections*, p. 214. **81** Webb, *Autobiography*, p. 56; F.S.L. Lyons, *John Dillon* (London, 1968), p. 253; Bessie O'Connor, *I Myself* (London, 1914), p. 142; Sophie O'Brien, *Golden Memories* (Dublin, 1930), p. 23, Bridget Boland, *At My Mother's Knee* (London, 1978), p. 136. **82** O'Connor, *Memoirs*, p. 65. **83** L.W. Brady, *T.P. O'Connor and the Liverpool Irish* (London, 1983), pp. 157–8. **84** John Redmond to John Dillon, 8 November 1907, Dillon Papers [DP], Trinity College Dublin, Ms 6747/229. **85** See Colonel Jameson to John Dillon, 27 March 1896, DP, Ms 6755/722; *FJ*, 27 March 1896, p. 5; Redmond memoranda, 3 March, 10 April, 1905, Redmond Papers [RP], National Library of Ireland, Ms 15,214 [3].

an MP.[86] Some members publicly disdained such offers,[87] while others decided on balance to put their reputations first. Justin McCarthy, for example, was offered £500 a year to join the board of a company dealing in Irish cattle; he refused because 'everybody here and in Ireland would know – must know – that I had merely sold my name for the money'.[88] Other members consulted the leadership before proceeding. William Abraham (1885–1915), for instance, wrote to John Dillon in 1897 asking if his involvement with a Brixton music hall company was compatible with his membership of the party.[89] As a director Abraham was to be paid £250 – no small sum, particularly for Irish members who tended to be poorer than their British counterparts. Although the vast majority of nationalist MPs who held directorships did so quite legitimately, inevitably some MPs were implicated in financial scandals.[90]

Such proposals were sometimes difficult to resist because parliamentary service often made working difficult. Indeed, both privately and publicly, Irish MPs testified to the damage being an MP could have on careers and professional reputations.[91] However, some Irish MPs (particular journalists and barristers) could and did benefit professionally from the prestige and useful connections Parliament provided.[92] Still, working two jobs was not easy. Stephen Gwynn had thought that 'it would not be difficult to combine my writing work with attendance at the House of Commons. Other people had done it – "T.P." and Justin McCarthy most notably.' But he later realized that '[n]o outsider can guess the strain involved by this double role.[93]' T.P. O'Connor himself remembered the difficulty of having to write a leading article to a dead-line of nine o'clock in the morning when 'it was a common if not a usual thing for me to be in the House of Commons till two or three o'clock in the morning'.[94] Justin McCarthy had similar 'grumbles'.[95] For some, the pressure was sometimes too much. As James O'Mara, a member of the London Home and Foreign Produce Exchange, wrote to a clerical friend in 1904, 'The doctor is not at all sure that I can stand the strain of a double career, but time will tell.'[96]

For those not of independent means or whose professions did not permit them to work during the session (such as farmers, shopkeepers and even solicitors) there was the parliamentary stipend.[97] This system of defraying the costs

86 MacDonagh, *Parliament*, p. 59; *The Times*, 25 May 1898, p. 3.   **87** *Kerry People*, 8 January 1910, p. 7.   **88** Justin McCarthy, *Our Book of Memories: Letters of Justin McCarthy to Mrs Campbell Praed* (London, 1912), p. 215.   **89** William Abraham to John Dillon, 7 October 1897, DP, Ms 6752/4.   **90** Maume, *Long Gestation*, p. 34; *The Times*, 30 April 1914, p. 4.   **91** For instance, see Boland, *Mother's Knee*, p. 42; *FJ*, 5 October 1910, p. 7; W.B. Wells, *John Redmond* (London, 1919), pp. 232–3; James Gibney to John Dillon, 11 April 1896, DP, Ms 6754/507; Michael McCartan to John Dillon, 21 November 1896, ibid., Ms 6756/974.   **92** Atherley-Jones, *Looking Back*, p. 146.   **93** Gwynn, *Literary Man*, p. 251.   **94** O'Connor, *Memoirs*, p. 258.   **95** Justin McCarthy, *The Story of an Irishman* (London, 1904), pp. 220–1.   **96** Lavelle, *O'Mara*, p. 59.   **97** For the history of the allowance, see O'Brien, *Parnell and his Party*, pp. 265–72; Alan O'Day, *The English Face of Irish Nationalism* (London, 1977), pp. 43–6; F.S.L. Lyons, *The Irish*

incurred by MPs incidental to their 'sitting, acting and voting' at Westminster was much criticised by the party's enemies, while for the party it not only constituted an enormous burden on its finances,[98] but for some members was simply not enough to live on.[99] Thus, it might be thought that the Irish Party would have welcomed the payment of MPs by the state introduced in 1911. But for the party, the main issue was not the impecuniosity of individual members, but whether acceptance of state payment compromised its self-denying ordinance of refusing position or patronage from the British government. Under pressure from its Liberal allies (and perhaps backbench discontent) the party leadership eventually discreetly capitulated.

But what difference did payment make to Irish members' quality of life? In fact, despite furnishing the party's critics with yet more ammunition in the years up to 1918, it seems that the receipt of the £400 paid by the state made comparatively little difference because there is evidence to suggest that the money was pooled and that members only took a subsistence allowance.[1] Furthermore, in 1911 the government did not make separate provision for the travelling expenses of members.[2] This was of particular concern to Irish MPs, for whom commuting between England and Ireland was a way of life. Indeed, so much was this so that it influenced the party's collective persona. As Harry Furniss, the parliamentary illustrator for numerous London newspapers and magazines, wrote when he recalled the introduction of the first Home Rule Bill:

> Some of the Irish MPs, so as to secure their seats, wrapped themselves up in their railway rugs and slept on the benches in the House, placing their cards in their places when they awoke the following morning ... a certain Tory wag entered the House when the Irish MPs were asleep – as they frequently are on the train journey backwards and forwards to Holyhead – and awoke them all by calling out: 'Tickets please! All change here for College Green,' and that a certain Member for Ireland, whose imagination had carried him into mid-Channel, was heard to murmur faintly, 'Steward!'[3]

As frequent commuters, Irish MPs had a great deal of experience of the rail network connecting the two countries and brought many of the problems they experienced to the attention of the government.[4] This political pressure, com-

Parliamentary Party, 1890–1910 (1951, Westport, CT, 1975), pp. 201–17. For a survey of Irish parliamentary finance in the nineteenth century, see William Gwynn, 'The finances of the Irish nationalist movement', in *Democracy and the Cost of Politics in Great Britain* (London, 1962), pp. 129–46. **98** John Redmond to John Dillon, August 1906, DP, Ms 6747/185. **99** John Redmond to Eugene Crean, 10 May 1903, DP, Ms 6747 /39; Laurence Ginnell to John Redmond, 10 September 1906, RP, Ms 15191 [3]. **1** *Report from the Select Committee on Members' Expenses,* Parliamentary Papers, 1920 (255) VII, 650. **2** *FJ,* 10 October 1912, p. 10. **3** Furniss, *Victorian Men,* p. 111. **4** 'M.A.' and J.F. Reid, *Life of William Field* (Dublin, 1918), p. 31.

bined with improvements in transportation, meant that by 1914 the London-Dublin journey took only nine hours.[5] Still for many it was physically demanding: a boat train from Euston to Holyhead, from there by ferry to Kingstown, and from Kingstown onwards to their destination. In fact, so demanding was the journey considered that to it was attributed the early deaths of numerous Irish MPs.[6] As the *Freeman's Journal* observed, when James O'Connor (1892-1910) died in March 1910, 'it can be said that in nearly all of [such instances] … the sad event [was] hastened by the strain of travelling to and attending at Westminster'.[7]

Of course, not all of such deaths should be attributed to the exigencies of parliamentary life; age (by 1910 an average of 50 for the party) was also an important consideration. F.S.L. Lyons considered this age low enough for the party to be an active one, but in terms of health and general fitness, it was certainly old enough for many members to have been suffering from the normal complaints associated with middle age.[8] However, while age was undoubtedly an influence on the health and well-being of Irish members, the life-style imposed on MPs by close attendance at Westminster was also a factor. The Palace of Westminster itself was reputed to be permeated with 'poisonous dust, probably charged with influenza germs'.[9] A more serious problem was the late nights and the fatigue this caused.[10] The long hours endured by parliamentarians, and the boredom which they endured, were sometimes relieved by the availability of subsidised tobacco and alcohol.[11] In fact, T.P. O'Connor wrote of how the Commons as a social environment could sometimes have deleterious effects on both individuals and whole parties,[12] and perhaps out of concern for this, Keir Hardie, during his leadership of the Independent Labour Party, 'laid down the rule that no MP should touch drink during Parliamentary hours'.[13]

While the claims of Edwardian nationalists that the lives of those members who died in parliamentary harness had been hastened by their selfless service were exaggerated, it seems clear that the health of a not insubstantial number of MPs was impaired, if often only temporarily, as a result of parliamentary service. John Redmond, for instance, was often exhausted at the end of the parliamentary session.[14] As he wrote to John Dillon in August 1906 from Ireland, 'We have had variable weather here, but have been out shooting every day and I feel

5 D.B. McNeill, *Irish Passenger Steamship Services* (2 vols, Newton Abbott, 1971), vol. 1, 13–14, 24–6. 6 *FJ*, 7 December 1909, p. 9. 7 Ibid., 14 March 1910, p. 7. Also see the obituaries of P.J. Power and P.A. Meehan, ibid., 9 January 1913, p. 7; 12 May 1913, p. 6. 8 Lyons, *Parliamentary Party*, p. 158. 9 Barnett Cocks, *Mid-Victorian Masterpiece* (London, 1977), p. 110. 10 Arthur Lynch, *My Life Story* (London, 1924), p. 248; A. Rainy, *The Life of Adam Rolland Rainy* (Glasgow, 1915), p. 357. 11 King, *Asquith Parliament*, pp. 86–7, 91. 12 O'Connor, *Memoirs*, p. 63. 13 Fenner Brockway, *Inside the Left: Thirty Years of Platform, Press, Prison and Parliament* (London, 1942), pp. 221–2. 14 John Redmond to John Dillon, 21 March 1905, DP, Ms 6747/133; John Redmond to John Dillon, 31 July 1906, ibid., Ms 6747/180.

quite recovered from London – the last month which nearly knocked me over.'[15] J.G.S. MacNeill (1887–1918) found that with the 'abruptness of the change from my tranquil life in Dublin to the strenuousness of party warfare in the House of Commons, my health gave way', and the biographer of Edward Blake (1892–1907) has written that 'There is no doubt that, from the material viewpoint, his Irish career was a losing battle, for his health was seriously impaired by overwork.'[16]

VII

The evidence considered here suggests that if the standard of living of Irish MPs after 1900 was better than that of their late Victorian predecessors, living in London and working at Westminster continued to pose significant financial problems for many Edwardian members.[17] Granted, it seems clear that Irish members were much more socially and culturally integrated within the House of Commons than in 1880, while beyond Westminster the substantial number of Irish MPs who were associated with the National Liberal Club illustrates the close political and social links between the Irish and Liberal parties. However, the image of these years which is most vivid is not the MP using the House of Commons 'as a kind of step ladder for climbing into the drawing rooms of London',[18] but of the often bored backbencher in his lodging-house 'looking at the four walls' or 'wandering aimlessly around the House striving to kill time'.[19] Such experiences should be acknowledged without immediately being juxtaposed with those of the men of 1916.

15 John Redmond to John Dillon, 17 August 1906, ibid., Ms 6747/183; *FJ*, 2 December 1912, p. 6.   **16** J.G.S. MacNeill, *What I have Seen and Heard* (London, 1925), p. 259; M.A. Banks, *Edward Blake: Irish Nationalist* (Toronto, 1957), p. 343.   **17** Jackson, *The Ulster Party*, pp. 92–3.   **18** *Hansard*, 4th series, vol. 116, col. 688 (20 December 1902).   **19** *Longford Leader*, 23 November 1912, p. 4.

White, black and green: racialising Irishness in Victorian England

CORA KAPLAN

'Race', wrote the anatomist and popular ethnologist Robert Knox in 1850, 'is everything: literature, science, art, in a word, civilization, depend upon it.'[1] Challenging the environmental and monogenetic explanations of human origin and difference that had dominated racial thinking in Britain in the first half of the century, Knox revised and elaborated older typological, polygenetic theories of race for the Victorians. His 'new sense' of race was less 'new' in its scientific detail than its comprehensive explanatory reach, its assertion that political and social explanations of intra-national and international conflict were redundant in the face of the determining, and unchanging, effects of racial difference and its equally natural corollary, racial antagonism. Races were fixed and immutable in known historical time in Knox's view, and he believed that each race was unique both in its character and its physiology. While he refused to order them hierarchically, it is perfectly clear from the attributes with which he endowed them that his own 'Saxon' or, as he preferred to call it, 'Scandinavian' race was top of the heap.

The Races of Men: A Fragment (1850) was a compilation of the lectures given by Knox at the 'Philosophical and Popular Educational Institutions of England', in Newcastle, Birmingham and Manchester in the mid-forties.[2] While Races of Men certainly reinforced the case for Saxon superiority and Saxon hatred of the 'Negro' and the 'dark races' more generally, its most provocative claims focused on the difference and disunity among the white races. In hindsight, he argued, the theories advanced in his lectures should be read as a prescient forewarning of the 1848 revolutions – a prediction of 'the coming war of race against race, which has convulsed Europe during the last two years.'[3] For at the core of Knox's displacement of political or national struggles with the rationale of race, was the reinterpretation of British and European conflicts as wholly racial in origin and effect. The opening chapters of The Races of Men led with the unyielding distinction and innate hostility between Saxon and Celt, whether the 'Caledonian' Celt of northern Scotland or those of France or Ireland. Dismissing environmental arguments for the development or alteration of racial

---

1 Robert Knox, The Races of Men: A Fragment (Philadelphia, PA, 1850) p. 7. This first American edition appeared in the same year as the English and has been reprinted in facsimile by Mnenosyne Publishing, Miami, FL). 2 Knox, Races of Men, p. 22. 3 Ibid., p. 20.

types as tired and discredited theories favoured by 'utopians' and 'universalists',
Knox argued for the self-evidence of the immutability of racial physiology and
character. 'To me', he insisted, 'the Caledonian Celt of *Scotland* appears a race as
distinct from the Lowland Saxon of the same country, as any two races can possibly be: as negro from American; Hottentot from Caffre; Esquimaux from
Saxon.'[4] 'Transplant him', Knox continued, 'to another climate, a brighter sky, a
greater field, free from the trammels of artificial life, the harnessed routine of
European civilization; carry him to Canada, *he is still the same*; mysterious fact.'
These Celtic emigrants, whether French, Scots or Irish, gave pioneers a bad
name, as being 'without self-reliance; without confidence. If you seek an explanation … go back to Ireland, and you will find it there: it is the race.'[5] The Irish
Celt presented the worst example of Celtic personality. 'Is Ireland civilized?'
Knox asks his implied 'English' audience rhetorically, early on in his introductory chapter, expecting a simple no.[6] 'I appeal to the Saxon men of all countries
whether I am right or not in estimate of the Celtic character. Furious fanaticism; a love of war and disorder; a hatred for order and patient industry; no
accumulative habits; restless, treacherous, uncertain: look at Ireland.'[7] Emigration
is no solution: the Celt remained 'a slave in mind' even in the free United States
… for the Celt does not understand what we Saxons mean by independence'.[8]

The address to 'we Saxons' was at the heart of Knox's appeal to the
common-sense prejudices of his provincial English audience. Constructing himself proudly as a Saxon from the Scottish lowlands, Knox, once one of the most
popular anatomy lecturers in Edinburgh, had been brought low by the Burke
and Hare scandal and, perhaps, by his own idiosyncratic views on religion and
medicine.[9] His post gone, he left for London and made a second career in the
forties, at once riding and leading the newly prominent conservative turn in
racial thinking, a turn that in part followed from the ending of colonial slavery,
but can by no means be reduced to its effects. Ireland, at the end of the decade,
was at least as urgent a matter to the English as the economic state of the West
Indies and its newly free population. Knox's brand of racial thinking provided a
biological explanation for the condition of Ireland, exculpated the English from
any blame for its starving poor, and, through its denial of any form of social
amelioration, encouraged a kind of political nihilism towards Ireland as well as
toward Celtic Europe (France) and the more distant outposts of empire. Knox's
view of his favoured Saxons was deliberately amoral and unsentimental,
designed to shock and flatter at once. Their attachment to freedom, for one
thing, was entirely selfish: 'No race perhaps – (for I must make allowances for

4 Ibid., p. 18. **5** Ibid., p. 21. **6** Ibid., p. 10. **7** Ibid., p. 27. **8** Ibid., p. 21. **9** See Adrian
Desmond, *The Politics of Evolution: Morphology, Medicine, and Reform in Radical London*
(Chicago, IL, 1989) pp. 77–81, 388–9 and passim for a good synoptic account of Knox's rise
and fall in medicine. His place in British racial theory is better analysed in Nancy Stepan, *The
Idea of Race in Science: Great Britain, 1800–1960* (Basingstoke, 1982), and in Robert J.C. Young
Colonial Desire: Hybridity in Theory, Culture and Race (London, 1995).

my Saxon descent,) – no race perhaps exceeds them in an abstract sense of justice, and a love of fair play; *but only to Saxons.* This of course they do not extend to other races.'[10] Empire, in Knox's brutal secular logic (his atheism set him apart from his age), could not be rationalised as a civilising mission, or only to the extent that it resulted in the extermination of other races and the unimpeded spread of an exclusive Anglo-Saxon empire. There were no loopholes through conversion or intermarriage. Religion was a property of race; for Knox, Catholicism was natural to the character of the Celt. Nor could interbreeding succeed in diluting or changing the characteristics of race where culture and education would inevitably fail. In persons of mixed race the 'stronger' racial type would prevail. But in any case the results of such unions, Knox thought, counterfactually, were often sterile. Miscegenation as a means of making a 'new' composite race was genetically doomed: 'Nature produces no mules, no hybrids, neither in man nor animals.'[11]

In the 1840s when, as Raymond Williams has argued, the English saw no solution to the social and political problems of their time, Knox's brutalist biologism, more crude rhetorical assertion than supported argument even by the standards of nineteenth century ethnology, did have an appeal. Perhaps more important, for few contemporary thinkers followed it literally, it marked an outer limit of racial logic which defined a more ethically troubled and confusing centre, altering the spectrum of debate and upping the ante for the explanatory power of racial thinking. In the ongoing discussion among historians today about whether and/or how the Irish were racialised by the English in the nineteenth century, it is important to emphasize how very available and au-courant the discourse of race had become in Britain at mid-century, both as an alternative to and a support for political arguments about policies at home and abroad.[12] A highly self-conscious rhetoric of race as the central element of both selves and others dominates the period. A much softer, much more idealized version of the Anglo-Saxonism espoused by Knox was increasingly adduced as the defining element of Englishness, but it was, confusingly, often complemented by something that was equally part of contemporary common sense and that wholly contradicted his thesis – a pan-European discourse of whiteness. Indeed as Knox points out early in his book, the monogenetic theories of his powerful adversary, James Cowles Prichard, who dominated British racial theory in the first half century, made race too exclusively a black and white thing, so that 'on the mere mention of the word race, the popular mind flies off to Tasmania, the polar circle, or the land of the Hottentot. Englishman [*sic*] cannot be made to believe, can scarcely be made to comprehend, that races of

---

10 Knox, *Races of Men*, p. 47. **11** Ibid., p. 53. **12** For a fascinating, provocative analysis both of the debate about whether or how the Irish were subjected to a racial discourse, and the question itself, see Luke Gibbons, 'Race against time: racial discourse and Irish history' in Catherine Hall (ed.), *Cultures of Empire: Colonizers in Britain and the Empire in the Nineteenth and Twentieth Centuries* (Manchester, 2000) pp. 207–23.

men, differing as widely from each other as races can possibly do, inhabit, not merely continental Europe, but portions of Great Britain and Ireland'.[13] Knox's project was to 'race' white Europe, to raise its differences once and for all to the same level of contemporary consciousness as the black-and-white paradigm he rejected, and in this aim he partly succeeded. Yet whiteness in the sense he addressed it, that is as a deeply embedded concept, the default of the blackness with which, as he said, the very word 'race' was associated, was a category that could exclude or include the Irish depending on its deployment. When exclusive it often resorted, although with major impediments, to the alignment of Irishness with one or another of the 'dark races'; when inclusive it disengaged the Irish from them. The Irish became the object of both these racialising terms; were caught, indeed, in their incommensurability. So too, however, were those that chose to use them.

In this essay I want briefly to explore some of the complicated, contradictory ways in which Ireland and Irishness was racialised in the writing and thinking of two of the period's popular social critics, the Reverend Charles Kingsley (1819–75) and Thomas Carlyle (1795–1881), suggesting the ways in which Ireland and the Irish present both a unique problem and an opportunity in their celebration of the Anglo-Saxon and their dreams of a Saxon nationality that was, in another of Knox's grandiloquent predictions, 'about to be the dominant race on earth.'[14]

Buried in the *Letters and Memories* of the Reverend Charles Kingsley, published by his wife Frances in 1876, the year after his death, on a page headed 'Ireland and the first salmon' is a disturbing – and disturbed – passage from a letter Kingsley wrote to her in July 1860 while holidaying with a friend in County Sligo. After proudly retailing his fishing exploits – 'I have done the deed at last – killed a real actual live salmon, over five pounds' ('a new and long coveted experience' according to Frances) – the letter's tone of boyish elation shifts to one of gothic horror. His pleasure in his retreat to the 'lovely' grounds of Markree Castle would be unalloyed, he confesses, except for the reminder of the poverty he had witnessed en route:

> But I am haunted by the human chimpanzees I saw along that hundred miles of horrible country. I don't believe they are our fault. I believe there are not only many more of them than of old, but that they are happier, better, more comfortably fed and lodged under our rule than they ever were. But to see white chimpanzees is dreadful; if they were black, one would not feel it so much, but their skins, except where tanned by exposure, are as white as ours[.][15]

13 Knox, *Races of Men*, p. 25. 14 Ibid., p. 15. 15 Frances Kingsley (ed.), *Charles Kingsley: His Letters and Memories of his Life* (2 vols, London, 1891), II, 111–12.

Politically and psychologically incoherent – guilt, fear and shame denied and avowed in almost the same breath – this passage by Kingsley, the Christian Socialist, novelist and social critic, is often cited by modern commentators as a shocking instance of mid-Victorian racial thinking, one in which, as it were, Irish and Africans are tarred with the same brush. The oxymoron of 'human chimpanzees' places the Irish in that unthinkable category caught between the animal and the human – the stuff of fantasy or nightmare, its gothic implications deepened when Kingsley confesses that the dread such monstrosity induces is as much due to their whiteness – the ineradicable sign that they are his fellow creatures. More interesting than its blatant racism however, is the way in which this passage highlights the difficulty of resolving the category confusion that the Irish poor induce by aligning them what contemporary ethnologists called 'the darker races'. Luke Gibbons, for example, reads this passage as a key instance of the psychic operation of the visually driven discourse of difference which is thrown 'into disarray' when the 'otherness' and 'alien character' of the 'native population' 'did not lend itself to visible racial divisions'.[16] For, as historian of science Nancy Leys Stepan has argued, Victorian anthropology 'had become, by mid-century, above all a science of the visible, physical body as it manifested itself in the marks of racial distinction', and these, she suggests, worked primarily as a 'contrastive concept' that relied largely on a binary difference between dark and light.[17] This hegemonic view is, indeed the one against which Knox was arguing. Kingsley's outburst, above all his childish wish that the Irish were black so that his unwilling response, an insupportable mixture of helpless sympathy and deep aversion, might be mitigated, simplified and distanced by clearer distinctions and hierarchies of race, both points towards the appeal of that contrastive idea of race, and its uneasy application to the Irish.

Yet that very lack of fit with the contrastive concept that results in the ambiguities of racial difference as applied to Irishness, were as useful as they were potentially unsettling to those Victorian Britons who chose to think of themselves as English, and who were interested directly or indirectly in redefining what it meant to be 'English' or 'British.' A colour-coded binary principle might be the dominant framework of racial thinking at mid century, as Stepan and others have persuasively argued, yet it was, for the self-identified English, consistently interrupted by the example of the Irish, as Kingsley's visual crisis with its phantasmagoric representation of the Irish rural poor suggests. The racial superiority of the Saxon, implied, as in Knox, or explicit, as in Kingsley and others, was impossible to make accurately through the difference of skin alone, and yet of all the visual signs of difference – hair, features, body shape and size – skin colour had become the leading and the indelible marker. Whiteness as the cutting edge of supposed otherness makes Ireland and the Irish indetermi-

16 Luke Gibbons, 'Race against time', p. 207–8. **17** Nancy Leys Stepan, *Picturing Tropical Nature* (Ithaca, NY, 2001).

nate referents in redefining Englishness and/or Britishness in terms of a racial imaginary, for, just as the Irish could dismissively be aligned with Africans – 'black-lead them and put them over with the niggers', in one impatient and not wholly ironic sally by Thomas Carlyle – an alignment meant to contract the racial limits of English sympathies – they could also, at convenient moments, be sympathetically appropriated. Carlyle could also, as we shall see, construct the Irish as the symbolic other whose inclusion, because of their whiteness, bound a newly imagined racial nation together.[18]

The nation, as Linda Colley points out, can be imaginatively construed as an organic and undifferentiated whole as against external rivals or enemies, while still remaining, in the minds of its subjects, a collectivity internally riven by hierarchies of all kinds. A 'growing sense of Britishness' in the eighteenth and early nineteenth centuries, Colley writes, did not meant that 'other loyalties' were 'supplanted and obliterated'. 'Identities are not like hats,' she adds, 'Human beings can and do put on several at a time.'[19] Humans also, we might add, play fast and loose with identities – their own and others. Less like costume perhaps and more like wild cards which can take on value and suit to aid the player in a game of identities, Ireland and the Irish often have radically contingent functions in which definitions and distinctions of class and gender, as well as religion and race play a part. Kingsley presents only one example of the sleight of hand through which both Ireland as a place and as a subject both shore up and undermine a brittle masculine identity, and it is his case which I will pursue initially.

Charles Kingsley had a colonial background which strongly conditioned his views of the Irish and of Britain's political role in Ireland. Kingsley's life-long love affair with all things Anglo-Saxon was the ground of his attitudes towards race and empire. These found their most notorious expression in his very public support for Governor Eyre's brutal handling of the Morant Bay Rebellion in Jamaica in the mid 1860s, but they were beliefs that were immanent in all of his work including his fiction.[20] Kingsley's mother, although brought up in England, was West-Indian born, the daughter of a judge in Barbados who was himself the last of five generations of West-Indian property owners. In the parlance of the day she might be considered, by birth at least, a white Creole – although quickly transposed to English soil. Her 'stock', to use the archaic, racially freighted lan-

18 Cited, but without reference, by Francis Hackett, *Ireland: A Study in Nationalism* (New York, 1919), p. 227. **19** Linda Colley, *Britons: Forging the Nation, 1707–1837* (New Haven, CT, 1992) p. 6. **20** My discussion of Kingsley is greatly indebted to Catherine Hall, *Civilizing Subjects: Metropole and Colony in the English Imagination, 1830–1867* (Cambridge, 2002), especially pp. 438–40. She neatly summarizes his career and its contradictions: 'Anglican clergyman, anti-Catholic, Cambridge professor, one-time Christian Socialist, heavily influenced by Carlyle and yet an admirer of Mill, enthusiast for cleanliness and sanitation, a lover of England, author of those paeans of praise to English masculinity, *Westward Ho!* and *Hereward the Wake*, supporter of the South and of Eyre, antagonist of women's campaigns for the vote, Kingsley was complex figure', p. 438.

guage of one of Kingsley's twentieth-century admirers, Elspeth Huxley, might be as 'solid and respectable' as Kingsley's father's 'sound old landed Cheshire' roots, but was presumably open to the common prejudice that Europeans long established in the colonies risked moral and physical degeneration.[21]

Unlike contemporaries such as Elizabeth Barrett Browning, who came to view her father's West Indian connection as a shameful inheritance, the sign of her family's complicity with slavery and imperialism, Kingsley admired from a safe distance his grandfather's 'tales of the West Indies, of the bravery and self-possession of white folks in the face of danger, of the romance of imperial conquest'.[22] Late in life, in 1869, he realized a long-held desire and visited the West Indies with his daughter, a visit that, predictably, confirmed his already settled views that blacks were inherently inferior, and, if human, barely educable, but which equally rewarded the romantic dreams of his childhood in his exuberant and boyish pleasure in the landscape, its fauna and flora.[23] Reading Kingsley on the West Indies, the source and structure of his colonial imagination emerges: its naïve hyperbole and pleasure in nature was joined to, perhaps even enhanced by, its desire for a strictly observed social order based on what he understood as biological inequality.

Seen through the lens of this long-held vision of a tropical, colonial 'paradise', in which 'nature' was ordered to delight but never threaten the European, the near hysteria that Ireland's contradictions induced in him, becomes more legible. For example, in his letter home, he used the verb 'killed' instead of 'caught' for his exploit with the salmon, and the next day he reported he 'killed' five more. His Irish holiday takes on the character of an imperial, possibly sub-Saharan, adventure – big game hunting rather than fishing seems the heightened analogy here – and one which, perhaps, by association leads him back to the image of 'chimpanzees', and hence the troubling absence of melanin in the skins of the Irish poor. But the fantasy of the hunter on safari cannot be sustained. Indeed, the more Kingsley tried to lessen his horror by wishing away the anomaly produced by his oxymoronic 'human chimpanzees', the more becomes wrong with his imperial scenario. Almost immediately a critical piece of political reality intervenes, one which suggests that the formal difference between the

---

21 Elspeth Huxley, *The Kingsleys: A Biographical Anthology* (London, 1973), p.7. See Charlotte Bronte's *Jane Eyre* (1847) for the best known fictional representation of European degeneration in the West Indies. **22** Hall, *Civilizing Subjects*, p. 439. **23** See Ibid., pp. 439–40. Kingsley's *At Last: A Christmas in the West Indies* (2 vols, London, 1871) is, like so much of his work, full of contradictions. Kingsley's belief that the 'Negros' were better suited to Catholicism, for the 'mere Negro … can no more conceive the true meaning of an average Dissenting Hymn book, than a Sclavonian of the German Marches a thousand years ago could have conceived the meaning of St Augustine's confessions.'The argument that 'Negros' could only be taught Christianity through their 'senses' is argued at length by a fictional Catholic priest, *At Last*, 226–30. But Kingsley stops just short of Knox's argument that Catholicism is a permanent effect of racial character; his argument is still developmental.

governance of Ireland and the rest of Britain's overseas empire was a central element of Kingsley's distress. His defensive comments highlight the fact that he
believed that the Act of Union and direct rule made the condition of Ireland and
the Irish an intimate and agonistic moral responsibility for British subjects.
Ireland was an indissoluble part of Britain whose continued economic plight,
thrown into stark relief by the relative prosperity of England in the eighteen-
fifties, could by many be ascribed to British policies and practices before, during
and after the Famine. Answering this accusation as if the dehumanized Irish poor
had spoken it, Kingsley explicitly rejects its genocidal and anti-humanitarian
implications – 'there are many more of them than of old, they are happier, better,
more comfortably fed and lodged under our rule than they ever were' – an
assertion that he immediately contradicts with the evidence of his own eyes: 'But
to see white chimpanzees is dreadful.' Seeking a refuge from his painful feelings
in a parallel world where the game hunter's healthy macho pleasure in 'killing'
lesser species protects him from false sympathies, and where whiteness is an
unambiguous mark of difference and hierarchy not the sign of human contigu-
ity, he attempts to re-enter the colonial fantasy. 'If they were black, one would
not feel it so much', a move which seems to exacerbate rather than dispel his
horror, forcing him to acknowledge an unwilling, even terrifying, consanguin-
ity: 'but their skins, except where tanned by exposure, are as white as ours'.

Kingsley's engagement with Ireland and the Irish poor, should not be construed as a simple set of binary racial antagonisms; the Irish are always, in this
passage and elsewhere in his writing, a shifting term which cannot be accommodated to a simple division of self and other. Indeed his attempt to imagine
the Irish as black leads Kingsley into a paradox that threatens sanity. For the critical last word of this passage – 'ours' – which should represent the secure Anglo-
Saxon identity of the dominant English culture – Knox's 'we Saxons', the racial
category that Kingsley and so many others thought was alone capable of
democratised self-rule – had become, through the hystericised logic of his letter,
biologically as well as politically joined to the sub-human. Whiteness was no
longer a purist refuge but a contaminated category.

Violence pervaded such English representations of the Irish, yet it is often
moot as to who is responsible for it. Kingsley's boastful phallic mastery of the
salmon, for example, may be understood as a kind of transparent, semi-pathetic
compensation for his political helplessness and disavowed guilt in relation to the
degradation he had seen, but a less sympathetic interpretation might see his
serial murder of the big fish as a harmless enactment of a more sinister, barely
suppressed wish, a final swift and Swiftian solution, robbed of its irony, to the
'problem' of Ireland.

Ireland and killing, yoked to questions of social justice, hovered also over
Kingsley's relationship to public issues involving class and racial antagonisms.
For all his supposed security in his Englishness, Kingsley was particularly thin-
skinned when his provocative public postures proved unpopular with the

masses, and the Irish in another role, as murderers rather than victims could conveniently be drawn in as third term in such controversies. When, in 1866, Kingsley appeared at a dinner in Southampton for loyal supporters of Governor Eyre, he was attacked by both local demonstrators and the press. He expressed anger and bewilderment at being 'cursed' for standing up for 'my noble friend, ex-Governor Eyre of Jamaica … cursed for it, as if I had been a dog, who had never stood up for the working man when all the world was hounding him (the working man) down in 1848-49'.[24] Here Kingsley used his very qualified defence of Chartism in the late forties as a reproach to his plebeian detractors in the mid-sixties, a reproach which implicitly criticized the rebellious English poor for making common cause with non-white rebels, and which, through the double metaphor of 'dogs' – as bestialized victim (himself) and baying hunter (the government of the 1840s) – suggests how easily hunter and hunted could change places in his paranoid rhetoric. Revolutionary violence was an international network, a ghastly, racially freighted, global fraternity. In his 'Letters to Chartists', Kingsley criticizes the 'unnatural alliance' of physical force Chartism with revolutionary Irish nationalism, and asks rhetorically: 'What brotherhood ought *you* to have with the 'United Irishmen' party, who pride themselves on their hatred to your nation, and recommend schemes of murder which a North American Indian, trained to scalping from his youth would account horrible?'[25] The Irish become the rogue element in a racialised spectrum of violence and potential violence. Irish revolutionary practices are represented as beyond the pale of even the racial/cultural difference that distinguishes the warrior customs of heathen North American Indians from those of whites. At one level the brotherhoods of vengeful violence or pacific resistance are above – or indeed below – race or ethnicity; at another, the introduction of the North American Indians as a comparator reduces violence itself to a racial attribute.[26]

In his fascinating study *The Infection of Thomas de Quincey*, which explores de Quincey's demonisation of the oriental, John Barrell argues that the introduction of a 'third term' is a characteristic move in nineteenth century racial discourse producing a rhetorical and psychic structure which strategically places a 'that' between 'the here' (the self) and 'the other' – the 'that', a kind of 'other' which 'can be made over to the side of the self – to a subordinate position on that side – only so long as a new, and a newly absolute "other" is constituted to fill the discursive space that has thus been evacuated.'[27] We can see this strategy at work in Kingsley's attempt to solicit Chartists on behalf of his version of radical reform. In his address, Kingsley enjoins the Chartists to remain on the side of Christianity, pacifism and order – his side – which he

---

24 Kingsley, *Letters and Memories*, vol. 2, 195. **25** Kingsley, *Letters and Memories*, vol. 1, 125. **26** See Gibbons, 'Race against time' for a discussion of the racial association of Ireland with North American Indians, rather than people of African descent. **27** John Barrell, *The Infection of Thomas de Quincey: A Psychopathology of Imperialism* (New Haven, CT, 1991) p. 10.

represents as that of the 'radical reformer' as against the 'hell broke loose' 'madness' of revolutionary Ireland, an Ireland conflated with, but in 'unnatural'
excess of, the innately savage Indian. The difficulty of this attempted appropriation and pacification of Chartism is highlighted by Kingsley's need to threaten
the Chartists with two discrete but linked versions of absolute otherness –
Irishmen and Indians. We might see his later rage at working-class opposition
to Eyre as generated in part by the retrospective failure of his rhetorical attempt
to separate Anglo-Saxon workers from an imagined political alliance with
black or Indian subjects, his failure to control in fact, the relations of affiliation
and antagonism within the nation and the empire in spite of his perceived
superior place in their hierarchies. At different moments, therefore, Ireland
could occupy different positions in Kingsley's imperial imagination. It could be
a kind of composite nightmare, the 'hell' of imagined retributive revolt of different kinds of oppressed or marginalized peoples – North American Indians,
Africans and West Indians – even the very Anglo-Saxon workers with whom
he had, however tentatively and patronizingly, made common cause. Or, con-
versely, as in the passage from his Sligo letter, it could represent a people so
degraded and destroyed by their rulers that their abjection provokes horror
rather than sympathy, and the recognition of complicity in their plight triggers
his relegation of the Irish peasantry to a space beyond the boundaries of the
human. When this does not alleviate his distress, they must – in fantasy – be
eradicated.[28] Kingsley's final image of Ireland in his visit of the 1860s, one of
death and mourning, eerily represents this fantasmatic act as already accomplished. Through his 'English eyes' he sees the country as a wholly depopulated
– a 'land of ruins and of the dead' – a vision which, in relieving his anxiety
about their liminal racial and human status, ironically allows the Irish to be
returned to the ranks of the human, embraced in absentia through a hackneyed
elegy to their 'ruined cottages' and 'unroofed hamlets.'[29]

The convoluted violence towards the Irish poor in Kingsley's writing is
overlaid, after 1848, with his denial of English responsibility for the worst
effects of the Great Famine. Yet Ireland's hunger and anger, and the urge to
erase it by finishing off the population for good and all, had a much longer history and is not restricted to Kingsley's idiosyncratic psychology. Indeed
Kingsley's death wishes may have been prompted by similar genocidal sentiments that appear years earlier in the blunter rhetoric of Kingsley's friend
Thomas Carlyle.

In two of Carlyle's 'Condition of England' polemics, *Chartism* (1839) and
Past and Present (1843), the Irish are given cameo roles as degraded and/or
murderous subjects. In *Chartism*, Carlyle acknowledges the long centuries of

---

28 See John Barrell, 'Death on the Nile: fantasy and the literature of tourism, 1840–60', in
Hall (ed.), *Cultures of Empire*, pp. 187–206, for a detailed analysis of this very common genocidal impulse in racial thinking in the period. **29** Kingsley, *Letters and Memories*, II, 112.

English injustice towards Ireland, an injustice deepened because, since God made all men, 'the Sanspotato is of the selfsame stuff as the superfinest "Lord Lieutenant"'.[30] Nevertheless, paradoxically the Irish 'brother man', who Carlyle sees fleeing to England at 'four-pence sterling' for the journey, are a residuum below any imagined 'Saxon' underclass – literally and figuratively a shadow lying across the nation:

> Crowds of miserable Irish darken all our towns. The wild Milesian features, looking false ingenuity, restlessness, unreason, misery and mockery, salute you on all highways and byways. The English coachman, as he whirls past, lashes the Milesian with his whip, curses him with his tongue; the Milesian is holding out his hat to beg. He is the sorest evil this country has to strive with.[31]

This imagined encounter with the Irish *en masse* in the town and on the highways of Britain is fully as sinister and as bizarrely skewed as Kingsley's account of the abject figures who line the Irish roads. The treacherous yet somehow transparent mobility of 'Milesian features' – a reference to the mythical Spanish origin of the Irish that associates them with the racial others of southern Europe – turns misery and inferiority into a mute but provocative mockery of the implied reader, the English, the 'Saxon', 'you'. To this deliberate challenge the 'you' responds in the person of the coachman, a figure not restrained by middle-class timidity or false sympathy, with 'a lash and a curse', both regrettable, involuntary and somehow deserved. Yet Carlyle stops short of arguing that the deformation of Irish national character, its 'degraded and disordered' state as he sees it, can be attributed to racial difference, although something of such difference is implied in his emphasis on the 'government and guidance of white European men' that has so significantly and disgracefully failed to halt 'the perennial hunger of potatoes to the third man extant'.[32] Instead he insists that 'long centuries' of English misrule have resulted in 'oppression' that 'has gone far farther than into the economics of Ireland; inwards to her very heart and soul' so that the 'wretched Irishman' is 'Immethodic, headlong, violent, mendacious.' Once the effects of oppression are particularized and individualized, Carlyle can, on the one hand, advise individual reform or a final solution to which 'all just men, of what outward colour soever in Politics or otherwise' will agree: 'This cannot last, Heaven disowns it, Earth is against it; Ireland will be burnt into a black unpeopled field of ashes rather than this should last.'[33] As the passage goes on, and the Irish become more like animals and less like humans, the temptation to incinerate Ireland, reducing it to 'unpeopled' blackened ground increases. For the Irishman is not only 'sunk from decent man-

---

30 Carlyle, *Chartism*, in Alan Shelston (ed.), *Thomas Carlyle: Selected Writings* (London, 1971) p. 169. **31** Carlyle, *Chartism*, p. 171. **32** Ibid., pp. 168–9. **33** Ibid., p. 169.

hood to squalid apehood', but, by pulling down wages threatens the Saxon native, whom he is driving out 'not by his strength, but by the opposite of strength' with the same fate, as he 'takes possession in his room', forcing the Saxon to emigrate. In their place 'abides he, in his squalor and unreason, in his falsity and drunken violence, as the ready-made nucleus of degradation and disorder.'[34] If English rule is starving the Irish, the Irish poor are getting their own back against the Saxon yeoman, in turn, degrading and dispossessing the rightful owners of English soil. It is not the fault of 'these poor Celtiberian Irish brothers, what can *they* help it? … not a straight or joyful way of aveng-ing their sore wrongs this; but a most sad circuitous one.' Carlyle's conclusion is that 'The time has come when the Irish population must either be improved a little or else be exterminated.'[35]

Two pages back, when extermination is first mooted, the rationale for the general razing of Ireland is the inability or unwillingness of its rulers to develop a policy that can confer social and economic justice. But by turning the effects of oppression into a national character that is a male figure of disorder and vio-lence, and by emphasizing its capacity both to 'infect' and displace the English, Carlyle shifts his discussion into a new register, one in which the Irish are both helpless and culpable, their guilt imagined without detailing a single act of phys-ical violence on their part. Their extermination at the hands of the English is the logical counter to the threat they pose by their very existence, their eco-nomic rivalry leaving the English poor no alternative but degradation, death or flight, and England itself razed and depopulated. Just as we seem to enter the land of ruins and the dead through the end logic of extermination, the argu-ment takes an unexpected and interesting turn. For although Carlyle does seem to play a 'race' card, naturalising the character of the English, he does so as a way of drawing back from the selective genocide of his modest proposal and offer-ing a different way of associating the English and Irish poor. His move to pre-serve the virtue of the Saxon from the contaminating degradation of the Irish also effectively undermines the supposed atavistic antagonism between Saxon and Celt, and thus weakens both parts of the double case he has offered for it brutal resolution.

Here, if not elsewhere, his argument most nearly approaches Knox's notion of immutable racial characteristics. The 'Saxon British' will not and cannot sink to the level of the Irish, for there is 'in these latter, thank God, an ingenuity which is not false; a methodic spirit, of insight, of perseverant well-doing; a rationality and veracity which Nature with her truth does *not* disown; – withal there is a "Berserkir rage" in the heart of them, which will prefer all things, including destruction, and self destruction to that.' This rage is importantly not negative but the very stuff of life, the sign of human superiority, of the liberal self's rejection of oppression: it is partly moralised as a 'genial central-fire' that

34 Ibid., p. 171.   35 Ibid., p. 172.

'deep-hidden' lies below the benign and pacific character of the English; a 'traditionary method, composed productiveness ... justice, clearness, silence, perseverance, unhasting, unresting diligence, hatred of disorder, hatred of injustice, which is the worst disorder, characterise this people.' The English are naturally resistant, genetically immune to the absolute fall that has afflicted the Irish, but their common wretchedness means that 'With this strong silent people have the noisy vehement Irish now at length got common cause ... the wretchedness of Ireland, slowly but inevitably, has crept over to us, and become our own wretchedness.'[36] The antagonisms and differences Carlyle has constructed in the chapter, and the rhetorical violence they induce — from the vision of a burnt-over land of the dead to the melodrama of the coachman's whip biting into the face and body of Irish duplicity and insolence, to the blunt announcement of 'extermination' — is dissolved into a sympathetic identification between abused Saxon and abused Celt, who become a single wretched body, the stoic silent Englishman borrowing noise and vehemence from his unwanted 'brother man'. The war between the Saxon and the Irish is replaced with a monstrous hybrid warrior created from mutual misery and extremity. While Kingsley, in 1848, warned the Chartists away from an alliance with murderous and vengeful Irish revolutionaries, Carlyle a decade earlier goes much further by imagining the alliance as already accomplished — the Saxon's saving 'berserker rage' psychically and dangerously joined to the Irish spirit of disorder.

Structurally considered, *Chartism* is a rambling and discursive book. Chartism loses much of its historical specificity in its pages and becomes the alarmist symptom of a world diseased and wrongly ordered from top to bottom. In Carlyle it is always style, the use of figurative and affective language, that appeals and persuades in place of more systematic or logical argument. As John Plotz has argued persuasively, *Chartism* is a very well-made work in rhetorical terms. It is, as he says, successful in its aim to delegitimise and silence Chartist speech and action by representing their strategies as dangerous, their pain, however real, as madness and delirium, their demands as beside the point and their voice as an 'inarticulate roar'.[37] At the same time as silencing the Chartist Englishman, Carlyle wants to preserve, at all costs, the essential virtue of the Saxon type, as well as warning of his imminent destruction. Carlyle's negative depiction of the Irish plays a central and complex role in this figurative strategy, starting with the parodic appropriation of Daniel O'Connell's stock phrase 'Finest Peasantry in the World' as the savagely ironic title for the fourth chapter of *Chartism*, which focuses on the Irish. Carlyle's negative depiction of the Irish plays a central and complex role in this figurative strategy. The Irish immigrant poor, symbolically the principle of degradation, irrationality and disorder when merged with the native born Saxon, produces but does not essentialise a com-

---

36 Ibid., p. 172. **37** See John Plotz, *The Crowd: British Literature and Public Politics* (Berkeley, CA, 2000).

positive figure of lower-class rebellion. From the spectre of this threatening hybrid and unnatural subject the virtuous Saxon can, through the alchemy of racial thinking, be separated out. Their racial residue of Saxon virtue, even the purer metal of their particular racial rage will survive untouched. While Carlyle argues that all men, including the degraded Irish are capable of some self-reform, his remaining hopes are focused on '*White-cliff*, Albion';[38] indeed, 'The Irish population must get itself redressed and saved, for the sake of the English if for nothing else.'[39]

The racial representations and narrative in *Chartism* are often convoluted and contradictory, but this, I am arguing, is not a sign of Carlyle's confusion about the use of contemporary racial discourse, but a deliberate strategy of moving between paradigms, a strategy which implies, without fully acknowledging, that the level of degradation that the Irish poor sink to, is only in part an effect of their oppression. In *Chartism*, which contains perhaps Carlyle's most extended assault on the Irish, it does not suit his purpose to 'black-lead' them or put them over with the 'niggers', for 'niggers' to him are subhuman and deserve no compassion whatsoever. Instead the Irish become, by implication, a lesser type in the spectrum of human races within Europe – a racial geography defined through whiteness and masculinity, with the 'white European man' as its figure – and a type whose fate is too closely tied to that of England to warrant the always threatened extermination that is the fail-safe if 'reform' in all its senses becomes impossible.

Perhaps the real scandal of Carlyle's representation of the Irish in *Chartism* is less the revival of the tired caricature of national character with its racial clichés, but the wholly instrumental role that Ireland and the Irish play in a drama which so obviously cares only about the fate of the English. Whether emblematically monstrous or merely miserable, the Irish in Carlyle's writing in the late thirties and early forties are present 'for the sake of the English' rather than for themselves. In *Past and Present* he picks up on the much circulated story of a case that came up in the Stockport assizes in 1841 in which an Irish 'Mother and a Father ... arraigned and found guilty of poisoning three of their children, to defraud a "burial society" of some £3 8s. due on the death of each child: they are arraigned, found guilty; and the official authorities, it is whispered, hint that perhaps the case is not solitary, perhaps you had better not probe farther in that department of things.' Ventriloquising the English common-sense response – '"Brutal savages, degraded Irish," mutters the idle reader of Newspapers' – Carlyle sees this incident as 'worth lingering on', since it is a classic example of English attitudes towards the Irish – 'the depravity, savagery and degraded Irishism being never so well admitted' – and a handy emblematic instance of the failure of British politics or economics to feed the poor. To rescue this hapless pair from the indifference of the thoughtless read-

---

38 Carlyle, *Chartism*, p.202.   **39** Ibid., p.172.

ers he brings them into a racial, religious and national fold: 'In the British land, a human Mother and Father, of white skin and professing the Christian religion, had done this thing; they, with their Irishism and necessity and savagery, had been driven to do it.'[40] As in *Chartism*, Carlyle makes the Irish represent the 'savagery' of a degraded and desperate poor – throwing an implicit *cordon sanitaire* around the English. At the same time, for the Irish in England to serve as exemplars of the extremity to which the poor in general are driven they must be included within a generously configured racial, religious and political nation, both white and Christian. For all Carlyle's tactical contempt for the unexamined prejudice of the 'idle reader of Newspapers', the passage relies for its effect by appealing to just such prejudices. The implication is that if such a crime were committed by black subjects in Britain, it could only represent a wholly innate savagery, all but outside the community of the European human, and therefore not worth lingering on. At the end of *Past and Present* Carlyle uses another 'Irish' vignette plucked from the media to illustrate the violence that follows from the denial, on ethnic or religious grounds, of human fellowship. A poor 'Irish Widow' in Scotland, denied help from all the charitable institutions comes down with typhus 'and infected her Lane with fever, so that "seventeen other persons" died of fever there in consequence'. The 'seventeen other persons' are implicitly British – 'Nothing is left but that she prove her sisterhood by dying, and infecting you with typhus.'[41] The victims of failed sympathy, the Irish remain, in *Past and Present*, agents, however passive, of contagion and death.

These representations of the Irish and Ireland precede the two visits that Carlyle made to Ireland later in the 1840s, visits triggered by the somewhat surprising relationship struck up in 1845 between leading activists in the Young Ireland movement, who had approached Carlyle because they admired *Sartor Resartus* and saw Carlyle's critique of English rule as making him a likely convert to the cause of Irish independence. Carlyle's friendship with Charles Gavan Duffy, and their sojourns together in Ireland in September 1846 and the summer of 1849, focused Carlyle's attention on Ireland's fate and future in its own right, but the trips did little to shift his earlier views of the Irish, and nothing to persuade him that independence would help their situation; indeed, his class, religious and racially-bound authoritarianism was deepened by his experience, although a visit to Lord George Hill's model farm at the end of his second trip, offered a gleam of hope for the improvement of the country's agriculture which was one of the main elements in his hope for change.[42] The ever-present sight of impoverished men, women and children during his travels distressed him greatly. But his distress – triggered by observing the degrading

---

40 Carlyle, *Past & Present*, in Shelton (ed.) *Thomas Carlyle: Selected Writings*, pp. 261–2. **41** Carlyle, *Past & Present*, p. 280. **42** See Fred Kaplan, *Thomas Carlyle* (Cambridge, 1983), chapter 13, for a brief account of these journeys and Carlyle's relationship to Young Ireland.

unproductive labour that the workhouse imposed on its inmates as well as the poverty – found, as ever, expression in the language of violence: it seemed better to 'shoot a man rather than train him (with heavy expense to his neighbours) to be a deceptive human *swine*'.[43]

Ireland and the Irish remain an unhappy issue for Carlyle. His role as social critic cannot quite exempt him from complicity with the misrule of the state that governs it or the state's proxy, capital's misguided economic managers – white European men all, like himself. Nor can Carlyle's invocation of the larger categories of whiteness and Britishness to include the impoverished Irish in Britain as brothers and sisters, while reserving an exalted space for the Saxon, quite exorcise the misery and rage induced in him by Ireland's predicament, which included the difference and inferiority of its Celtic population, a difference that is always figured as in excess of the recognized effects of centuries of mismanagement and oppression. Never willing to blame the Irish for their plight, nor to let them off the hook, nor to leave them to their own devices, too willing to credit them with all the vices of men and none of their resources or virtues (all allocated to the Saxon people), the paradox that results cannot be psychically managed, but became for Carlyle, as for Kingsley, the internal as well as the external signs that all was not well not only within England but within that masculine self-construction, the English self.

1849 was not only the year of Carlyle's trip to Ireland with Duffy, it was the year of the writing and publication of Carlyle's most notorious expression of his racial views, the 'Occasional Discourse on the Negro Question' which appeared in *Fraser's Magazine* at the end of the year, and was later retitled, republished and aggressively circulated by him as 'Occasional Discourse on the Nigger Question'. The two issues – Ireland and the West Indies – were for him deeply connected. The rage at the immiseration of 'white Christians' in Britain, including those lesser types of Celtic Catholics with their 'Irishisms', and the residual guilt that it induced, becomes projected outward in 'The Negro Question' onto idle 'Quashee', the caricatured Jamaican freedman who refuses the discipline of plantation labour.[44] 'Quashee' was a racial construct both ethnically and physically at a safe distance from Great Britain. His new freedom to sell or withhold his labour incited in certain elements of the white metropolitian imagination a guilt-free, murderous fantasy of order undemocratically imposed, of rebellions brutally suppressed – of violence, in short, that can go

43 Thomas Carlyle, *Reminiscences of My Irish Journey in 1849*, ed. J.A. Froude (London, 1882), pp. 175–6. 44 The frustrated Carlyle could concede that if the landlords seized all the crop for rent, it was 'understandable that the Irish peasants declined to work *and* starve also.', Kaplan, *Thomas Carlyle*, p. 340. The independence of the free black peasantry in contrast received no such acknowledgement and their idleness was attributed to their near animal status, see 'Occasional Discourse on the Negro Question', *Fraser's Magazine*, 40 (December 1849), or its revised version 'Occasional Discourse on the Nigger Question', reprinted in *English and Other Critical Essays* (London, 1964).

unpunished, that does not somehow miss its mark and shoot the shooter. Carlyle and Kingsley's defence of Governor Eyre is anticipated in their writing from the late 1830s forward. As for Kingsley, Carlyle's racialised representation of Ireland and the Irish poor was bound up with a retro-romance with England as a 'Saxon' land, a romance joined to their frustration with the failure of the resistant and rebellious poor within England to listen to the advice of leading intellectuals. Carlyle's *Chartism* ends with a hymn to the spread of empire through Saxon emigration.[45] Carlyle and Kingsley shared a vision of a future empire run by Saxons in which supposedly inferior races were properly disciplined and subordinated. A very wide range of public figures from the broadest political spectrum admired Carlyle. Engels and Duffy, from their different standpoints, mistook his ferocious anti–utilitarianism as part of a progressive critique of capitalism and colonialism. In fact it was often a reactionary modernity that Carlyle espoused – one that depended in its view of home and empire on both vertical and horizontal hierarchies of racially defined subjects, whose own rational as well as embodied assessment of the injuries of capitalism, class and colonialism must be rejected and silenced. That Ireland and the Irish, for Knox, Carlyle or Kingsley, could not, first or finally, be conflated with what they regarded as the subhuman African, does not lessen the centrality of race in their representation of them.

'No race interests us so much as the Saxon',[46] wrote Knox in his introduction to *The Races of Men*, and perhaps that ethnically solipsistic statement is the guiding principle to understanding the engagement of the English or at any rate English-identified Victorians with the plight of the Irish, whether in Ireland or in Britain and with the racial attributes of Irishness. Yet the repeated imputation of 'disorder' that clings to the description of Irishness, and not only to the Irish poor, whether conceived as innate or cultural, or, more commonly as I have suggested, a bit of both, is one that seems to return to trouble but not necessarily to disempower the very racialised discourses that seek to locate its sources, spirit and practice anywhere but in Saxon England. English thinking about the racial status of the Irish and the Saxon is partly hostage to the 'contrastive concept' that Stepan sees as the ruling paradigm of the age: Knox's argument acquires much of its energy from his attempt to disprove it with a racially purist theory that, for Carlyle at least, would have rendered England and Britain ungovernable. What I have tried to suggest in this short piece on the varieties and continuities in such thinking is that while Knox's exaggerated claims for race as the monocausal explanation for Ireland and Europe's history and present state were key to his self-promotion as a prophetic voice, his instinct that

---

45 Knox's vision was more contradictory. Although he saw the Saxon character as best exemplified in the United States where he was free from the Norman yoke, he also argued that races, including the Saxon did not thrive when removed from their region of origin. **46** Knox, *Races of Men*, p. 15.

Victorian society was ripe to accept racial thinking, if not quite his extreme version, as a central causal explanation in part as a replacement for a misguided
'utopianism' or 'universalism' – registered as a naïve ameliorative, humanitarian
vision of an earlier generation – was largely correct. Nor was he on the wrong
track when he insisted that 'race' as an idea was not only a black and white
affair. His 'new sense' of race was a symptom of an expanding and bleakly conservative modernity that provoked and permitted the 'deniable genocidal fantasy'[47] which all three of the writers discussed above entertained for racial
others, the Irish among them.

---

47 Barrell, 'Death on the Nile', p. 202. Barrell sees this fantasy, among other strategies, as a
way of 'wishing away' the uncertainty that racial difference and relations throw up in this
period, by 'wishing away' the raced group that causes it.

Music hall Unionism: Robert Martin and the politics of the stage-Irishman

PATRICK MAUME

Robert Martin (1846–1905) is remembered now only because of his sister Violet (1862–1915), the 'Martin Ross' of the authorial partnership 'Somerville and Ross'. Yet in his time he was a prominent Unionist political activist and, as 'Ballyhooly', a comic journalist and stage performer. In 1911 the journalist John McGrath recalled how, around 1890, the Dublin Corinthian Club banqueted Martin as 'Ireland's foremost man of letters'. McGrath suggested W.B. Yeats deserved this title, but the Corinthians knew nothing of him.[1] Edith Somerville reprinted verses by a tenant suggesting Robert had received a magic flute from the fairies ('He got it by great intrest as a favour from the gintry/ It was sint to him by finvarra the rular of Nockma').[2] One narrator in the 'Cyclops' episode of *Ulysses* sneers at 'a fellow with a Ballyhooly blue ribbon badge spiffing out of him in Irish'.[3] This paper sketches Martin's life and relates his worldview to the hedonistic Tory image of landlord-tenant relations popularised by Charles Lever and exploited by Unionist and landlord spokesmen, to the anti-domestic fantasies of male audiences, and to the image of Queen Victoria as imperial matriarch.

Robert Martin was born on 16 June 1846, eldest son of James Martin and his second wife Anna Selina Fox. The Martin estate at Ross in Connemara was mortgaged because of famine relief expenditure and never fully recovered. James Martin had five daughters by his first marriage – one virtually sold to a wealthy husband to help family finances – five by his second, and two younger sons, and kept afloat by leader-writing for a London Conservative paper, and becoming a Poor Law auditor (a classic case of nineteenth-century official patronage as outdoor relief for the gentry). Violet Martin's memoir of her brother suggests his attachment to the estate reflected adolescent memories of horse-racing on the strand or roaming the mountains with dog and gun, while his attitude to the tenantry recalled, with nostalgia or bitterness, deference to 'the young master'.

1 John McGrath, 'W.B. Yeats and Ireland', *Westminster Review*, July 1911, pp. 1–11. For McGrath and his relationship with Yeats see Warwick Gould, John Kelly and Deirdre Toomey (eds), *The Collected Letters of W.B. Yeats, Volume 2: 1896–1900* (Oxford, 1997), pp. 10, 14, 21, 35, 118. **2** Edith OE Somerville and Martin Ross, *Irish Memories* (London, 1918) pp. 165–8. **3** James Joyce, *Ulysses: The Corrected Text*, ed. Hans Walter Gabler (London, 1986) p. 255. Martin's song 'Ballyhooly' celebrates the 'Ballyhooly Blue Ribbon [temperance] Band' whose 'temperance drink' is whiskey punch, 'Ballyhooly' [Robert Martin], *Bits of Blarney* (London, 1899).

Robert Martin attended Trinity College, Dublin, then entered the London Bohemian journalism which absorbed many impecunious Irish gentry and their younger sons. Martin wrote for the Tory evening paper the *Globe* and the *Sporting Times*. His life centred on newspaper offices and theatrical first nights; despite nostalgia for Ross he was always restless there. When James Martin died in 1872 (allegedly from trauma when 'ungrateful' tenants voted for the Home Ruler Colonel Nolan in a by-election), Robert leased out the house, only occasionally visiting to shoot woodcock.

In 1877 he returned to Dublin, becoming active in journalism and amateur theatricals. His fine voice, musical ability and physical presence (he stood over six feet tall) captivated audiences. He composed and performed comic songs (accompanying himself on the piano), activities which became the mainstay of his subsequent career. He also composed humorous pantomimes, including travesties of Aladdin and Faust; the elderly Faust, as played by Robert, resembled Gladstone. Martin also raised funds for charitable organisations which tried to relieve distress in the west; these organisations attracted nationalist denunciation as aristocratic patronage aimed at perpetuating deference. For the rest of his life he was 'Bob' to friends, 'Master Robert' to tenants and 'Ballyhooly' to audiences, readers and casual acquaintances.

The Land War and agricultural depression extinguished Martin's rental income; his agent embezzled rents, despoiled the property, and eventually absconded to Canada. His exposure had been delayed because Martin accepted the agent's claim that the tenants could not pay.[4] Martin worked for pro-landlord groups as an emergencyman, organising labour and supplies for boycotted individuals and caretakers for evicted farms, and narrowly escaped assassination. Violet believed the unpopularity and isolation associated with these events matured him.[5]

In 1886 he married Constance Roche, widow of a Cork landowner. Connie was somewhat older and wealthier than him; his family thought she had Jewish blood (her maiden name was Schmidt). They had one daughter, Barbara. The marriage was troubled by Robert's flirtations and Connie's drinking; although she was on friendly terms with Violet, Robert's mother disliked her, and she remained an outsider in the wider Martin family circle.[6]

Robert's household moved to London and resided in Bayswater. Besides his theatrical and literary work (he helped his sister and cousin with publishers), Robert addressed Unionist by-election meetings. A Liberal obituarist commented ironically that he inherited the oratorical talent of his anti-Union great-grandfather Charles Kendal Bushe.[7] In March 1887, when he spoke 'as a boy-

---

4 Maurice Collis, *Somerville and Ross: A Biography* (London, 1968), pp. 50–1. **5** Violet Martin's fragmentary memoir (*Irish Memories,* pp. 3–40) breaks off with the early 1880s. **6** Collis, *Somerville and Ross,* p. 74; Gifford Lewis (ed.) *The Selected Letters of Somerville and Ross* (London, 1989) pp. 156, 213. **7** *Galway Express,* 16 September 1905 p. 3, 23 September 1905

cotted man and on Land League topics' at a Derbyshire by-election, 'He actually reduced the miners to tears'.[8] A speech to the Lincoln Primrose League drew denunciations from the New Ross Town Commissioners:

> Mr Martin recited many incidents showing the cruel character of boycotting ... at New Ross in Wexford, where being unable to secure a vehicle on account of the boycotting, he had to walk eleven miles with food for starving men, and when he got there he found them without water, as the National League had poisoned the wells. After great difficulty he got some barrels of water sent to the men, and by that means the decrees of the League were set at naught (applause).

The (National League) Town Commissioners denied wells had been poisoned, quoting reports by the local JPs, the RIC district inspector, and the clerk of petty sessions. One member commented, 'This Bob Martin must have as much strength as he has the power of lying, when he says he carried food eleven miles'; another referred to 'the means which the ILPU are employing against Home Rule, in England ... He was introduced ... as "Honest Bob Martin"... he should be called "Bob the Liar".'[9] Others reacted differently. Martin was elected to the Carlton Club for his political services, and considered this the greatest honour he received.[10]

In spring 1888 Robert's mother and two unmarried sisters (including Violet) returned to Ross. The tenants became outwardly deferential, and Robert visited regularly, sang comic songs and physically expelled drunks at the tenants' New Year dance. He thought of establishing part-time residence but soon grew bored.[11] In February 1891 Martin oversaw governmental famine relief in Connemara. On 13 April Lady Zetland, spouse of the lord lieutenant, passed Ross while inspecting relief works, accompanied by Robert. The Martins organised a torchlight welcome by their tenants, and a local singer rendered Robert's comic songs. Robert led cheers for the Zetlands, Balfour, the Martins, and the queen; one newspaper subsequently praised 'a Galway landlord and his tenants [who] united to give a true Irish *caed mille failthe* [*sic*] to an illustrious visitor'.[12] When Parnell and the Conservative Cabinet Minister W.H. Smith died on the same day, Martin composed sententious verses contrasting Smith's honoured record with the Luciferian fall of Parnell.[13]

---

p. 3, 30 September 1905 p. 3. **8** Violet Martin to Edith Somerville, 27 March 1887, in Lewis, *Selected Letters*, p. 39. **9** Irish Press Agency Leaflets, No. 42, *Irish 'Unionist' Tactics in England and Scotland: An Astounding Falsehood and its Exposure* (published by the London-based Irish Press Agency for circulation to newspapers and as election leaflets); *Wexford People*, 29 February 1888. **10** *Galway Express*, 30 September 1905 p. 3 (article reproduced from *Sporting Times*). **11** Collis, *Somerville and Ross*, pp. 73–4, 76–82. **12** Lewis, *Selected Letters*, pp. 170–4. **13** *Bits of Blarney*, pp. 80–1.

Lever's earlier picaresque novels end with the exiled heir's triumph over his supplanters. Martin's fantasies followed a similar pattern; to his sister's dismay he spoke of redressing his father's electoral humiliation. In 1895 Violet wrote to Edith Somerville, 'I believe two constituencies in England are open to him, and I do wish he could go in for one, instead of this rotten and humiliating game. In '72 Captain Trench ... polled six hundred votes against Nolan's three thousand and when one thinks of the altered franchise and the complete loss of influence on the landlords' side I should say that if Robert got two hundred he would be lucky.'[14]

Martin did not become a candidate, as ultimately his financial well-being depended on a stage career which was incompatible with parliamentary life. He remained, however, a member of Oughterard Poor Law Guardians and Petty Sessions (his experiences as a JP provided humorous dinner-party anecdotes), and frequently came over to vote with Unionists on these local bodies, perform at local charitable concerts, use official contacts to obtain favours for locals, and judge the Oughterard Races. He wrote for the pro-landlord *Dublin Daily Express* (as 'Ballyhooly'), electioneered and attended annual meetings of the Irish Landowners' Convention, but his life centred on London.[15]

Early in 1905 Robert Martin developed kidney disease and retired to Ross, and within a year his weight dwindled from fifteen to seven stone. He spent his last months reminiscing about politics and the Land War. Humorous to the last, he called his nonagenarian mother 'the little girl that brought me up'. He wrote a formal last letter to the Carlton, but was unable to write to his *Sporting Times* colleagues as he was too weak. Robert Martin died on 13 September 1905 in Oughterard. Tenants dug his grave and carried his coffin. He chose to be buried in Oughterard rather than the family vault at Killannin, annoying tenants who had expected funeral festivities.[16] His widow Connie lived at Ross until her death in 1914, when Barbara sold the house.

II

The Martins of Ross, like many of their counterparts, imagined landlord–tenant relations as a familial connection, with their inherently irresponsible tenants consigned to perpetual childhood. The moralist version of this ideology was exemplified by evangelical landlords, such as Lord Farnham, whose 'moral agents' supervised tenant behaviour. Robert Martin preferred the hedonistic version popularised by Lever's novels, where tenants and landlords share a semi-libidinal bond cemented by indiscriminate largesse, mutual drunkenness and, ultimately, military service. This Tory idyll was supposedly threatened by calculating upstarts

14 Lewis, *Selected Letters*, p. 222. 15 *Galway Express*, 16 September 1905, p. 3, 23 September 1905, p.3, 30 September 1905, p. 3. 16 Collis, *Somerville and Ross*, pp. 136–8.

driven by naked economic rationality, allying with 'patriotic' demagogues and naive English rationalists to present self-aggrandisement as reform.

Lever's preference for aristocratic spontaneity and amateurism over bourgeois calculation and foresight was shown by his working methods. Issuing his novels in instalments, he wrote each episode as its predecessor appeared, with no margin for delay. When offered a bonus for a full text, he declared himself incapable of writing material in advance.[17] Similarly, Martin lived by his fluent journalistic pen, priding himself on never correcting proofs. Much of his material, delivered semi-spontaneously to coteries of family and friends, never saw print.[18]

Lever's books were widely read. Thackeray's Lever parody, *Barry Lyndon*, assumes familiarity with the originals; when advocating land reform to English readers in 1868 George Sigerson felt obliged to refute Lever's claim that Ireland's problems could be solved by compelling absentee landlords to renew their personal bond with their tenants, who as a naturally 'feudal' race allegedly desired personal rule unfettered by law.[19]

Of particular relevance to Robert and Violet Martin is Lever's *The Martins of Cro' Martin* (1856), loosely based on the Martins of Ballinahinch, whose massively-indebted Connemara estates went bankrupt during the Famine, relief efforts hastening the final collapse. The heiress Mary died in childbirth after emigrating to Canada, where her descendants made a new life. Later, a visiting Canadian Martin inspired Somerville and Ross's first novel, *An Irish Cousin*.[20]

Echoes of this plot occur in some of Robert Martin's stories. In 'St Patrick's Day in the Morning', the Ballyblake estate (its Connemara location indicated by placenames) is acquired by an English insurance company, as was Ballinahinch under the Encumbered Estates Court. In Martin's tale, 'English remedies for Irish grievances' such as whitewashing cottages, fitting them with glass windows and removing pigs to sties, give way to strict rent enforcement and eviction when tenants prove unresponsive. In 'The Submerged Shamrock', indebted aristocrats emigrate like the Ballinahinch Martins, selling out to a publican's widow turned temperance reformer; the story celebrates tenant resistance to her attempts to make them 'drown the shamrock' in water.[21] Some of Martin's sketches are miniature Leveresque tales, notably 'The Kerry Recruit', where a Ribbonman who inadvertently joins the army while drunk stays in the force from loyalty to the young master who enlisted after gambling losses; both die in the Crimea.[22]

Robert's most easily accessible literary work comprises two small volumes. The 1882 verse collection *Days of the Land League* reflects the violence of the early Land War. 'The Irish Tenant' is a Browningesque monologue, in which a

17 Lionel Stevenson, *Dr Quicksilver: The Life of Charles Lever* (London, 1939); Tony Bareham (ed.) *Charles Lever: New Evaluations* (Gerrards Cross, 1991). For examples of these themes in Lever's novels see *Charles O'Malley* (1841) and *The Knight of Gwynne* (1847). **18** Martin, *Irish Memories*, p. 37. **19** An Ulsterman [George Sigerson], *Modern Ireland: Its Vital Questions, Secret Societies and Government* (London, 1868), pp. 11–18. **20** Lewis, *Selected Letters*, p. 61. **21** *Bits of Blarney*, pp. 199–204. **22** Ibid., pp. 63–71.

tenant getting drunk in a shebeen mixes slogans about oppression with memories of 'the Masther's' benevolence and 'the Misthress' nursing the tenant's
dying son:

> That's the way that she robbed and crushed us, and the Masther's a great
> deal worse.
> They were sayin' above at the meetin', he desarves all the people's curse.
> And as one Miss Parnell was statin', that the landlords should all lie flat
> Through makin' manure of our fathers, and talk that's the like of that.

Father Mick's exhortations that 'all the money he gave to my childers, was cash
that he stole from me' and 'while the misthress had silks and satins, it was rags
that my childers wore' appear as demagogic incitements. The revolt of the tenants produces a moral inversion, displayed when the Master is murdered outside
the shebeen and his murderer seeks refuge:

> Give me some drink, more, slantha! Sorry? I cannot tell,
> This new way that leads to heaven, seems the ould way that led to hell,
> Come give me some more whiskey, 'sorry' how can it be,
> How on earth can I ever be sorry for the man who was good to me?
>
> Is it give you just one night's shelther, and you've brought to a bloody
> ind,
> The man you and I, Ned Moran, were proud once to call a frind?
> You've killed a desperate oppressor? well maybe you've said what's right,
> And the man who murthered his masther, shall sleep in my house to-
> night.[23]

'One Who Knew Better Days' describes a landlord's widow – perhaps the 'misthress' of 'An Irish Tenant' – dying of 'famine' in English lodgings, while her
children cry for food and she bitterly recalls helping the 'robber band' of tenants who dispossessed them. This was a standard theme of Unionist propaganda,
based on the plight of landlords' female relatives dependent on payments from
the estate and drawing on established imagery presenting the famine through
the sufferings of landed families.[24] Martin presents tenants as children killing
their fathers and exiling their mothers; the destruction of the landlord family
mirrors the wider attack on aristocratic paternalism.

Despite these parricides, Martin presents the familialist moral order incar-
nate and inviolate in the monarchy. 'Lady M—' celebrates Victoria's assistance to

23 *Days of the Land League* (Dublin, 1882, reprinted 1884, adding some formal verses written
for Martin's Dublin dining club), pp. 5–6. The reference is to Fanny Parnell's poem 'Hold the
Harvest'. The title parodies a pro-Land League collection *Lays of the Land League*, see
Margaret O'Callaghan, *British High Politics and a Nationalist Ireland: Criminality, Land and the
Law under Forster and Balfour* (Cork, 1994), p. 123. 24 *Days of the Land League*, pp. 8–9.

the widowed Lady Mountmorres, boycotted after the shooting of her impecunious husband during the Land League agitation in Connacht. Here the queen reasserts domestic virtues and Christian Beatitudes threatened by unmanly peasants who hunt women.

Martin presents emergencymen and magistrates in the classic colonial image of the solitary British hero facing down native rabble, standard imperial mythology recurring in Unionist literature from Trench's *Realities of Irish Life* to Marjoribanks' life of Carson.[25] The coloniser's solitary determination shows his self-sufficiency and right to rule; the failure of the colonised to enforce their threats justifies their subordination. Martin's 'Irish Cowards!' assimilates assertion of landlord authority to the deeds of Anglo-Irish imperial soldiers, while the Land Act reflects the threat to Empire from Gladstonian appeasement:

> 'Cowards!' a Society forming in defence of their lives and lands,
> Trying in vain to strengthen the Government's trembling hands
> Upholding the law of England in the midst of a desperate game,
> That's how the Irish landlords have come by the cowards' name …

> See how the thieves' agitation with the Government ably copes,
> Rewarded at last with a plunder exceeding their wildest hopes;
> And they buy off the traitors with money which they steal from the loyal few,
> And say to the landlords, 'Be thankful for the little that's left to you' …

> It was one of those Irish 'cowards' who in Afghan won the day,
> It was one of those loyal Irish who showed the British the way;
> It was Gladstone gave back the position won by many a glorious feat,
> It was Roberts won the battle; it was Gladstone who said, 'Retreat' …

> The fight it may be too heavy, the odds of ten thousand to one
> May beat down those Irish cowards, – it may be their day is done;
> If so, in the day of rebellion Old England may count the cost,
> And sigh for the loyal 'cowards' her Premier has ruined and lost.[26]

Days of the Land League ends with a bitter epigram on the Kilmainham Treaty:

> The Irish 'twixt moonlight and moonshine
> The difference now understand:
> The law of the Land League is moonlight
> And moonshine the law of the land.[27]

25 William Stuart Trench, *Realities of Irish Life* (London, 1869), pp. 70–7; Edward Marjoribanks, *Life of Lord Carson* (2 vols, London, 1932), vol. 1, 107–10; Kathryn Tidrick, *Empire and the English Character* (London, 1990). 26 *Days of the Land League*, pp. 3–4. 27 Ibid, p. 12.

Bits of Blarney, an anthology of humorous sketches, short stories and songs, reflects the anti-Gladstonian campaigns of 1886–92. 'A Parliamentary Candidate' is supposedly the diary of a Conservative landowner, Harry Largeman, parliamentary candidate for the borough of Shackleberry. Like other right-wing Bohemians on the make in the metropolis, Martin adopts the persona of a deep-rooted English gentleman beset by cosmopolitan adventurers mouthing un-English Radical slogans: 'My opponent is Adolphus Dryberger, a Radical Jew, whose programme is redolent of the Land of Promise. His territorial possessions consist of a doubtful carpet bag, while his acquaintanceship with Shackleberry dates from his becoming the Radical candidate … a week after the vacancy occurred.' Martin attacks Gladstonian claims that Liberal by-election victories after 1886 indicated growing British support for Home Rule. The election turns on anti-vaccination and Largeman's alleged failure to employ Shackleberry tradesmen ('my ancestors employed Shackleberry tradesmen before Dryberger's progenitors escaped from Judea'). Dryberger denounces Largeman's Catholic grandmother; Largeman's references to the Liberals' Catholic allies are dismissed – 'the Irish are Irish and therefore excusable'. Just before polling a Liberal clergyman falsely accuses Largeman of adultery. Martin concludes ironically:

> The result of the poll was described as a GREAT RADICAL VICTORY – DRY-BERGER 3,360: LARGEMAN 3,325. This is the 'flowing tide', 'the nation's voice', 'the condemnation of the Government', etc. And yet the Government or the Opposition had nothing whatever to do with the result.[28]

In a comic song, 'Donegal', a bath (lost by an English tourist) is discovered in Ireland, and the corporation, lord mayor and city marshal gaze in bewilderment. A councillor uses it and catches cold; the bath is denounced as unnatural and its owner savagely chastised. This satirises nationalist use of civic ceremonial (when tried for sedition in September 1887, T.D. Sullivan, lord mayor of Dublin, processed to court accompanied by the robed corporation and civic officers). Martin's audience are assured that these titles and accoutrements conceal unwashed savages.[29]

Somerville and Ross were acutely aware of their semi-marginalised position as unmarried women within an extended family that was both supportive and stifling, and this influenced their suffragism. Martin, in contrast, revelled in headship of the family without taking its responsibilities too seriously. The sporting press and music halls lay beyond Victorian respectability and favoured humour more risqué than that found in mainstream publications.[30] Consciously addressing a male audience, Martin voices misogynistic suspicion of domesticity.

---

28 Ibid., pp. 37–41. **29** Ibid., pp. 116–18; Marjoribanks, *Life of Carson*, vol. 1, 117–18. **30** Donald Thomas, *The Victorian Underworld* (London, 1998), pp. 184–8

The identification of Liberalism with Protestant nonconformity and temperance drove brewers, publicans and music-hall habitués to Tory defenders of aristocratic and proletarian hedonism against self-righteous bourgeois interference. Such Tories feared enfranchised women would extend domestic values into the political sphere, endangering havens of male camaraderie and self-indulgence. If Martin's images of carefree drunkenness, dirt and violence discount nationalist claims to equal citizenship, they also fantasise escape from social constraints. His imagined Ireland is conflated with the alcoholic nirvana desired by male music-hall listeners and readers of sporting papers, threatened by a common enemy.

Bits of Blarney features misogynistic ridicule of female Radical activists and temperance reformers. Miss Sarah Jenkins, a Liberal platform speaker 'found that a little personal knowledge of the Emerald Isle would be decidedly useful when she was taken to task in her geography by a man of Unionist politics, who suffered from the disadvantage of having lived in Ireland the greater part of his life'. She leaves Peckham Rye for Ennis, assuming that Clare, as the most disturbed part of Ireland, is most visibly oppressed. After mishaps on the ramshackle Irish railways and an uneasy perch on an outside car whose jarvey tries to ingratiate himself by praising the suffering landlords, she arrives at the Liberator's Arms Hotel, Ennis. The food, beds, and ginger-beer ('Miss Jenkins was a teetotaller') are 'archaeological unpleasantries'; local nationalists exude 'an atmosphere of whiskey hateful to her soul'. Martin continues:

> Feeling sad and extremely dirty, Miss Jenkins walked by the seashore, when suddenly she beheld an establishment which bore the label of 'Sea Baths'. Here, then, at last was cleanliness, and Miss Jenkins was not slow to avail herself of the chance. In she went, and soon found herself enjoying a large and thoroughly comfortable bath.
>
> Miss Jenkins was a happy woman for the first time since she had left home. She rolled in the water in delight, and, suddenly seeing a string above her, in her old-maidish joy she pulled what she believed to be the string of a shower-bath, and a dash of water came which missed her. She pulled again, this time without result. Then a third pull was equally ineffectual. At last she looked. Through the open trap she saw a man with a bucket of water in his hand gazing at her nude form.
>
> 'If you keep pushing to the westward', he said, 'I'll give ye the full body of the strame'.

* * *

Miss Jenkins has left the Liberator's Arms for England.[31]

---

31 *Bits of Blarney,* pp. 187–91.

The male reader is invited to share the physical sensations of Miss Jenkins, to visualise her – participating in her symbolic violation – and feel she deserved it as a meddling prig. The story also foreshadows Somerville and Ross's humorous emphasis on Irish dirt and disorder and satire on visiting English reformers.

Alcoholic jocularity becomes sentimentality when the maternal Queen Victoria is evoked. 'Hearts around the Queen' cites Victoria's charitable appeals for survivors and dependents after naval and military incidents and industrial accidents while inviting its audience to mourn her son-in-law Prince Henry of Battenberg, dead of fever in 1896 during the conquest of Ashanti:

> Only a woman after all –
> The poorest understand,
> Only a woman after all,
> The Queen who rules the land.
> And, therefore, must all hearts be true,
> Who know what sorrows mean;
> The song goes up, 'God comfort you!'
> From hearts around the Queen.[32]

Royal visits to the central imperial military hospital at Netley, overlooking Southampton Water, symbolise the familial bond uniting her subjects:

> The sight that to some most joy affords
> Is the old Queen sitting in Netley wards
> With her wounded soldiers around her;
> It shows how our Queen played a woman's part
> And the good deeds born of a noble heart
> Are the gems with which Fame has crowned her.[33]

This imagery extends to the prince of Wales in 'The Old Woman of Elbow Lane'. During the prince's 1885 visit to Ireland the Dublin sanitary officer, Sir Charles Cameron (a member of the Corinthian Club) showed him a Dublin tenement. Martin contrasts nationalist stridency with the old woman's recognition of the prince's kindness and concern.[34]

III

Many 1880s Unionists employed a Leveresque idiom to present the Irish as a race of clowns who neither desired nor understood equal citizenship. They even

---

32 Ibid., pp. 110–11. **33** Philip Hoare, *Spike Island: The Memory of a Military Hospital* (London, 2001), describes how Victoria's visits were assimilated to the 'Lady with the Lamp' iconography established by Florence Nightingale. **34** *Bits of Blarney*, pp. 225–6; Sir Charles Cameron, *Autobiography* (Dublin, 1921).

projected themselves in these terms. Margaret O'Callaghan notes that the memoirs of the Kerry land agent Sam Hussey present a Leveresque 'broth of a boy', while his business papers display ruthless economic rationality. The Ulster Unionist leader Edward Saunderson presented himself as a stage-Irishman to English visitors and engaged in calculatedly 'Irish' taunting of nationalists in parliament, provoking angry responses which 'proved' Irish infantilism.[35]

Robert Martin celebrated the backwoods Irish country gentleman while living in London; his popular song 'Killaloe', about the attempts of 'a French Mossoo' to teach Irish peasants French, celebrates the narrator's vigorous refusal to be civilised – but its jokes presuppose knowledge of French.[36] Leveresque humourists exploited modern forms of cultural consumerism, a mass print audience and a widespread awareness of world events, which Martin could celebrate or travesty. One song parodies Stanley's 'Through Darkest Africa' – after searching 'Darkest Ireland', Ballyhooly decides to 'colonise the nearest public house'.[37] *Bits of Blarney* evokes Connemara ('the Western Highlands') like a tourist brochure. The inhabitants, whom Martin knew to have been involved in violent land agitation, become apolitical equivalents of Scottish ghillies:

> They wish nothing better than to spend the day with those who work in the Western Highlands with rod or gun ... A couple of sporting lodges ... which are inhabited at this time of year, supply them with any notions they may have about the rest of the universe. Wars, foreign policy, elections ... are things as unknown to them as carriages or cathedrals. But if you want to spend a time amongst good and faithful fellows, you will find few better than these Gaelic-speaking Irishmen who live miles from anywhere.[38]

Martin could only maintain his feudal fantasies as a tourist in the land of his ancestors.

Robert Martin did not enter the Unionist pantheon. A planned memorial volume fell through, and Violet, a professional writer whose time cost money, never completed her memoir.[39] He was too southern to interest later Ulster Unionists. His humour was too coarse and aggressively Unionist to be cherished like the wittier and less political Percy French.

Martin's combination of Unionism and stage-Irishness did, however, influence nationalist Ireland. The *Freeman's Journal* denouced the *Irish RM* stories as a prose version of the Ballyhooly Ballads.[40] Arthur Griffith execrated 'a thing

35 Reginald Lucas, *Colonel Saunderson, MP: A Memoir* (London, 1908), pp. 15, 193, 199–202; Alvin Jackson, *Colonel Edward Saunderson: Land and Loyalty in Victorian Ireland* (Oxford, 1995), pp. 96–102, 112, 189–90. **36** *Bits of Blarney*, pp. 34–6. **37** Ibid., pp. 167–9. **38** Ibid., pp. 140–4. **39** Martin, *Irish Memories*, p. 3; Martin to Somerville 10 July 1906, in Lewis, *Selected Letters*, pp. 277–9. **40** Violet Powell, *The Irish Cousins*, (London, 1970), p. 115.

called Robert Martin, which has done more to slander Ireland than any man alive'.[41] He depicted Martin celebrating the Wyndham Land Act with landlord shylocks in 'the Rabbi Ben D'Israeli Habitation of the Primrose League'.[42] Politics may have divided Martin and Griffith, but they had antisemitism in common.

Griffith's denunciations, like Martin's fantasies, had older roots. Catholic and Young Ireland writers imagined the Irish peasant as ideal citizen, exemplifying domestic virtue and patriotic heroism, in conscious counterblast to the Leveresque. Nationalists retorted to invocations of starving gentlewomen and disrupted aristocratic families with images of homes destroyed by eviction and emigrant daughters forced into prostitution; the maternal image of Victoria became Maud Gonne's 'Famine Queen'.

Frank Hugh O'Donnell accused Yeats' *Countess Cathleen* of fabricating antecedents for the grotesques of 'Ballyhooly'.[43] Nationalists who disrupted Synge's *Playboy*, which (like 'An Irish Tenant') depicted a murderer lionised in a Connacht pub, saw it as a stage-Irish caricature of drunken and amoral lawlessness; Trinity students who cheered it as insulting nationalists echoed Robert Martin.

---

41 *United Irishman*, 24 October 1903, p. 5.   **42** Ibid., 31 October 1903 p.5.   **43** Lionel Pilkington, *Theatre and the State in Twentieth-Century Ireland: Cultivating the Nation* (London, 2001), p. 24. See also Gould, Kelly and Toomey, *Collected Letters of W.B. Yeats*, vol. 2, p. 677.

'God Save the Green, God Save the Queen, and the usual loyal toasts': sporting and dining for Ireland and/or the queen

TOM HAYES

'God Save Ireland!' said the heroes;
'God Save Ireland!' said they all:
Whether on the scaffold high
Or the battle-field we die,
Oh, what matter, when for Erin dear we fall![1]

The 1867 ballad commemorating the 'Manchester Martyrs' Allen, Larkin and O'Brien, executed for their part in a botched attempt to free a Fenian prisoner during which a policeman was shot dead, was an early expression of a philosophy of dying for one's country that reached a kind of apotheosis, half a century later, in the rhetoric of Pádraig Pearse.[2] It was a philosophy mocked in the works of James Joyce, whose hero, Stephen Dedalus, as Benedict Kiely has noted, cared not for dying for his country, but wanted his country to die for him.[3] Three quarters of a century later, a much more confident Ireland, in 1990 the holder of the presidency of the European Community, produced diplomats and politicians with wags among them who could say they were 'dining for Ireland'. Obviously rich sauces, fine meats and Montrachet were taking their toll on diplomatic girths. Such remarks came, interestingly, only a decade after the Republican hunger strikes of 1980 and 1981 – when dying for Ireland meant eschewing dining for Ireland (if you'll excuse the strained pun).[4]

Beyond the semantics and word games of treating together dying, dining and 'anti-dining' for Ireland, there was a significant connection between the dinner table and nationalist politics that was especially notable in the nineteenth century. For Gary Owens the banquets that followed O'Connell's Repeal monster meetings were the third act of an elaborate dramatic performance and possessed immense political significance.[5] Similarly, British political dinners of the early

---

1 T.D. Sullivan, 'God Save Ireland', *Nation*, 7 December 1867. 2 Ruth Dudley Edwards, *Patrick Pearse: the Triumph of Failure* (London, 1977); Declan Kiberd, *Inventing Ireland* (London, 1996). 3 Benedict Kiely, 'Joyce's Legacy', in Augustine Martin (ed.), *James Joyce, the Artist and the Labyrinth* (London, 1990), pp. 41–63. 4 David Beresford, *Ten Men Dead* (London, 1987). 5 Gary Owens, 'Nationalism without words: symbolism and ritual behaviour in the Repeal "monster meetings" of 1843–5', in James S. Donnelly, Jr., and Kerby A. Miller (eds), *Irish*

nineteenth century were, for Peter Brett, as much a part of the political process
as public meetings, petitioning and press agitation.[6] This essay sets out to investigate the connections between nationalist politics and dining in Limerick in the
second half of the nineteenth century. To further refine the focus it will also consider the relationship of both to a key element of elite and popular culture –
sport. The political significance of sport does not need elaboration here; one
vignette from William Bulfin's *Rambles in Eirinn* is, however, apposite. Observing
a Shannon regatta, Bulfin noted what he termed the 'Union Jackery' and
denationalisation that seemed to inspire its organisers. With no less attention to
detail he noted also the people chatting, eating, smoking and refreshing themselves – many of them oblivious to the actual racing.[7] In considering the relationship between these two phenomena, I have interpreted dining loosely, to
include all meals, refreshments and drink attached to sporting events.

As Bulfin's example shows, eating, drinking and refreshments continued to
be integral to the sporting experience, even in the wake of the influence of
muscular Christianity and commercialisation in the late nineteenth century.[8]
Dennis Brailsford's analysis of late eighteenth and early nineteenth-century
English sport and leisure highlighted the contribution of refreshment and catering to sport's appeal, particularly to women. The place of food in the festival
atmosphere of nineteenth-century sports can be seen in the comments of
Limerick's own 'Robin Hood' (no less) who noted of a proposed archery meeting that 'A refreshment tent on the ground would not be out of place, and the
sweet strains of a military band would add greatly to the pleasures of the day.'[9]
Archery was the mid-century sport with the highest rate of participation by
women and was very often a majority female affair. Food remains an essential
part of the modern sporting experience, and inadequate or excessive provision
arouses as much passion as it did more than a century ago.[10]

If food and drink were essential to viewers of sporting events, they were no
less important to the participants. Breakfasts were notable parts of the sporting
day for Limerick's first organised hunt clubs.[11] However, one meal was not

Popular Culture, 1650–1850 (Dublin, 1998), pp. 242–69. **6** Peter Brett, 'Political dinners in early
nineteenth-century Britain: platform, meeting place and battleground', *History*, 81:264 (1996),
527–52. **7** William Bulfin, *Rambles in Eirinn* (Dublin, 1907), pp. 60–7. **8** The 'refreshment
pavilion' at the 1884 Limerick regatta was unable to serve alcohol until the caterer obtained
a temporary licence – which proved not to be until the races were half over – leaving many
people without a 'soothing draught', *Limerick Chronicle,* 22 July 1884. **9** Dennis Brailsford,
A Taste for Diversions: Sport in Georgian England (Cambridge, 1999), p. 133; *LC [Limerick
Chronicle]* 11 August 1866. 'If a racecourse were without them [stalls] it would lose half the
charms for the crowd', ibid., 18 September 1866. **10** See, for example, the complaints about
food and drink facilities at Lille for the Munster versus Stade Francais European Rugby Cup
semi-final game on 21 April 2001, *Limerick Leader,* 23 April 2001; the complaints by doctors
that modern stadia are 'glorified beer tents' (ibid.) were also redolent of 1880s debates about
the Limerick Races. **11** 'Sumptuous champagne breakfast for County Limerick Hunt', *LC,*
7 January 1871; Muriel Bowen, *Irish Hunting* (Tralee, 1955); W.H. Wyndham-Quin, *The*

always sufficient for the day – luncheons and post-hunt repasts provided by the hosts were matters of considerable pride.[12] Lucius O'Brien's poetic account of a day's shooting on his County Clare estates pays great attention to the three square meals that punctuated a sporting day. Regarding breakfasts, O'Brien encouraged a hearty appetite to 'nerve your arm' and recommended that eating should accompany talk of previous shoots and of the shoot to come. Come mid-day, despite sportsmen's claims not to eat lunch, all did so. There then followed more talk and an opportunity for guns to be cleaned. Concluding the sporting day, O'Brien versified:

> At dinner time the subject is renewed
> And after dinner all the day reviewed.
> At tea, the same employ beguiles the time
> Told for the ladies now in terms sublime.[13]

Hunting and shooting were not the only day-length pursuits that had to include breaks for food. Cricket was another sport that had to provide meal intervals (and which additionally offered post-event meals), while horse racing and regattas could not reasonably be held without the provision of on-site catering.[14] The sources for hunting and shooting reveal the pre-occupations of society's elite, which, while long on society and sport, are short on political matters, ideologies and tactics.[15] Limerick's elite was mostly Tory, though leavened with some Liberals and the occasional maverick supporters of the idea of an Irish legislature.[16] With such a homogeneous make-up it was unsurprising that the tensions of politics would not impress themselves unduly upon the cream of gentry sporting society.[17]

Political tensions associated with sport were more obvious when the homogeneity of the organising and dining group began to be undone. As the Roman Catholic and Home Rule-supporting middle class increasingly took control of sports events in the 1870s and 1880s from their original organisers, the gentry,

---

Foxhound in County in Limerick (Dublin, 1919). **12** Hoppen noted the 'lavish hospitality' at many hunting meets, K. Theodore Hoppen, *Elections, Politics, and Society in Ireland, 1832–1885* (Oxford, 1984), p. 120. **13** Lucius O'Brien, *Directions for a Day's Shooting at Dromoland* (Ballinakella Press, Co. Clare, n.d. – text dated to early 1830s). **14** See, for example, advertisement for Turret Restaurant at Limerick Races, *LC*, 16 September 1865, and reports of cricket match dinners, ibid., 27 August 1851, 20 July 1878. **15** See reports of hunt dinners, ibid., 1 April 1869, 17 February 1870. **16** Robert Cussen, 'Caleb Powell, High Sheriff of County Limerick 1858, sums up his Grand Jury', in Etienne Rynne (ed.), *North Munster Studies: Essays in Commemoration of Mons. Michael Moloney*, (Limerick, 1967), pp. 401–25; Thomas Hayes, 'The Response of Loyalism in Limerick to the New Departure, 1880–1886' (Unpublished undergraduate thesis, Mary Immaculate College, Limerick, 1996); Limerick County Club, *The Limerick Club Centenary: a Short History of a Hundred Years of Club Life* (Dublin, n.d.), probably published to mark the centenary in 1913. **17** See, for example, Shannon Yacht Club meeting and dinner report, *LC*, 8 May 1884.

political differences were expressed in contrasting attitudes to the symbols of Union and monarchy. In 1860 an advertisement for the Limerick regatta included the initials VR and the exhortation 'God Save the Queen', however, by 1887 the finale to the musical programme played by the Boherbuoy Band at the Limerick Races was *God Save Ireland*. This choice would have been unthinkable two decades before, not just for the omission of *God Save the Queen* – an expression of anti-Union feeling even Home Rulers could live with – but for the adoption of the anthem of advanced nationalism to ritualise a gathering of official and popular Limerick.[18]

The two key areas where food and sport were combined in a setting with latent or overt political significance were celebratory functions such as Harvest Homes and formal occasions such as testimonials, dinners to mark the end of season and post-event receptions. Celebratory functions included Harvest Homes, parties on occasions of some importance to a landlord such as births and marriages, Christmas and New Year festivities and, for the Protestants of Limerick, Sunday School excursions.[19] Many functions involved sports as a sideline, often of an unorganised character. There was a routine to many of these celebrations. Following a welcome from the master and mistress of the house, an address on behalf of the children or tenants was read out in thanks. After a meal, groups scattered about the grounds playing games, dancing, singing, or simply engaging in conversation. Frequently at the end of the day, children in particular were gathered to cheer for their hosts and to sing *God Save the Queen*. The anthem thus ritualised the event for a particular political tradition and contributed to the politicisation of sports that had previously been either absent or understood without question. The highest point of the acculturation of children via organised garden parties, though in this case not associated with sport, occurred on the occasion of the queen's 1900 visit, when a children's day in the Phoenix Park was mirrored by a nationalist counter-party at Clonturk Park.[20]

There is scant evidence for the overt attachment of symbols of crown and Union to sports in the period before formal organisation. Sport was initially a local affair, which, as the processes of rationalisation and organisation developed, came to signify something greater in political and popular definitions of the nation. The *Irish Sportsman and Farmer* asserted confidently in its first editorial of 1870 that 'there is a clear link between a country's history and its sports', and that those sports represented 'the sunniest aspects of its history'.[21] This assertion, coming in the same year as the formation of the Home Government Association

18 Ibid., 25 October 1887. **19** 'Castle Lough, North Tipperary, novelty sports, banquet for 450, fireworks, dancing and singing', ibid., 12 December 1882; 'Kilscannell Sunday School dinner and games', ibid., 15 August 1865; ibid., 31 March 1852. **20** Janette Condon, 'The Patriotic Children's Treat: Irish nationalism and children's culture at the twilight of empire', *Irish Studies Review*, 8:2 (August 2000), 167–78. **21** *Irish Sportsman and Farmer*, 19 February 1870.

to pursue Home Rule for Ireland within the Union, immediately posed the questions, whose history? whose sports? and whose country?[22] The reaction to the attachment of overt political significance to sports events was already underway – in 1866 Fenians encouraged racegoers in Cork not to attend a gentry-sponsored race meeting with the exhortation 'God Save the Green!'[23]

The fact that the anthem and symbols of monarchy and Union were no longer uncontested meant that an important change had occurred. When political elites feel the need to explain themselves and their rituals it points to a growing lack of deference. One correspondent in 1864 noted the sham nature of many such celebrations, denouncing the behaviour of the recipients of landlord largesse as the 'mean crouching of a pack of slaves, under the lash of their master'.[24]

Formal dining occasions, such as testimonials, dinners to mark the end of season and post-event receptions, were more structured affairs where the presence or absence of symbols may be seen as indicators of a complex of negotiation, agreement, dispute and compromise.[25] Post-regatta suppers and banquets were among the most significant in terms of understanding the impact of politics upon sporting society in Limerick. The tensions involved in reconciling men of common sporting interests, but of opposing political, religious and class backgrounds, can be seen in the accounts of those events and of the post event meals.

The Limerick Boat Club (LBC), formed in 1870, adopted a crest, membership policy and set of values that marked it out as an essentially Anglo-Irish institution.[26] In a fit of ebullience a local paper once mistakenly referred to it as the Limerick Royal Boat Club.[27] Though it included both Protestant and Catholic members, it was viewed locally as a Protestant and class-exclusive club.[28] The designation 'Royal' was not deserved because a warrant would have

22 For political background, see Alan O'Day, *Irish Home Rule, 1867–1921* (Manchester, 1998). **23** *LC*, 17 April 1866. **24** Ibid., 9 February 1864; W.E. Vaughan, *Landlords and Tenants in Mid-Victorian Ireland* (Oxford, 1994), pp. 103–4. **25** For examples, see '70 of Lord Fermoy's sporting friends to put on a dinner for him', *LC*, 24 March 1866; 'Dinner for Marquis of Waterford from his sporting friends', ibid., 10 May 1851; '38 County Limerick Hunt members to give a dinner for MFH', ibid., 2 November 1865; 'End of season hunt dinner', ibid., 1 April 1869; 'Annual hunt dinner', ibid., 17 February 1870; Post-regatta banquets, ibid., 2 September 1871, 8, 10 August 1872; LBC Annual Banquet menu cards [microfilm in possession of author]; Post-race meeting balls and suppers, *LC*, 21 September 1865, 11–20 September 1866. **26** Ibid., 5 February 1870. The club crest contains two panels of three lions rampant – historically associated with England. Military officers posted to the city did not have to submit their names to be balloted for admission. **27** Ibid., 16 April 1870. **28** The *Chronicle*, evidently drawing back from the royal tag, later sought to portray the club as neutral in political and religious matters. Following an incident involving the flying of Italian and Austrian flags to celebrate the visit of the lord lieutenant to the town, some locals interpreted the gesture as support for the Italian state and thus a snub to the pope, ibid., 15 June 1871. The paper noted that allowing this interpretation to become common would work only to 'make the club unpopular'. The exclusive membership policy of the LBC (and of the SRC) led to the formation of a third rowing club (Commercial Rowing Club) in the city, formed mainly by

been necessary, but the pretension that it should be so designated was revealing. The LBC's rival, the Shannon Rowing Club (SRC) represented the commercial middle-class, Catholic and Home Rule section of Limerick.[29] Both the competing aquatic clubs also had roots in department stores in the city, many LBC men coming from Murray & Todd and the SRC men from their retail rival, Cannock, Tait & Co.[30] To emphasise the position of each club as the centre of their own particular interest communities both sports clubs also held regular Christy's Minstrels shows.[31] The rowing clubs had, therefore, political, religious, commercial, musical/dramatic and sporting rivalries. One Harbour Board member, discussing the proposal to grant a site for the SRC clubhouse on a pier also occupied by the LBC, expressed a fear that the rival crews might resort to fisticuffs to resolve their differences, such was the atmosphere on occasions.[32]

Regatta dinners were significant affairs at which both clubs were represented for a formal purpose. When the event was solely run by the LBC, the first toast, to 'Her Majesty the Queen', was given signal importance, but, when organised by the SRC, the indication was that the 'usual loyal toasts' were observed. As the SRC was an elite Catholic and moderate Home Rule institution no overt snub was offered to the monarchy, yet the cursory passing of the toast was not without significance. Nor was such a lack of enthusiasm unprecedented. William Thackeray's 1842 accounts of farming society dinners in Leinster similarly reveal the perfunctory approach to the early dinner toasts. Thackeray noted that in Naas, although there was cheering for the health of the monarch and her husband, the toast to the lord lieutenant was received coolly, and, perhaps most importantly, only after these formalities did the 'real business of the night begin'.[33] Later events organised solely by Home Rule or nationalist societies would excise the loyal toasts. Dinners which loyalists also attended sometimes included a toast to the queen, but the gesture would be undermined by a call to toast the pope – perhaps a case of parity of (dis)esteem.

---

men unable to gain admission to these clubs, ibid., 5, 12 June 1880. **29** The SRC entered a boat called *Home Rule* in the first race of the 1873 regatta, ibid., 2, 5, 7, 9 August 1873. The club also marched in a large nationalist demonstration in 1887 along with the GAA and other voluntary associations, ibid., 1 November 1887. **30** The young men participating for their various establishments at the 1866 regatta subsequently became prominent members of the two clubs, see regatta report, ibid., 28, 30 August 1866. **31** 'LBC Minstrels', ibid., 1 April 1872; 'SRC Minstrels', ibid., 10 January 1871. **32** Ibid., 2, 4, 16 August 1870. For more on their rivalry see 'Regatta ructions', ibid., 20 July 1876. Contrariwise, the joint participation of political, religious, and commercial rivals in the sport of rowing did have the potential to reduce the divisions between rowers, ibid., 13 January 1872. This apparent rapprochement was at best short-lived, witness the deep bitterness between the clubs in 1874, when both sought to organise it solo, resulting in two rival regattas being planned, ibid., 17 March to 4 August 1874. **33** William Makepeace Thackeray, *The Irish Sketch Book, 1842* (facsimile of 1925 edition, Belfast, 1985), pp. 271–2.

The degree of attachment of Home Rule Limerick's most important sporting institution, the SRC, to the monarch cannot only be inferred from by the absence of overtly loyal banquet toasts. There are numerous examples of the rejection of loyal symbols by middle-class Catholic Limerick. The riotous scenes following the playing of *God Save the Queen* at a cross-community hospital fund-raising concert in 1884 were a more middle-class response than the earthier country folk's destruction of a Union flag and riot at a regatta in Glin.[34] The thoroughly respectable Young Men's Society dinner in the early 1850s, at which hundreds were seated, saw only a dozen rise for the toast to the monarch, with a considerable number not simply remaining neutrally silent, but actively hissing the gesture. The political outcome of this anti-monarchical feeling was the rejection of an opportunity to present an address to the prince and princess of Wales during their tour of the south-west in 1885. This reflected a considerable increase in antipathy towards the crown and Union compared to the occasions two decades earlier when the addresses to the monarch on the births of her children were merely scrutinised to temper more effusive loyalist texts with less sentimental, more practical expressions of congratulation.

Even before the emergence of the Gaelic Athletic Association in 1884 the process of attaching ideas of the worth of sport to the nation had long begun; the rise of the GAA would simply bring that reaction, literally, to a higher pitch. Limerick at song, at play, at the table was anything but Victoria's family, and became steadily less so as her long reign advanced.

---

34 *LC,* 22 July 1884.

Britishness as an imperial and diasporic identity: Irish elite perspectives, *c.*1820–70s

JENNIFER RIDDEN

In so far as the term 'Britishness' was used in Victorian Ireland, it had strong imperial connotations, especially among Protestants. The importance of empire in the construction of Irish Protestant identity, particularly among evangelical Protestants, has long been recognised. Some Irish historians, such as Donal Lowry, have gone so far as to conclude that 'Ulster's Britishness was and remains primarily an imperial, not a metropolitan variety of Britishness'.[1] However, in general historians have been slow to recognise that many Irish Catholic people saw the empire in positive terms too. Perhaps even more important, historians have been slow to recognise that Irish support for the empire reflected perspectives that were varied, and that were often quite different from English perspectives. Irish perspectives (both Protestant and Catholic) were shaped by various political ideologies and attitudes, by Irish pragmatic goals, and by various non-English senses of identity. Furthermore, Irish colonisers, both Catholic and Protestant, played important roles in shaping British identity in the colonies. The varied forms of Irish participation in the imperial project allow us to assess how ideas about empire affected the construction of British identity both in Ireland and among Irish members of colonial societies.

Irish emigration to America vastly outweighed Irish emigration to the settlement colonies throughout the nineteenth century, and this has encouraged us to forget that between 1815 and 1910 about one-third of the population of white settlers in the British empire were Irish, and that this figure does not include those Irish people who were active in the empire as missionaries, soldiers, or who were in temporary colonial postings.[2] The Irish were undeniably significant and active participants in the 'British' empire, whether this participation was as 'internal others', as junior partners in empire, or as 'enthusiastic imperialists'. To varying degrees they became conscious of their role in the imperial project and they took part in the construction of the identities involved, which ranged from senses of diasporic Irish identity, emerging colonial national identities, and a sense of British imperial identity. Because this empire was not in general controlled from the metropolitan centre by the

---

1 Donal Lowry, 'Ulster resistance and loyalist rebellion in the empire', in Keith Jeffery (ed.), *An Irish Empire? Aspects of Ireland and the British Empire* (Manchester, 1996), pp. 208–9. 2 D.H. Akenson, *The Irish Diaspora: a Primer* (Belfast, 1996), p. 56.

British state, but was instead driven by the efforts of individuals and diverse groups on the spot (although often calling upon the British state for assistance and protection), the perceptions and experiences of Irish colonists played an important role in the development of a British imperial identity, and a role that was quite different from that played by English colonists.

This essay focuses in particular on the roles played by liberal members of the Irish elite in the development of a liberal model of empire, which had quite different implications from those of conservative Protestant approaches to empire. This liberal view of empire made it possible for Irish (and other non-English) people, whether Protestant or Catholic, Unionist or nationalist, to find a place as colonisers within the empire and at the same time retain a sense of their Irishness. Whether the Irish subscribed to Britishness in the colonies as a national identity or as a form of imperial patriotism varied, just as it varied among Scottish, Welsh, and English colonists. Nevertheless, during the nineteenth century it became possible and even advantageous for many Irish people to subscribe to a broad and flexible notion of imperial Britishness, and a notion of the empire as a loose British framework characterised by local variation and the rule of law, within which might fit their colonial aspirations. Furthermore, the network of connections and movements of Irish people throughout a 'British world' in this period (not only between Ireland and the colonies, but also between different colonies, America, and back to Ireland) meant that Irish people at home also became increasingly aware of the ways in which the language of imperial Britishness could be turned to their advantage, and in particular could be used to frame aspirations toward self-government in Ireland. Debates about identity were concerned with pragmatic benefits and power relations, as well as with issues of emotional and cultural attachment.

Ireland provides an interesting case for consideration within both British and imperial discussions of 'centre' and 'periphery', because the Irish seem to shift places from 'periphery' to 'centre' and back again, depending on the context. Irish historians have consistently resisted the notion that Irish history should always be seen in relation to British history, and have preferred to study Irish history in its own right. But they are now beginning to consider the implications of this 'centre' and 'periphery' debate in British history, and in particular for the reassessment of Irish emigration to England.[3] This work connects with the vision of Irish history developed by postcolonial scholars and literary critics in particular, and it links Ireland with other postcolonial societies, whose experiences and approaches to Britain were similar because of their shared experience of being colonised. In this reading, nineteenth-century British or English identity was framed against an Irish 'other'.[4] Catherine Hall uses this

---

3 See, for example, Mary Hickman's chapter in Roger Swift and Sheridan Gilley (eds), *The Irish in Victorian Britain: The Local Dimension* (Dublin, 1999), and Graham Davis, *The Irish in Britain, 1815–1914* (Dublin, 1991). **4** For example, see David Cairns and Shaun Richards,

work to develop a wider assessment of the cultural impacts empire had upon metropolitan Britain. She argues that the way the Irish were perceived within Britain was shaped by the emergence of a racial conception of British identity from the 1830s, which developed in response to British experiences of race in the empire. As a result, the Irish were an 'internal other' in the British metropolitan centre, and were only one step above the black African 'external' other which were so prominent in mid-Victorian discussions of parliamentary reform and of the Morant Bay rebellion.[5]

Some Irish historians have noted difficulties with this interpretation, especially with its tendency to focus on the working-class Catholic Irish rather than on the whole range of Irish emigrants.[6] This forms part of a long-running debate in Irish historiography, but there is also growing awareness that Ireland's involvement in the United Kingdom ran parallel with her involvement in the empire, and that these focuses of Irish involvement in the United Kingdom and in the empire were inter-related.[7] One of the main positive aspects of the Union between Britain and Ireland was that it widened Irish access to imperial opportunities in the nineteenth century, for the Protestant elite and also for Irish Catholics. This awareness of the benefits that flowed from Irish activities in the empire, pursued as colonisers and not simply as a colonised people, created the possibility of a much more favourable view of empire. As a result, Tom Bartlett argues, there was much more widespread and conscious identification with the empire, among both nationalists and Unionists in Ireland, and among both Catholics and Protestants, than identification with the Union.[8] Gearóid Ó Tuathaigh has also recently argued that Irish identity in the nineteenth century was not only constructed within the framework of the Union in the nineteenth century, but also that both British and Irish identity were closely connected with a favourable view of the British empire, as an arena within which the Irish could prosper.[9]

Writing Ireland: Colonialism, Nationalism and Culture (Manchester, 1988); Seamus Deane, 'Imperialism/Nationalism', in F. Lentricchia and T. McLaughlin (eds), *Critical Terms for Literary Study* (2nd edn, Chicago, 1995), pp. 354–68; David Lloyd, *Anomalous States: Irish Writing and the Post-colonial Moment* (Dublin, 1993); Luke Gibbons, 'Race against time: racial discourse and Irish history', in his *Transformations in Irish Culture* (Cork, 1996), pp. 149–63. See also exchanges between Steven Ellis, Nicholas Canny, and Brendan Bradshaw in Ciaran Brady (ed.), *Interpreting Irish History: The Debate on Historical Revisionism 1938–1994* (Dublin, 1994). **5** Catherine Hall, Keith McClelland, and Jane Rendall, *Defining the Victorian Nation: Class, Race, Gender and the British Reform Act of 1867* (Cambridge, 2000). For another interpretation of 'peripheral' impacts upon the metropolis, see Stuart Ward (ed.), *British Culture and the End of Empire* (Manchester, 2001). **6** See G. Walker, 'The Protestant Irish in Scotland', in T. Devine (ed.), *Irish Immigrants and Scottish Society in the Nineteenth and Twentieth Centuries* (Edinburgh, 1991). **7** Stephen Howe, *Ireland and Empire: Colonial Legacies in Irish History and Culture* (Oxford, 2000). **8** Thomas Bartlett, 'This famous island set in a Virginian sea: Ireland and the British Empire', in P.J. Marshall (ed.), *The Oxford History of the British Empire. III: The Eighteenth Century* (Oxford, 1998), pp. 256–7. **9** Gearóid Ó Tuathaigh, 'Ireland under the

As a group, the elite and gentry were particularly significant in empire, not just as settlers, but also as colonial administrators, policemen, members of the armed forces, professionals, and clerics and missionaries. They developed extended networks throughout the empire which provided further opportunities for them, and also provided a conduit through which attitudes and experiences of empire flowed back to Ireland. Because they were frequently in colonial postings or in the army, they were more likely to return to Ireland than were settlers or poorer Irish people. This essay considers a particular group of intermarried liberal Protestant families that emerged in counties Limerick and Clare (including an inner circle of Spring Rices, Bourkes, de Veres, and O'Briens, and a second tier of connected families including the Quaker Harvey and Fisher families). All were involved in a network that spanned the imperial world, and many spent time in one or more of the colonies, or were deeply involved in colonial and emigration policy. This group was Whig-Liberal and Unionist in political terms, they were liberal in religion, and they emerged as prominent opponents of the evangelical crusade in the 1820s and as supporters of Catholic emancipation. They were reformers who saw British and Irish identities as nested and compatible within the framework of the Union. This was possible because they saw Britishness as broadly Christian rather than specifically Protestant, and as an inclusive or umbrella identity. Because members of this group were prominent in debates in Ireland, at Westminster, and in the colonies, it is possible to see how their understandings of Britishness in each of the three contexts interacted.

This essay considers two members of this group of intermarried families – Sir Richard Bourke and William Smith O'Brien. They emerged from a shared cultural and political milieu, and both spent time in the Australian colonies before returning to Ireland, but their political ideas and perspectives on Ireland came to diverge quite dramatically by the 1850s. Sir Richard Bourke was an officer in the British army during the Napoleonic Wars and took part in the Peninsula War, and then retired to County Limerick where he became a landlord and a well-known liberal Protestant reformer in Limerick politics. Between 1818 and 1820 he was election manager for Thomas Spring Rice (MP for Limerick 1820–31, then MP for Cambridge and Whig-Liberal chancellor of the exchequer in the late 1830s). Bourke went to the Cape Colony as lieutenant governor between 1823 and 1826, and then to New South Wales as a reforming governor between 1831 and 1837, before returning to Ireland in retirement. In contrast, though William Smith O'Brien emerged into adulthood in the 1820s and 1830s as a religious liberal and a liberal Tory in political terms; in 1843 he joined the National Repeal Association which sought to repeal the Act of Union; and then he became one of the founding leaders of the Young Ireland movement and was transported to

Union: a critique', unpublished paper presented to the Cambridge Group for Irish Studies, Queens' College, Cambridge, 13 March 2001.

Van Diemen's Land for his role in leading the Young Ireland Rising in 1848. While a gentleman convict, he wrote anonymous articles on colonial politics in the local newspaper. He also wrote a two-volume treatise entitled *Principles of Government*,[10] which outlined his thoughts on legitimate government in general, and on legitimate government in Ireland and the Australian colonies in particular. He was eventually pardoned and returned to Ireland, and then undertook speaking tours in America and Canada, travelled in Europe, and continued a low-key participation in Irish political debate. While there has been much research on O'Brien's ideas in the 1840s and in particular on his role in Young Ireland, the periods beforehand and especially afterward, are not so well known. As a result, the consistency of his support of British imperialism before and after his emergence as a revolutionary nationalist has been poorly understood.[11]

In the 1820s and 30s moderate reformers such as those in this Limerick group usually used the term 'empire' in a number of different but related ways. First, they used it to indicate Ireland's membership of the British core, and to argue that Ireland could use the Union for its own gain. According to Thomas Spring Rice in his 1834 speech in support of the Union, Ireland was as much an equal partner in this 'United Empire' as was Scotland, Wales, and England. The 'Imperial Parliament' provided 'easier redress for many local evils, than [either Scotland or Ireland] could have found in separate Legislatures of their own, swayed as those Legislatures would have been by conflicting interests'.[12] As a result, Spring Rice repudiated O'Connell's assertion that the Union represented the attempted imperial annexation and domination by a foreign English state, and that the Irish were a subjugated people akin to slaves in colonies such as Jamaica.[13] On the contrary, it was the 'Parliament of the United Kingdom; not the Parliament of England' that legislated for Ireland, and Irish MPs were well represented in that Parliament.[14] As a result, Spring Rice and other Irish liberal Protestants argued that the Irish lost none of their identity as a 'separate people' by becoming British, but they gained the opportunity of participating in a powerful British state which gave them the capacity to affect

---

10 William Smith O'Brien, *Principles of Government; or Meditations in Exile … in 2 Volumes* (Dublin, 1856). 11 A recent exception is Richard Davis, whose *Revolutionary Imperialist: William Smith O'Brien, 1803–1864* (Dublin, 1998) also deals with some of the issues raised in this essay. 12 Spring Rice's Speech in the House of Commons debate on the Repeal of the Union, *Hansard's Parliamentary Debates*, 3rd series, vol. 22, col. 1194 (24 April 1834). 13 There is not sufficient space to consider the question of race directly, but the historical debate about this is far from settled. See discussion in Jennifer Ridden, '"Making Good Citizens": National Identity, Religion, and Liberalism among the Irish Elite, *c.*1800–1850' (unpublished PhD dissertation, Kings College, London, 1998), chapter 6; Noel Ignatiev, *How the Irish Became White* (New York and London, 1995); Stephen Howe, *Ireland and Empire*, chapter 4; Graham Walker, 'Old History: Protestant Ulster in Lee's Ireland', *Irish Review*, 12 (1992), 66; and D.H. Akenson, *If the Irish Ran the World: Montserrat, 1630–1730* (Liverpool, 1997), pp. 174–5. 14 Spring Rice's speech in the debate on the Repeal of the Union, *Hansard*, 3rd ser., vol. 22, col. 1179 (24 April 1834).

both domestic English affairs and in the colonies overseas. And so, Spring Rice warmly congratulated Emerson Tennent on his 1834 speech in support of the Union, when he said that,

> [the Irish MP] sits [in Parliament] to legislate … for the interests of the most opulent and powerful empire in the universe … [he helps to extend] the blessings of freedom from the confines of India to the remotest shores of the Atlantic; to liberate the Hindoo, and to strike off the fetters of the African … these are honours which enable us, whilst we pride ourselves upon our birth-place, as Irishmen, to add to our distinctions the glory of being Britons.[15]

One example of the way Limerick liberal Protestants participated in legislating for the empire was the key role they played in shaping the schemes for assisted emigration. Thomas Spring Rice was colonial under-secretary for a short time and was instrumental in the development of the assisted emigration schemes along with his son Stephen, William Smith O'Brien, and Stephen de Vere. In New South Wales, Richard Bourke organised the colonial lobbying for Irish assisted emigrants, and made preparations for their reception. Thomas Spring Rice took personal advantage of these schemes, which provided new opportunities for his tenants as colonial settlers in Canada and Australia, and at the same time he used the schemes to clear his estates.[16] A common Irish liberal justification for this activity was used by Aubrey de Vere, when he argued that Ireland was owed these imperial opportunities as recompense for centuries of mistreatment by the British State. As he wrote in 1850, colonisation

> supplies at critical periods … the "means of amendment" – that is, a blank slate to remould an individual or national "estate" burdened by the original sin of accumulated pauperism.[17]

15 Sir James Emerson Tennent's speech in the debate on the Repeal of the Union, ibid., cols 1297, 1313, 1314 (24 April 1834). As the Liberal member for Belfast from 1832, Tennent was an enthusiastic supporter of moderate reform and of Spring Rice; however, in 1834 he was one of the few Irish Liberals to join Lord Stanley's defection on the appropriation of Church revenues question. **16** Christopher O'Mahony and Valerie Thompson, *Poverty to Promise: The Monteagle Emigrants, 1838–58* (Darlinghurst, 1994). Spring Rice's and de Vere's sons played an important role in collecting information for parliamentary Inquiries into Irish emigration, and Stephen de Vere's evidence to the House of Lords Select Committee on Colonisation from Ireland in 1847 (which was chaired by his uncle Thomas Spring Rice, now Lord Monteagle) was crucial in reforming the Passenger Act. See also Stephen De Vere's diary of his voyage to Quebec, 1847–1848 America Journals, Trinity College Library, Dublin, Manuscripts Department, MSS 5061–5062; Ruth-Ann M. Harris, '"Where the poor man is not crushed to exalt the aristocrat": Vere Foster's programmes of assisted emigration in the aftermath of the Irish Famine', in Patrick O'Sullivan (ed.), *The Meaning of the Famine* (London, 1997), pp. 172–93; and Ridden, "Making Good Citizens", chapter 7. **17** Aubrey de Vere, *Colonisation*

Irish Liberals like Sir Richard Bourke were also active in colonial administration. When Bourke went to New South Wales as a Whig-Liberal governor in 1831, he took with him a well-developed notion of the empire as a framework which provided opportunities for the Irish as well as the English and Scots, and a notion of Britishness that was non-denominational and could encompass diverse groups of people, and was therefore transportable around the empire. He saw his role as one of overseeing the transformation of New South Wales from a penal colony to a colony of free settlement, where the inhabitants would be morally improved to the extent that they could participate in free political institutions. He aimed to make sure that Australia's emerging political and social institutions were constructed within a non-denominational British model, rather than a narrowly English Protestant one, because he thought this would ensure that a corrupt and illegitimate Protestant ascendancy like Ireland's would not develop in the Australian colonies. Consequently, he prevented the Church of England from becoming the state church in Australia, and forced a measure through the legislative council in 1833 which guaranteed funding for all the major churches.[18] He also tried to create a non-denominational education system in New South Wales based on the model of the Irish National Schools system (which he had helped to design), arguing that it would 'alleviate religious and national conflicts … soften social discontents … and eradicate moral vices.'[19] His efforts to allow ex-convicts to sit on juries gained him the support of the Emancipist Party, which was campaigning for political rights for convicts whose terms had expired, but who had previously found it difficult to answer the charge that they had foregone their rights as freeborn Englishmen when they were convicted of crimes. Bourke's view of British civilisation, which involved the belief that convicts could be reformed and morally improved, gave ex-convicts a basis for negotiation with the British state by allowing them to claim Britishness without having to conform to stringent English social norms and models.

However, Governor Bourke's vision of colonial Britishness was contested by other British groups within the colony. Despite his status as the colony's most senior representative of the British state, his activities attracted virulent opposition from the Anglican church in Australia, from colonial dissenters from Ireland, Scotland and England, and from colonial conservatives.[20] These varied critics found they had a shared weapon, namely, the accusation that Bourke was un-British because he undermined the colony's Protestantism and because he

(London, 1850), pp. 54–5. **18** Bourke to Lord Stanley, 30 September 1833, *Historical Records of Australia*, Series 1, vol. 17, p. 227. **19** Bourke to Dick Bourke jnr, 28 July 1836, Bourke family papers, State Library of New South Wales, Mitchell Library, ms 403/9. See also Roger Therry, *An Explanation of the Plan of the Irish National Schools* (Sydney, 1836). **20** For example, Henry Cavendish Butler (St Helliers, Hunter River) to John Butler Danvers of Swithland Hall, Leicestershire, 20 August 1838, quoted in Patrick O'Farrell (ed.), *Letters From Irish-Australia, 1825–1929* (Sydney, 1984), pp. 33–4. Butler was a Presbyterian from County Cavan, where he later returned to the life of a substantial landlord.

favoured Irish radicalism in New South Wales. Thus, the conservative *Sydney Herald* warned that Bourke's education schemes fostered an 'O'Connellite Tail faction' in New South Wales, and that he favoured his Irish 'com-*Pat*-riots'. His education proposal would give ascendancy in the colony to 'the children of the present race of transported Irish papists, at the expense of the Protestant land-holders of this country'.[21] This is ironic, considering Irish liberal Protestants like Bourke were involved in a bitter competition with the O'Connellites for status as the legitimate elite in Ireland during the 1820s and 1830s. But these subtleties were lost on the *Sydney Herald* which argued merely that Bourke was trying to turn New South Wales into an Irish rather than a British colony. Bourke's answer to these kinds of charges was that New South Wales should develop toward a non-denominational form of self-government in order to guarantee that it could develop institutions that reflected its particular character, which was neither wholly English nor wholly Protestant. The Church of England in Australia should not be responsible for education because it was not the estab-lished church in the colony. Bourke argued that 'the interests of Religion would be prejudiced by [the Church of England's] Establishment' in the Australian colonies, and by allowing the Church to control education, because 'the incli-nation of the colonists, which keeps pace with the Spirit of the Age, is decid-edly averse to such an Institution'.[22] In his view, British colonies should not be confined to narrow English and Protestant conventions, unless this reflected both the demographic make-up of their inhabitants and the practical conditions in which they operated. This was certainly not the case in New South Wales, where Catholics formed between one-quarter and one-third of the population during the whole of the nineteenth century.

Even among the Irish in New South Wales, perspectives on Britishness as an imperial identity were varied, but they varied in ways that did not map precisely to perspectives within Ireland. Many Protestants felt an affinity with the British empire as an extension of their Unionism, and empire was also seen as a wider mission of civilisation and Protestant evangelism. Thus in the settlement colonies (especially Canada and Australia), the Twelfth of July was transformed into Empire Day, which drew in a broad coalition of British Protestants across the whole empire in celebration of the spread of Protestantism, and loyalty to the Protestant constitution and to the Protestant monarchy, which surmounted the differences between colonies.[23] Yet, despite the widespread assumption that

---

21 *Sydney Herald*, 21 January 1836. This disparaging recognition of the Bourke family's Irishness was important in female 'society' as well; Fanny Macleay somewhat cattily com-mented that Anne (Bourke's daughter) was 'a stout plain, common looking person quite *Irish* but a most admirable songster', Fanny Macleay to W.S. Macleay, 8 January 1832, Fanny Macleay letters, cited in Steven G. Foster, 'Edward Deas Thomson and New South Wales' (unpublished PhD thesis, University of New England, 1975), p. 99. See also *Sydney Herald*, 4 July, 1 August, 13 October 1836. **22** Bourke to Lord Stanley, 30 September 1833, *Historical Records of Australia*, Series 1, Vol. 17, pp. 224–33, especially p. 227. **23** For example, see Lowry,

empire, monarchy and Protestantism were an indissoluble triplet that formed the basis of British identity, many Irish Catholics in the settlement colonies displayed a sense of connection to an imperial form of identity, which was linked with the monarchy and the rule of law, but which was distanced from Protestantism, from a sense of domination by a foreign imperial state, and in particular from direct rule by the British state. This was especially prevalent among middle-class Irish Catholics who sought respectability and power within the colony. Thus, at the 1881 St Patrick's Day banquet in Sydney the toasts offered were (in order of priority):

The Queen;

The Prince of Wales and the rest of the Royal family;

The Governor;

The Day we celebrate [i.e. St Patrick's Day];

The Land we live in;

The Parliament of NSW; and finally,

Ladies, Press and Chairman.[24]

Similarly, the paraphernalia of St Patrick's Day processions in the Australian colonies expressed the desire to avoid contentious and divisive contemporary politics in Ireland, to reaffirm Irish-Australian loyalty to the crown, and to assert Irish claims to civilisation that paralleled English civilisation, and could therefore claim equal standing with it. Middle-class Catholics were particularly vociferous in combining their claim to a sense of separate Irish-Catholic cultural identity with their claim to full membership and citizenship within this British colony. As a result, Catholics in Australia were hostile to attempts to set up Land League branches in Australia, but they were much more supportive of Redmond when he toured New South Wales. His perspective on Home Rule fitted more easily with their own hopes that, like the Australian colonies, Ireland could be self-governing within a loyal and loosely British imperial framework.[25]

Bourke's views on the development of a loose British model of empire in the 1830s meshed with a more generalised liberal notion of empire after the loss of the American colonies. Victorian Liberals promoted a notion of Britishness in the United Kingdom and in the empire which can be best conceived as a framework within which relationships between groups and between localities could be negotiated, and within which various contending identity claims were made. This framework was defined by a few key elements including the rule of law, mixed government, the sense that inclusion in a community was neither geographically nor ethnically defined, and a notion of civilisation that was Christian rather than specifically Protestant. However, beyond the basic criteria

'Ulster resistance and loyalist rebellion in the empire'. **24** Quoted in P.J. O'Farrell, *The Irish in Australia* (2nd edn, Sydney, 1992), p. 225. See also James H. Murphy, *Abject Loyalty: Nationalism and Monarchy in Ireland During the Reign of Queen Victoria* (Washington, DC, 2001). **25** O'Farrell, *Irish in Australia*, pp. 219–23.

for belonging, there was very little sameness throughout the 'British' community worldwide, because the nineteenth-century United Kingdom and the
British empire were nothing if not pluralistic. Britishness remained a significant
tool in contests between colonial interest groups, because it allowed them to
make legitimacy claims, and thus could be used to justify various schemes for
restructuring relations between interest groups within colonies, and between
the colonies and the British state. Colonial political power relations were structured in very different ways from those in the United Kingdom, and involved
clientage relations with the governor, lobbying of Westminster and the Colonial
Office, parliamentary inquiries, and so on, and this affected the kinds of arguments used.[26] This meant that debates about identity in the colonies did not
simply replicate or even necessarily derive directly from those in the United
Kingdom, even though colonial groups that claimed Britishness frequently used
their connectedness to Britain to claim legitimacy for their demands.

By the 1830s and 1840s the liberal conception of Britishness was considered
particularly relevant to the demands for 'Responsible Government' or devolu-
tion in political institutions from the British state to the settlement colonies, as
well as to Ireland and Scotland, because it allowed a degree of variation between
regions whose populations could be considered broadly 'British' but which had
different requirements and senses of identity. Colonies of settlement such as
Canada and Australia were considered improvable despite large Catholic or convict populations, because their populations were largely European and could
therefore not be reasonably denied British liberties. Yet, according to Liberals, the
attempted incorporation of French Catholics into a British colony in Canada,
and Irish Catholics into the British colonies in Australia, required a degree of
relaxation in the three usual criteria for full Britishness, namely that colonies
must conform to British norms, that they must accept the direct authority of the
British state, and that they must be Protestant.[27] As James Stephen put it in the
1860s, the right course of action for settlement colonies had been that of

> cheerfully relaxing, one after another, the bonds of authority, as soon as the
> colony itself clearly desired that relaxation … no national pride wounded,
> or national greatness diminished, or national duty abandoned.[28]

On the other hand, those colonies with large native populations or slaves were
deemed unimprovable and could therefore be ruled directly and with force.
Thus, in Stephen's view, 'The rest are unfit for it – detached islands with het-

---

26 J.B. Hirst, *Convict Society and its Enemies* (Sydney, 1983), pp. 169–72. **27** For example, Lord
Durham, 'Report on the Affairs of British North America' (1839), in Arthur Berridale Keith
(ed.), *Selected Speeches and Documents in British Colonial Policy, 1763–1917* (Oxford, 1929). **28**
Quoted in Kenneth N. Bell and W.P. Morrell (eds), *Select Documents on British Colonial Policy,
1830–1860* (Oxford, 1928), p. xxiv.

erogeneous populations – wretched burdens which in an evil hour we assumed and have no right to lay down again.'[29] This liberal model of empire was further developed by John Stuart Mill in the 1840s and 1850s, and an increasingly hard line was drawn between those colonies and native peoples that were capable of improvement, and those that were not.[30] The liberal conception of empire required an acceptance of regional variation, and it was allied with the development of an emphasis on self-government within a loose British framework.

Ireland occupied an ambiguous position in this liberal model of empire. It was ruled by force for much of the nineteenth century and many Irish nationalists, including Daniel O'Connell and John Mitchel, argued that Ireland had been annexed by a foreign English state. The escalation of racialised attitudes toward the Irish from the 1840s onward, also suggests that Ireland fitted on the 'imperial domination' side of the equation and, in the minds of many English observers, the Irish were uncivilised, un-Saxon, and were therefore unfit for self government. According to Thomas Carlyle, for example, the Irish shared their savagery with black people, but 'having a white skin and European features, [they] cannot be prevented from circulating among us at discretion, and to all manner of lengths and breadths'.[31] Even English Liberals like John Stuart Mill felt they could not take for granted which side of the liberal divide the Irish fell. He argued that India and Jamaica were clearly not ready for self-government because their peoples were not sufficiently civilised to make them fit for liberty, and thus their government was necessarily and to 'a considerable degree despotic'. Similarly, the Irish had not yet demonstrated 'a measure of the qualities which fit a people for self-government', but he argued that they must be incorporated into the Union despite their backwardness, because they were white, because many of them now lived in England and Scotland, and because many could vote.[32] In general, Irish Liberals did not challenge the liberal model of empire, but they focused instead on contesting Ireland's place within that model. Furthermore, once the Irish became directly involved in imperial expansion, the need to defend their place on the white 'civilised' side of the imperial and racial divide, and to defend themselves against accusations of disloyalty and religious inferiority, became even more acute.

The Irish were part of the United Kingdom by virtue of the Union, and after Catholic emancipation in 1829 removed political disabilities from Catholics, it was easier to argue that the Irish were British citizens with a legitimate claim to British liberty. The experiences and roles of Irish colonisers, administrators and professionals in the empire added further weight to this case.

29 Ibid.   **30** Uday Singh Mehta, *Liberalism and Empire: a Study in Nineteenth-Century British Liberal Thought* (Chicago, 1999).   **31** Quoted in Hall, *Defining the Victorian Nation*, p. 213.   **32** John Stuart Mill, *Considerations on Representative Government* (1861), reprinted in J.M. Robson (ed.) *Collected Works of John Stuart Mill, vol. 19: Essays on Politics and Society* (Toronto, 1977), p. 377, and Mill, *England and Ireland* (1868), in ibid., *vol. 6: Essays on England, Ireland and the Empire* (Toronto, 1982), pp. 524–6. See also Hall, *Defining the Victorian Nation*, pp. 188–91.

As a result, it became more viable for Irish nationalists to argue that Ireland was a civilised and improvable society which could legitimately demand British lib-erty and self-government within a broad British imperial framework. By the 1880s this argument was being made by many constitutional nationalists in the Irish Home Rule movement, including John Redmond and Charles Stewart Parnell.[33] For example, Parnell told his audience in 1885 that

> We can show the powers that have been freely conceded to the colonies – to the greater colonies [that is, the settlement colonies] – including this very power to protect their own industries against and at the expense of those of England. We can show that disaffection had disappeared in all the greater English colonies, that while the Irishman who goes to the United States of America carries with him a burning hatred of English rule, … the Irishman coming from the same village, … equally mal-treated, … who goes to one of the colonies of Canada or one of the colonies of Australia, and finds there another and a different system of English rule to that which he has been accustomed to at home, becomes to a great extent a loyal citizen and a strength and a prop to the com-munity amongst whom his lot has been cast; … He no longer continues to look upon the name of England as a symbol of oppression, and the badge of the misfortunes of his country *(cheers)* … The English statesman who is great enough … to give to Ireland full legislative liberty, full power to manage her own domestic concerns, will be regarded in the future by his countrymen as one who has removed the greatest peril to the English empire *(hear, hear).*[34]

The ambiguity of Ireland's place in the United Kingdom and in the empire produced double standards among many English speakers, but it also produced opportunities for the Irish (both nationalists and Unionists). In the Victorian period it became possible for nationalists and Unionists to manipulate the lib-eral model of empire to suit their own purposes, and the Irish were not averse to turning the imperial language used by English Conservatives against them. Thus, Irish participation in empire multiplied the possibilities of using imperial language for Irish purposes, whether nationalist or Unionist, especially when this aim was combined with growing public awareness of colonial affairs within domestic Britain.

When Irish liberal Protestant reformers drew comparisons between Ireland and the overseas colonies in the late 1840s and 1850s, they were more likely to group Ireland with the colonies of settlement than with colonies like Jamaica

---

33 C.A. Bayly, 'Ireland, India and the empire: 1780–1914', *Transactions of the Royal Historical Society*, 6th series, 10 (2000), 377–97; Ó Tuathaigh, 'Ireland under the Union: a critique'. **34** Charles Stewart Parnell, 'Speech at Wicklow', *Freeman's Journal*, 6 October 1885.

or India, on the grounds that Ireland was improvable and its people were legitimate claimants of British liberties. This did not stop them from using the language of empire when accusing the British state of misrule, but they used it for
a different purpose from many Irish nationalists. For example, when Aubrey de
Vere published his *English Misrule and Irish Misdeeds* during the Famine, he used
the language of empire which was being popularised in the *Nation*, but he
deliberately used it to argue an opposite case. He concluded that if Britain
abandoned illegitimate 'empirical [i.e. empire-ical] legislation, … prejudiced discussion, and … contemptuous and capricious benevolence', then England and
Ireland could 'bury past animosities' and have a

> union of mutual respect, good-will, and good deeds … May the imper-
> ial nation thus built up be worthy of its destinies, and show to the infe-
> rior nations of the earth for what cause nationalities exist.[35]

Irish Liberals such as de Vere, Bourke, and Spring Rice, used imperial language
to help them define that Union in ways that were advantageous to Ireland, or
to argue for a change the terms of that relationship within the existing constitutional framework. But they were not willing to forego Ireland's place in the
United Kingdom under the Union for two main reasons. This constitutional
relationship could be used to protect their own leadership within Ireland against
challenge from below, and they believed that the Union provided them with
greater opportunities both within the United Kingdom and in the empire.

William Smith O'Brien provides an interesting contrast to Richard Bourke
and other Irish liberal reformers, despite the fact that they emerged from a
shared Limerick liberal Protestant circle, and despite the fact that their
approaches to empire and their political ideology during the late 1820s and
1830s were very similar. Like other Irish liberals, O'Brien was well aware of
benefits of a British imperial identity which could encompass and serve the
needs of Irish Catholics as well as Protestants, and which allowed Irish people
unfettered access to imperial opportunities and spoils. When in 1840 he put forward a private member's bill proposing a state-funded scheme of assisted emigration to the settlement colonies, he argued that this would:

> At once … relieve the necessities of the population of the mother coun-
> try [in which he included Ireland], and, at the same time, [would] …
> extend the resources and promote aggrandisement of *our* colonial
> empire, … thus converting the involuntary idler into an active and pros-
> perous colonist.[36]

35 Aubrey de Vere, *English Misrule and Irish Misdeeds* (London, 1848), pp. 263–4. **36** William
Smith O'Brien, speech on emigration, *Hansard*, 3rd series, vol. 54, cols 832–3, 848 (2 June
1840) [italics mine].

In this speech he reminded the House of Commons that 'almost all of the evils under which Ireland still suffers have been, either remotely or immediately, occasioned by English misgovernment'.[37] The clear implication was that he viewed the British state's mishandling of famine relief as the most recent example of misgovernment, but Ireland's membership of the United Kingdom now allowed her MPs to claim financial support that would redress these evils. Significantly, though, he went further and argued explicitly that helping the Irish poor to participate in the empire would teach them to identify with an imperial form of British identity. He explained,

> There is no more legitimate kind of national pride than that which exults in viewing our country [the United Kingdom] as the parent of many nations, whose future greatness is destined to bear witness to the wisdom and the energy of the people who founded them ... No, Sir, instead of circumscribing [the Irish poor's] patriotism within the limits of a parish or a province, we ought rather to teach them to indulge the more expansive nationality of regarding every portion of the British empire as the home of the enterprising and the free.[38]

By early 1843 he had become so disillusioned with the Union that he called it a 'system of misgovernment', which was 'unjust, exclusive, overbearing, and an anti-national system of domination by which Ireland has been oppressed for 600 years', and which had resulted in the illegitimate use of force.[39] The Irish Liberals' failure to persuade the British government to push Irish reforms through parliament prompted O'Brien to abandon the O'Connellite reform movement in favour of the Young Ireland and then the Irish Confederation movements.[40] Yet there is no indication in 1840 that O'Brien thought the British empire as a whole was illegitimate in principle. This comes as a surprise from someone who led a revolutionary nationalist rising eight years later, who wrote for the revolutionary nationalist newspaper the *Nation*, and who was connected with John Mitchel during the 1840s (although Mitchel was always more radical than O'Brien). It was O'Brien's liberal ideology that provided a framework that allowed him to maintain consistent support for British imperial endeavours in the settlement colonies. Like other liberals, O'Brien differentiated between legitimate colonisation through settlement under the rule of law where 'wealth was produced ... by the labour of [European] emigrants upon the virgin soil of a fruitful territory', and the illegitimate imperial domination of civilised peoples by force.[41] As he explain in the *Principles of Government*,

---

37 Ibid., col. 837. **38** Ibid., cols 833, 851. **39** *Dublin Evening Mail*, 14 June 1843. **40** Robert Sloan, 'O'Connell's liberal rivals in 1843', *Irish Historical Studies*, 30:117 (1996), 47–65. **41** *Hansard*, 3rd series, vol. 54, col. 849 (2 June 1840).

A constitution which produces the happiest results amongst a community of Americans would lead to nothing but confusion if conferred upon an Asiatic population accustomed to despotic rule … a paper constitution – however perfectly devised, never gave, nor ever can give, liberty to a people who are indisposed to exercise self-government … Neither legislators nor writers on the theory of government can create public spirit in the minds of a people to whom this sentiment is unknown, [however,] they can effectively aid in developing it where it exists. [Thus,] Peculiarities of national character, traditional ideas, feelings, and habits, as well as local circumstances of various kinds, must be taken into account in moulding the political institutions of each country.[42]

Consequently, he supported the notion of a generalised division between civilised societies that were capable the 'public spirit' upon which liberty and citizenship depended, and uncivilised societies that were incapable of liberty.

His support for 'legitimate' colonial expansion through Wakefieldian settlement remained consistent throughout his life, both before and after the Young Ireland rising in 1848; in fact, it actually intensified as a result of his observations in the Australian colonies. As he explained in 1858, 'When I was in Australia I met many hundred Irishmen who had realised more than a competency – and in a few instances some who had acquired enormous wealth, though they had left Ireland unprovided with capital and impelled by a desire to escape indigence.'[43] Furthermore, while in Van Diemen's Land, he wrote an anonymous article in the *Launceston Examiner* in support of 'Responsible Government', on the grounds that Van Diemen's Land was improvable and that it required local political institutions in order to develop in ways that reflected its particular circumstances. His proposal of a 'loose confederation' of Australian colonies within a liberal imperial framework was workable because it allowed for local variation and self-government.[44]

Although he consistently differentiated between 'legitimate colonisation' in the colonies of European settlement and imperial domination in non-white, uncivilised colonies, in fact his views on the latter underwent important shifts during his lifetime. In 1830 he was an active supporter of campaign to have the East India Company's charter renewed, on the basis of Britain's civilising mission. In his 1830 pamphlet on the subject, he wrote that, 'In contemplating this vast [Indian] empire … it is impossible not to glow with exultation at the glorious prospects which its acquisition has opened to Great Britain'. Imperial rule in India would achieve 'the dethronement of a benighted religion', education

---

42 *Principles of Government*, vol. 1, 1–3.   43 *Nation*, 22 May 1858.   44 His model constitution for Van Diemen's Land, first published in the *Launceston Examiner*, 31 August 1853 (cited in Davis, *Revolutionary Imperialist*, p. 322), was later reproduced as an appendix in *Principles of Government*, vol. 2, 369–80.

would eliminate 'the impurer rites and extravagant doctrines of a debasing creed' and replace them with 'the pure morality and exalted spirit of Christianity ... In learning our language, and reading our books, the natives of India will imbibe their spirit, and exchange the feelings and ideas of Asia for the juster notions and more elevated principles of Europe.'[45]

However, in later life he accused the British state of consistently mistreating civilised non-white people in the empire. For example, his 1858 in response to the British invasion of Afghanistan and to the Indian Rebellion, he wrote in the *Nation* that, by supporting the East India Company in its intrigues and violence, the British state had pursued a policy of imperial annexation by force which had originated in Ireland, and that it was now applying the same illegitimate policy to the New Zealand Maoris.[46] It is notable that his two examples of illegitimate imperialism outside Ireland were both borderline examples in the liberal binary scheme and were societies which could lay some claim to being civilised and improvable and which did not fit neatly into the tropical 'unimprovable' category in the liberal model of empire. It is significant that he does not comment on British imperial rule in those colonies with large African populations, beyond the statement that the growing need for labour in British Guiana, Trinidad, Mauritius and Jamaica should be met by encouraging the immigration of free black labourers, rather than by Europeans.[47] That is, they were not seen as suitable destinations for civilised Irish settlers.

His conclusion that the Irish, Indians and New Zealand Maoris were all subjugated people who suffered under illegitimate British imperial rule was designed to make a political point which stemmed from Irish issues, namely, that Britain consistently undervalued the civilised qualities of the non-English people which it governed overseas and used this as an excuse for mistreatment. This fits neatly with his argument in the *Principles of Government*, that violence had been justified in Ireland because of its history of mistreatment by the British state. In the false belief that the Irish were uncivilised, the British state had illegitimately withheld liberty from the Irish, and had ruled Ireland against the interests of its inhabitants. O'Brien saw republican revolution as a legitimate response to this mistreatment, but it was a last resort. The demand for self-government and limited autonomy on a Canadian or Australian model within a liberal empire of settlement colonies was far preferable, and it would allow the Irish to 'enjoy, under an Irish Parliament and an Irish Ministry, the practical advantages of self-government'.[48] Furthermore, self-government within the

---

45 William Smith O'Brien, *Considerations Relative to the Renewal of the East-India Company's Charter* (London, 1830), pp. 16–17, 29, 35, 55–7. **46** *Nation*, 22 May 1858; *Principles of Government*, II, 224–7. **47** William Smith O'Brien, speech on emigration, *Hansard*, 3rd series, vol. 54, col. 841 (2 June 1840). **48** We cannot ignore the possibility that his writing after 1848 was tied up with his efforts to gain a pardon, and was thereafter motivated by a desire to rehabilitate his reputation in Britain and among the Irish elite. However, his *Principles of Government* is far too sophisticated an exploration of political philosophy, and his support for

imperial framework was likely to develop into an even better constitutional structure, namely, an 'international connection between Great Britain and Ireland' that was federal in style.[49] Thus, even though O'Brien participated in a revolutionary nationalist rising in 1848, within eight years he was proposing a form of Irish Home Rule that placed Ireland firmly within a British imperial framework, in ways that foreshadowed the arguments used by constitutional nationalists in the Irish Parliamentary Party thirty years later.

Although O'Brien shifted his political stance from what we might call liberal Unionism in the 1830s to liberal nationalism in the 1840s, both were conceived within a liberal British imperial framework which allowed scope for both Irish pragmatism and principled thinking. Thus, there was substantial common ground with other Irish Liberals like Bourke and Spring Rice in the 1830s and 40s, and nationalists such as Parnell and Redmond in the 1880s. These elite Unionists and nationalists all accepted the liberal division between civilised and non-civilised, or predominantly white and non-white colonies; but they objected to the assumption made by some English Liberals that the Irish should be classified with the uncivilised peoples, and they quite deliberately set about turning Ireland's ambiguous status and British imperial language to Irish advantage.

Queen Victoria's reign was an age of imperial expansion and the establishment of a new 'world order', and the Irish played some rather unexpected roles in that process which in turn played a part in re-shaping the way Irish issues were conceived at home. It is thought provoking that an Irish colonial governor and Irish gentleman convict transported for revolutionary activities could share very similar approaches to empire, and this highlights the complexity of identity formation in the 'British world'. British imperial identity within the empire was not fostered by a centralised state and unified elite in any straightforward manner, and then transmitted outwards into the empire and downwards to the popular level. Instead, it was contested, it was highly politicised, and it was adapted in response to changing circumstances and pragmatic political strategies. Consequently, imperial forms of Britishness can still be best understood as an overarching political and cultural framework within which identity claims were contested, and within which various cultural and interest groups negotiated both with each other and with the British state. This is compatible with Catherine Hall's conclusion, namely, that difference was mapped across nation and empire in many different ways, and subjects were constituted across multiple axes of power. However, it was this process of mapping that provided 'the basis for drawing lines as to who was inside and who was outside the nation or colony', and for what forms of cultural or political belonging were possible at any given time.[50] Where we perhaps differ is on the question of how this mapping related

colonisation far too consistent, to allow this explanation complete sway. **49** *Nation*, 20 March 1858. **50** Catherine Hall, *Civilising Subjects: Metropole and Colony in the English Imagination 1830–1867* (Cambridge, 2002), p. 20.

to English or British identity. In the nineteenth century many elite interest groups, especially non-English elite interest groups, found that British identity could be used to achieve strategic advantage in political contests in their localities, and in the metropolitan centre as well, whereas Englishness was less amenable. This encouraged the development of various and competing forms of Britishness which were associated with debates about the relationship between different local communities within a 'British world', and about their relationships with the British state. Identity contests in the empire were not simply transplanted from England or Ireland. They varied because the interest groups, their relationships, the circumstances and the power structures within which they operated, were different. And these mapping episodes in various historical moments and places affected each other in complex ways, not least because the people involved moved from place to place around this 'British world'.

For many Irish nationalists the American model remained dominant. However, many other Irish people, whether Protestant or Catholic, Unionist or nationalist, saw the notion of a loose-fitting and liberal British imperial framework as an alternative to the American or earlier French models of republican nationalism. It was attractive because of its flexibility, which suited Irish colonisers who sought to defend their place as civilised white people, in an empire in which race was becoming increasingly important. A loose-fitting British imperial identity (as opposed to a more exclusive English Protestant form of imperial identity) had particular advantages for those Irish people who migrated to the settlement colonies in the nineteenth century, because it allowed them to pursue their own individual aims, supported by British imperial structures. As a result, Irish people were active participants in the construction of an imperial form of British identity in the colonial setting, and they frequently contested the narrower vision of British identity which was exclusively Protestant and English.[51]

51 I am grateful for the support of Lucy Cavendish College, University of Cambridge, where I was a research fellow when the original conference paper was written, and the School of History, Keele University, where I was a lecturer when the chapter was revised.

Fenian rebels and Cretan insurgents, 1866–1869: unlawful subjects or 'lovers of freedom'?

PANDELEIMON HIONIDIS

In September 1866 the *Irishman*, in an article entitled 'Another fight for freedom', remarked:

> Irishmen are believed to have a lurking sympathy with rebellion everywhere; and we are sure they will sympathise with a rebellion which is now going on in a historic island of the Mediterranean against the brutal tyranny of the effete Turkish Government ... [Crete] is the centre of many mythical and historical traditions; and it shares with Ireland the reputation of being free from all noxious reptiles, except the human ones – the Turks being the Orangemen ... of poor Crete.[1]

This article was one of the first responses of the Irish press to the Cretan insurrection. However, the *Irishman's* attempt to draw a parallel between the Cretan difficulties and the Irish case was only one of the positions that Irish papers adopted in dealing with the insurrection. This study argues that diverse opinions on the Cretan question and varying degrees of sympathy for the Cretan insurgents should be accounted for mainly within the framework of different approaches to Ireland's difficulties and Irish nationalism. Moreover, the comparison between the Cretan problem and the Irish case, which was one (if a rather marginal) aspect of the debate on Crete in England, provides an interesting insight into the impact of the contemporary Fenian movement and established notions of the Irish 'character' on English opinion in the late 1860s.

After some brief introductory remarks on the Cretan insurrection of 1866 and Britain's policy during the crisis, the arguments developed in this essay are based on a detailed examination of the Irish press and the study of statements in parliament and articles in London newspapers, which illustrate, in contrasting and complementary ways, the English understanding of the Cretan and the Irish cases.

II

Crete, under Turkish rule since 1669, experienced a period of chronic unrest in the nineteenth century and repeatedly became the scene of unsuccessful upris-

1 *Irishman*, 1 September 1866, p. 153.

ings. Economic problems combined with national claims, especially after the
establishment of the independent Hellenic kingdom in 1830, to form a pattern
of discontent, culminating in a number of insurrectionary movements among
the Christian population, which constituted two thirds of the entire population
of the island. In the summer of 1866 the insurgents at first argued that they had
revolted for the redress of local grievances regarding taxation and education, but
soon issued a declaration of independence from the Ottoman empire and for
union with Greece. Despite some initial successes, in the second half of 1867
the Turkish army forced the insurgents to retreat and take refuge in the mountains. By 1868 the insurrection had degenerated into occasional attacks on
Turkish military positions, and was largely sustained by money, ammunition and
volunteers from Greece.[2]

Apprehension over the possible complications that an insurrectionary
movement in a Christian province of the Ottoman empire could generate
remained the prevailing concern in Britain throughout the crisis. The government and the majority of the London political press agreed on the need for a
policy of non-intervention in Crete, and this stand remained unaffected by the
return of the Liberal Party to power in December 1868.[3] The English press
expressed surprise and anxiety at what seemed to be an unexpected revival of
a problem, which, 'of the many difficulties which for the last half century have
disturbed the peace of Europe … is the most complicated, the least capable of
solution', and attacked the Hellenic kingdom 'for fanning the flame of the
Cretan revolt, and supplying the fuel which keeps it burning'.[4] Finally, British
attention was decisively directed to the conduct of the Greek state in
December 1868 and January 1869, when Turkey issued an ultimatum virtually
denouncing the Greek government for violating international law by its action
in Crete. The imminent possibility of a Greek-Turkish war that could lead to
a general conflagration in the East alarmed the Great Powers, which gathered
in Paris to deal with the question.[5] In Britain the Cretan crisis was regarded,
throughout its various phases, mainly in connection with the Eastern
Question, the revival of which in 1866–1869 was held to be detrimental to the
political interests of Britain in Europe.

---

2 On the Cretan insurrection of 1866 see T. Tatsios, *The Megali Idea and the Greek-Turkish War
of 1897: the Impact of the Cretan Problem on Greek Irredentism, 1866–1897* (New York, 1984), pp.
29–39. 3 For the policy of Stanley, who held the office of foreign secretary between 1866
and 1868, and his successor, Clarendon, on the Cretan insurrection, see Kenneth Bourne,
'Great Britain and the Cretan Revolt, 1866–1869', *Slavonic and East European Review*, 35:84
(1956), 81–7. 4 *Daily Telegraph*, 10 January 1867, p. 5; *Daily News*, 10 December 1866, p. 4.
Also see *Examiner*, 6 October 1866, p. 625; *Saturday Review*, 6 October 1866, p. 407; *Morning
Post*, 11 October 1866, p. 4; *The Times*, 10 December 1866, p. 8. 5 For the Paris conference
and its outcome, see Maureen Robson, 'Lord Clarendon and the Cretan Question', *Historical
Journal*, 3:1 (1960), 46–55

III

The reaction of the Irish press to the Cretan insurrection presents a complicated case, as divergent opinions on the question were expressed, which even a simple distinction between Protestant and Catholic papers does not adequately describe. To start with, Irish Protestant newspapers accepted the analysis of the majority of the English press of the Cretan insurrection, in regarding the movement with apprehension for its possible repercussions on the Eastern Question and the peace of Europe. Papers such as the *Dublin Evening Mail*, the *Irish Times* and the *Warder* questioned the motives and the intentions of the insurgents and castigated Greece for its involvement in the conflict.[6] Towards the end of the crisis, in December 1868, the *Dublin Evening Mail* reminded its readers of the paper's earlier verdict: 'we have pronounced Greece to be in the wrong'.[7] A month later the *Irish Times* declared that the 'vain ambition of one of the weakest kingdoms of Europe' had caused all the troubles in Crete and that this should be restrained by the joint military intervention of the Great Powers in the Hellenic kingdom.[8] These remarks summarized the Protestant papers' comments throughout the Cretan insurrection. Even when Turkish rule over Christian subjects was unfavourably described, the outbreak and the course of the Cretan revolt were still attributed to the aggressive policies of Greece or the intrigues of Russia, or even the United States, in the area.

The shift of emphasis from the international implications of the Cretan insurrection to its character as a 'national struggle' becomes apparent in examining the articles of the *Cork Examiner*, the *Dublin Evening Post* and the *Freeman's Journal*. The *Cork Examiner* – 'a nationalist paper with a Catholic outlook … constitutional and moderate in politics' – depicted the Cretans' feelings as part of 'that sentiment of nationalities now acquiring such immense momentum' and justified the assistance offered by the Greeks of the independent kingdom who apparently shared 'the same faith, the same language, and the same glorious traditions' with the islanders.[9] The *Dublin Evening Post*, a paper 'liberal in politics … and friendly to Catholics', and the *Freeman's Journal*, 'the most important journal in the country', a 'very respectable constitutional paper', concurred with their

6 The *Dublin Evening Mail* has been described as 'the organ of Orangeism and Toryism in their more intransigent forms', the *Irish Times* as 'the organ of the Protestant interest in Ireland' and the *Warder* as 'steadily opposed to Catholic claims and national movements', Stephen J. Brown, *The Press in Ireland: a Survey and a Guide* (Dublin, 1937), pp. 28, 34.   7 *Dublin Evening Mail*, 19 December 1868, p. 2.   8 *Irish Times*, 13 January 1869, p. 2; 19 January 1869, p. 2.   '9 Brown, *Press*, p. 156; *Cork Examiner*, 25 August 1866, p. 2; 1 October 1866, p. 2. John Francis Maguire, the paper's proprietor, was acquainted with members of the Greek community in London. In 1862 Maguire defended in the House of Commons the business interests of Stefanos Xenos and in 1863 he became vice-president of a short-lived Philhellenic Committee; see respectively: *Hansard's Parliamentary Reports*, 3rd series, vol. 167, cols 814–31 (20 June 1862); *The Times*, 12 October 1863, p. 9.

contemporary in identifying the Cretan crisis as a question of nationality and displayed a spirit of understanding for the 'Greek sentiment of nationality', even confessing that 'it is impossible not to respect the feeling that prompted a small and poor state to make such sacrifices for a common nationality.'[10]

However, while these three papers were prepared to concede that Cretans and Greeks had acted in the pursuit of a noble cause, they all criticized the means that Greek nationalism employed in order to achieve its objectives. The *Freeman's Journal*, in two leading articles published in December 1868 and January 1869, argued that internal improvements and peaceful reform would enable the Hellenic kingdom to become the nucleus of the Greek nation in the future: 'if the Greeks would settle down, work more, and dream less, they would be more likely to reach the goal of their ambition than by lavishing their slender resources in expeditions and armaments'.[11] Was this recipe for national success, offered to the Greeks in late 1868 and early 1869, a reflection of the recent experience of Irish revolutionary nationalism and that particular paper's commitment to constitutional action in Irish affairs? This is a tempting hypothesis, however the *Freeman's Journal*, as well as the *Cork Examiner* and the *Dublin Evening Post*, abstained from drawing a clear parallel between the Cretan struggle and Irish problems. Only the *Freeman's Journal* compared English policies in Italy with English indifference towards Crete, censuring the government and the English people for hypocrisy and fanaticism against the Pope.[12]

Whether as a foreign conspiracy menacing the peace of Europe, or as an ill-timed national struggle doomed to fail, the Cretan insurrection as reported and commented upon in the columns of the majority of the Irish press, both Protestant and Catholic, seemed an event hardly relevant to the affairs of Ireland. Nevertheless, for a number of papers advocating 'advanced national principles', the Cretan crisis, far from being an isolated episode in the Eastern Mediterranean, was seen as an opportunity to discuss the history and present state of Anglo-Irish relations. The case of three weekly papers, the *Irishman*, the *Nation* and the *Flag of Ireland* is suggestive from that point of view. The *Irishman* and the *Nation* were 'devoted to nationalist policies', the first 'rejecting parliamentary agitation in any form', while the latter 'advocated parliamentary agitation … in independent opposition form'.[13] The *Flag of Ireland*, a short-lived paper that published long reports of Fenian activities in the United States and attacked Britain on every occasion, notably through a political cartoon on its front page, has been described as 'a Fenian organ'.[14]

The three papers underscored the national as well as the religious dimensions of the Cretan insurrection and commented in emotional terms on the gallantry

10 Brown, *Press*, p. 19; Robert Kee, *The Green Flag: a History of Irish Nationalism* (London, 1972), p. 314; *Dublin Evening Post*, 17 December 1868, p. 2; *Freeman's Journal*, 19 December 1868, p. 3. 11 *Freeman's Journal*, 22 January 1869, p. 2. 12 Ibid., 19 December 1868, p. 3. 13 R.V. Comerford, *The Fenians in Context: Irish Politics and Society 1848–1882* (Dublin, 1985), p. 95. 14 Brown, *Press*, p. 36.

of the Cretans and the ferocity of their Turkish opponents. The 'brave fellows' in Crete were 'struggling on with a heroism worthy of the proudest epochs in Grecian history', aiming at national unity, which they had failed to achieve in 1830 when they had been 'betrayed by the base diplomatists of England and her allies'.[15] The patriotism manifested by the Cretans, 'who constituted themselves a sacrifice … on the altar of nationality', secured the sympathy of Irishmen for the insurgents; 'all lovers of freedom must heartily wish them success', according to the *Irishman*.[16] The *Flag of Ireland* added another reason why 'the discontented Irishman' should wish the Cretans success, namely 'the humiliation of the power that wronged him [the Irishman] with unsparing hand'.[17]

It was exactly this emphasis on identifying the combatants involved in Cretan affairs with the parties concerned in the Irish question that differentiated the comments of these nationalist papers from those of their Irish contemporaries. The interpretation of the Cretan insurrection as a typical case of an oppressed nationality fighting against its oppressor made the events of 1866–9 in Crete particularly attractive to the three papers under consideration. The Cretans, revolting against political and religious oppression, resembled the Irish people: 'we who have passed through the fiery ordeal of persecution and still live to testify to the miseries of persecution', the *Nation* argued in June 1867, 'can comprehend their [the Cretans'] fidelity and sympathise with their sufferings.'[18] Furthermore, Cretans, like Irishmen, were daily confronting the harsh reality which a conquered people experiences: 'Cretan grievances, no more than Irish, we'll be bound, have little foundation in the legends of historic romance'.[19] In January 1869, when Turkish rule was finally restored over Crete, the *Flag of Ireland* pitied 'the descendants of PERICLES and PELOPIDAS', and praised the Irish nation's great power of endurance: 'but one of the most powerful European nations after seven hundred years' trial of strength upon her, can only rule unarmed Ireland, to all intents and purposes, in the conditions of a stage of siege'.[20]

If painful experience familiarized Irishmen with the sufferings and patriotic enthusiasm of the Cretans, British policy in the Cretan crisis provided an opportunity for a bitter criticism of Britain equating Turkish with English practices and tactics of war. Why was it that 'on the continent … the only power which wishes England well is the Turk[?]', the *Irishman* asked in January 1869.[21] The *Flag of Ireland* complemented the question by enquiring why 'England is horrified at the possibility of a burst of battle' in Europe, and the *Nation* wondered whether in Crete 'the real criminal was England, pious Protestant England, who … sacrificed a noble Christian people to the brutal murderous despotism of Turkey'.[22] The answer to these questions was plain and simple. In a world

---

15 *Nation*, 4 May 1867, p. 586; 20 April 1867, p. 554. **16** *Irishman*, 1 September, 1866, p. 153. **17** *Flag of Ireland*, 23 January 1869, p. 5. **18** *Nation*, 8 June 1867, p. 665. **19** *Irishman*, 17 November 1866, p. 330. **20** *Flag of Ireland*, 2 January 1869, p. 4. **21** *Irishman*, 30 January 1869, p. 489. **22** *Flag of Ireland*, 23 January 1869, p. 5; *Nation*, 8 June 1867, p. 665.

divided between oppressors and their victims, England was decidedly enlisted among the former. Ireland itself had witnessed both the viciousness of England's force and the feelings of hostility which such experiences had helped to foster. The *Flag of Ireland* claimed that 'England's guilty conscience is its own accuser … [S]he fears foes upon every side … with discontented colonies, with Ireland in such a condition for revolt'.[23] The *Nation* portrayed the Turks in Crete as imitators of 'the Saxon system' of warfare: 'Change the names of persons and places, and the account of his [Omar Pasha's] late exploits might be substituted for a chapter in the history of Ireland in 1798, or the recent episode in Jamaica.'[24]

While the three papers unreservedly supported the cause of the Cretan insurgents and exploited the occasion to make allusions to the situation in Ireland, the role of the Hellenic kingdom in the crisis attracted limited attention and the broader claims of the Greek state for a leading role in the East were more cautiously received. In fact, during the Cretan insurrection the *Irishman* and the *Nation* followed their English contemporaries in commenting on the internal condition and the failures of the Hellenic kingdom.[25] This attitude towards the claims of the Greek state corroborates the view that Irish papers embraced the Cretans' struggle solely as an episode that offered a good example of an oppressed people's patriotism and an opportunity for criticizing England.

The view that the Cretan insurrection attracted the attention of the *Flag of Ireland*, the *Irishman* and the *Nation* because of the 'persecutor–victim' analogy they could draw between Crete and Ireland is further supported by the papers' hesitation to exploit the analogy to its logical conclusion. If the Irish people had suffered under English rule as harshly and unfairly as the Cretans had under the Turks, should the former follow the latter's example, rise into rebellion and demand the separation of Ireland from Britain? Articles about the Cretan crisis published in Irish papers of 'advanced national principles' throughout the years 1866–9 paid scant attention to the ultimate aim of the Cretan insurrection – independence and union with Greece – and did not make any direct suggestions as to its application to the Irish case. With the exception of the Fenians, armed rebellion and the advocacy of separatism lay outside the framework of even the most self-conscious expressions of Irish nationalism in the late 1860s.[26]

IV

While a portion of the Irish press utilized the Cretan insurrection as an exercise in nationalistic rhetoric, in England statesmen and newspapers dealing with the Cretan crisis employed the more familiar Irish and especially Fenian paral-

23 *Flag of Ireland*, 23 January 1869, p. 5. **24** *Nation*, 1 June 1867, p. 670. **25** See for example, *Irishman*, 26 December 1868, p. 408; *Nation*, 22 June 1867, p. 697. **26** See Patrick O'Farrell, *England and Ireland since 1800* (Oxford, 1975), p. 27.

lels to support their arguments and justify their policy on Crete. Any comparison between Turkish difficulties in Crete and England's troubles in Ireland could of course whitewash Turkish rule and justify Turkish practices in suppressing the insurrection by recalling the common problems facing all imperial powers.[27] However, such a comparison could also challenge the prevailing notions regarding England's presence and role in Ireland and therefore it could not and did not have any wider appeal beyond the circles of a few devoted supporters of the Ottoman empire. On the other hand, the representation of Irish Fenians and Cretan insurgents alike as somewhat misguided but still extremely dangerous rebels provided a safer option to British commentators who co-examined the difficulties in Ireland and Crete.

The case of Sir Henry Layard, who referred to England's position in Ireland in order to defend the Turkish presence in Crete in the House of Commons, testifies to the exceptional, if not offensive, character of such a comparison. Layard's early archaeological exploits and long stay in Turkey, his leading role in the radical pro-interventionist Administration Reform Association during the Crimean War and his extensive writings in the periodical press, gained him a reputation as an authority on Eastern affairs and an ardent Turcophile.[28] In March 1867, after a lengthy reference to the difficulties that the Ottoman empire was facing and its ability to overcome them, Layard argued that the Turks in the East were not mere conquerors, who could be easily expelled from Europe, but owners of land permanently settled in territories for centuries under Ottoman rule. At that point, Layard cited the case of English presence in Ireland: 'the Turks in Europe were very much what the English were in Ireland, and if there was a difference it was in their favour.'[29] The reaction of the *Daily News*, the leading Liberal organ, to Layard's remarks was prompt and plain; his argument was attributed to the peculiarity of his Eastern sympathies since 'there can be no rational comparison between the conditions and circumstances of the Ottoman domination in Candia and those of the British rule in Ireland.'[30]

Most appropriately in the light of future developments, the Duke of Argyll argued the case against mentioning British presence in Ireland in treating Turkish rule over the Christians of Crete. Argyll, variously described as a 'life long Whig' and 'a Peelite with Palmerstonian sympathies ... close to Gladstone', began his ministerial career in 1853 at the age of 29 and thereafter participated

---

27 The imperial argument was the main point invoked by the defenders of Turkish rule in Crete; see Ann Pottinger Saab, 'The doctor's dilemma: Britain and the Cretan crisis, 1866–69', *Journal of Modern History*, 49:4 (1977), 1399–1404. 28 A member of Gladstone's first administration, in 1877 Layard was appointed by Disraeli to the embassy at Constantinople, only to be recalled when Gladstone returned to power in 1880. See Gordon Waterfield, *Layard of Nineveh* (London, 1963); J.P. Parry, *Democracy and Religion. Gladstone and the Liberal Party, 1867–1875* (Cambridge, 1986), p. 72; R.W. Seton-Watson, *Disraeli, Gladstone and the Eastern Question: a Study in Diplomacy and Party Politics* (London, 1962), pp. 363–4. 29 *Hansard*, 3rd series, vol. 185, col. 432 (11 March 1867). 30 *Daily News*, 12 March 1867, p. 4.

in all Liberal governments until his resignation in 1881 over Irish policy.[31] During the Cretan insurrection, Argyll became the main apologist for the Cretans in parliament, stressing the alleged atrocities committed by the Turkish troops and Britain's failure to discharge its duties as the protector of the Christian populations of the Ottoman empire.[32] In March 1867 in the House of Lords, the earl of Kimberley criticized Argyll for slating the Turkish authorities' naval blockade of Crete by suggesting that Britain would react in a similar manner 'if the United States sent ships at this moment to the coasts of Ireland to remove any foreign insurgent volunteers who might be found there.'[33] The analogy was forcefully dismissed by Argyll:

> There was no analogy between what was being done by this country in Ireland and what the Turks have been doing in Crete. Women and children were not in need of conveyance from the shores of Ireland. No one suspected that Irish women and children would be ill treated by our troops. There was no argument so false as that founded on false analogy.[34]

What provoked an immediate response to Kimberley's and Layard's reasoning on the Cretan question was its implicit challenge to the legitimacy of British rule in Ireland. More significantly, these remarks could question the notion of England's benevolent, tolerant, civilised and civilising influence in Ireland by equating English administration with the infamous sway of an Oriental power over its unwilling subjects. If the comparison between English and Turkish rule was embarrassing and could potentially offend English sensibilities, the simple identification of the Cretans with the Fenians posed less problems, since it was based on commonly accepted notions of Irish nationalism and Irish 'character'.

The fact that English commentators in 1866–9 mentioned Fenianism in their remarks on the Cretan insurrection can be cited as evidence of the deep sensation aroused by the Fenian movement in Britain. What has been described as 'Fenian fever' or 'Fenian panic' in Britain, a sense of Irish danger that captured the imagination of the English public mainly in 1867, a year marked by the uprising in March, the Manchester episode in September and the Clerkenwell explosion in December, is clearly traceable in comments on the Cretan insurrection. English papers criticized politicians who defended the Cretans; 'the moment', as a London paper observed in March 1867, 'was not particularly well chosen for expressing sympathy with insurgents when we had a Fenian insur-

31 John W. Mason, 'The Duke of Argyll and the land question in late nineteenth-century Britain', *Victorian Studies*, 21:2 (1978), 151; Parry, *Democracy*, p. 75. **32** See, for example, *Hansard*, 3rd series, vol. 185, cols 1513, 1517, 1529 (8 March 1867); vol. 188, col. 158 (20 June 1867); vol. 191, cols 809–11 (3 April 1868). For Argyll's role in the Bulgarian atrocities agitation in the late 1870s, see his own account, *Autobiography and Memoirs* (2 vols, London, 1906), vol. 2, 122–5. **33** *Hansard*, 3rd series, vol. 185, col. 1541 (8 March 1867). Kimberley was colonial secretary, 1870–4. **34** Ibid., col. 1544.

rection to deal with at our doors.'[35] Even the appeal to the British public on
behalf of the Cretan refugees, which seemed to have all the merits of a charitable undertaking, could be dismissed by referring to the Fenians; 'we might as
wisely and morally unite with Irish servant girls in clubbing our money for the
relief of distressed Fenians', a correspondent in *The Times* replied to a letter rec-
ommending to the British public a Cretan Refugees' Relief Fund.[36] The well-
documented tendency of the English press to attribute Fenianism to foreign
instigation was also reflected to remarks on the causes of the Cretan revolt: 'the
disaffected Cretans were urged to revolt, just as the Fenians were stimulated by
the enemies of England'. The United States in particular was directly accused of
'sympathy with Ireland and Candia, or, in other words, with possible Fenian
rebels and with actual Cretan insurgents'.[37]

However, it is important to notice that the comparison between Ireland and
Greece both predated the Cretan crisis and, even during the years 1866–9, was
not confined to drawing parallels between Irish and Greek displays of revolutionary nationalism. It was the failure of the Irish and the Greek people to meet
English criteria of civilisation and progress that called forth critical comments
and a comparative approach towards both cases. Already in the first half of the
century the taunting pen of Thackeray ridiculed modern Athens by compar-
ing it to a ready example of 'barbarity': 'The shabbiness of this place actually
beats Ireland's and that is a strong word'.[38] The almost simultaneous outbreak of
disturbances in Crete and Ireland in the late 1860s led to an enquiry into the
particular subject of the two peoples' propensity for self-government and representative institutions. Just as the Irishmen's violent 'character' and their tendency towards endless political debates and dreams prevented the investment of
English capital in the island, the 'Hellenic Fenians', as the *Saturday Review* called
the Greek politicians in July 1866, 'act very efficiently as scarecrows for fright-
ening away labour and capital from the soil of the Greek kingdom.'[39] On the
other hand, for a committed philhellene such as Arthur Arnold the establishment of the difference between the Irish and the Greek 'characters' was an integral part of his attempt to exonerate the latter.[40] Arnold, 'a staunch radical',
editor of the London *Echo*, and later Liberal MP for Salford (1880–5), visited
Greece in 1868, and dismissed as prejudice unfavourable remarks on the Greeks'
political maturity by assuring his readers that his own fear that 'Greek election

---

35 *Daily News*, 12 March 1867, p. 4.   **36** *The Times*, 26 August 1868, p. 10.   **37** *Daily Telegraph*,
26 July 1867, p. 6; *Saturday Review*, 20 April 1867, p. 486. On English papers' comments on
the foreign origin of Fenianism, see O'Farrell, *Ireland*, p. 40.   **38** M.A. Titmarsh, [W.M.
Thackeray], *Notes of a Journey from Cornhill to Grand Cairo by Way of Lisbon, Athens,
Constantinople, and Jerusalem* (London, 1846), p. 72.   **39** *Saturday Review*, 21 July 1866, p. 77.
40 On the meaning of 'character' and 'national character' in Victorian Britain, see Stefan
Collini, 'The idea of "character" in Victorian political thought', *Transactions of the Royal
Historical Society*, 5th series, 35 (1985), 31–3, 41–3.

would be at least as riotous as a similar ceremony in Ireland', had been happily disappointed.[41]

Towards the end of the Cretan crisis, in February 1869, the *Morning Star*, which throughout the insurrection had agitated in favour of the Cretans, criticised its contemporaries' understanding, or rather lack of understanding, of the Irish and the Greek people, manifested in the advice to both to emulate the English ideal, that is to 'be frugal and sober; to encourage English capital; to avoid acts of violence and political agitations which keep English capital away … in a word, to be virtuous in order to be happy.'[42]

V

Far from being indifferent to continental national movements, as some have argued,[43] at least the most advanced Irish nationalist writers were eager to exploit an insurrection in a remote island of the Mediterranean in order to construct and present an 'England versus Ireland framework' representing English rule in Ireland as a hostile external force. On the other hand, English comments on the Cretan insurrection and Greek nationalism suggest that the anxiety caused in Britain by Fenianism reinforced rather than challenged prevailing notions of Irish nationalism and Ireland's problems.

This essay has sought to show that the study of Irish nationalism and British perceptions of Ireland in the nineteenth century can advance further if the contacts of the former with the national movements in continental Europe, and British commentary and judgemental pronouncements on other nations, are recognized as fields of historical inquiry with which the study of the Irish case should communicate.

---

41 *Dictionary of National Biography. Supplement 1901–1911* (London, 1920), pp. 57–8; Arthur Arnold, *From the Levant, the Black Sea, and the Danube* (2 vols, London, 1868), I, 192. Arnold became chairman of the executive of a Greek Committee in 1880. **42** *Morning Star*, 8 February 1869, p. 4. On the political views of the paper, which was established in 1856 by Cobden and Bright, see Stephen Koss, *The Rise and Fall of the Political Press in Britain* (2 vols, London, 1981), vol. 1, 107–11. **43** See Nicholas Mansergh, *The Irish Question, 1840–1921: a Commentary on Anglo-Irish Relations and on Social and Political Forces in Ireland in the Age of Reform and Revolution* ([1965], London, 1975), p. 81.

Michael Davitt, Irish nationalism and the British empire in the late nineteenth century

CARLA KING

The traditional assumption that Irish nationalism was by its nature anti-imperialist has been effectively challenged by various historians, among them Stephen Howe, who argues in *Ireland and Empire: Colonial Legacies in Irish History and Culture* that the history of Irish anti-imperialist discourse is 'a surprisingly thin subject'.[1] However, Howe's assertion that 'Early Irish nationalists hardly ever identified their situation or case with that of other, non-European subject peoples in the British Empire or beyond',[2] and Bernard Porter's claim that 'The Nationalists rarely looked further than their Irish noses; they saw everything from the point of view of the Anglo-Irish dispute',[3] appear to overstate their case. There were a few Irish MPs in the House of Commons, among them Frank Hugh O'Donnell, J.C. McCoan, Alfred Webb and Michael Davitt, whose interventions show them concerned both to challenge the British empire as an institution, and to denounce various instances of injustice or misgovernment in a manner that was neither designed simply to harry the government nor to make points that were essentially about Irish politics.[4] The focus of this essay will be an examination of Davitt's critique of the British empire and his activities in opposition to it.

Michael Davitt's life has sometimes been seen as dividing into an early phase, up to the end of the Land League in 1882, when he was primarily concerned with Irish affairs, and a second period of his life when he drew closer to the British labour movement and focused more on international affairs. While this is broadly true, there is some evidence that his interest in world events dated from his youth.[5] Examination of the Davitt's first long manuscript, 'Jottings in Solitary' – written while he was imprisoned in Portland in 1881–2 – demon-

---

1 Stephen Howe, *Ireland and Empire: Colonial Legacies in Irish History and Culture* (Oxford, 2000), p. 43. 2 Ibid., p. 44. 3 Bernard Porter, *Critics of Empire* (London, 1968), p. 312, quoted Howe, *Ireland and Empire*, p. 46. 4 Other party members who spoke out frequently on imperial issues included J.J. O'Kelly, T.P. O'Connor, Justin McCarthy and later John Dillon, William Redmond and Swift McNeill. See, for the period 1880–86, Alan O'Day, *The English Face of Irish Nationalism: Parnellite Involvement in British Politics, 1880–86* (Dublin, 1977), pp. 158–66. 5 For example, in 1885 he referred to the Hungarian leader Lajos Kossuth as 'one of my favourite heroes when doing my boyhood reading', Davitt Papers, Trinity College Dublin, MS 9544, Diary, 24 January 1885. I should like to thank the Board of Trinity College Library, Trinity College Dublin for permission to quote from the Davitt Papers.

strates that, even before the demise of the Land League, he was addressing himself to a broad critique of British colonial policy. Here he commenced by asking:

> Of all the races which are known in history as 'Conquerors,' that is, robbers and murderers on a gigantic scale – the one which has most signally failed in impressing either its civilization or religion upon the victims to its lust of power is the Anglo-Saxon. This is all the more surprising from the fact of their form of government, institutions and administration of justice *in England* being infinitely superior to those which obtained in Spain and Portugal when these latter countries commenced their career of conquest; as well as from the additional circumstance of their religion – the Protestant – being, if I may use the expression, a more *palatable* one to force upon a vanquished nation, than that of the Roman Catholic faith; with its mysterious ritual, sacramental obligation, and rigid exaction of implicit belief in the infallible teachings of its Church. What then, is the explanation of this defect in the conquering career of the Anglo-Saxon Race?[6]

His answer was that British policy, both in international relations and with respect to its colonies, was dominated by considerations of 'British interests', narrowly conceived. In illustration he cited the examples of India and Ireland. The fate of India's inhabitants had been 'left in the hands of the rapacious East India Company', whose employees proceeded to plunder it on a vast scale. British rule proved far more repressive than 'the petty despotism and rapacity of the native rulers of India', and was characterised by acts of violence and bad faith. In Ireland, too, any attempts to win Irish support for 'English civilisation' were vitiated by repressive policies. Resistance was not due to

> any inherent antagonism of Keltic blood in the composite race of the Anglo-Saxon, as probably most of our countrymen flatter themselves into believing – but from the seemingly inseparable relationship of English conquest to all that sordid selfish lust of power, sleuth-hound unerring pursuit of object and remorseless disregard of every humane feeling toward a defeated but unbending victim, or fear of moral responsibility in carrying out a pitiless policy of extermination towards him if he yield not a willing submission[.]

He concluded:

> had the national land code been … left intact and the people allowed to remain the owners, instead of the creation of the plantation scheme – from which Irish Landlordism is derived – and permitted also the same enjoy-

---

6 Davitt Papers, MS 9639, 'Jottings in Solitary,' fol. 20. An edition of *Jottings in Solitary* was published by University College Dublin Press in 2003.

ment of their religious creed, there is every probability that Ireland would
be today in reality and not in name, 'an integral part of this British Empire,'
and my countrymen as submissive to English rule as those of their kilted
and Cambrian race north of the Tweed and west of the Severn.[7]

It is important to note that Davitt's quarrel with British rule is not a racial one:
on the contrary, he suggests that had British imperialism been less repressive it
might have been successful. His strongest arguments against British rule in
Ireland were, firstly, that the British government propped up a parasitic landlord
class as a 'garrison' in Ireland, which leached money from a needy economy.
And, secondly, that while the British political system was an admirable one as it
functioned in Britain, British rule in Ireland was not an extension of the British
system there but a mechanism to promote British, rather than Irish, interests.
Dominated by Dublin Castle and its apparatus, it was profoundly anti-democ-
ratic, self-serving and corrupt. He used the device of imagining the situation
reversed, of an Irish clique ruling of Britain through Whitehall (a model he later
employed in speeches and in his pamphlet, *The Castle Government of Ireland*).[8]
These were important insights. The first point linked the imperial system to the
perpetuation of landlordism. The second observation contradicted the argument
often made for British rule overseas, that it extended the benefits of liberal
democracy across the world. Davitt, while he admired liberal democracy as
practised in Britain, claimed that this was not what the empire exported to its
colonies. His arguments were broadly economic and political, rather than cultural or religious. His brand of nationalism was intrinsically anti-imperialist, as
he believed that the people of each nation knew their own best interests and
were therefore best fitted to rule themselves.

   Through most of the nineteenth century there was a strand of Irish nationalist opinion that opposed the empire. O'Connell had criticised the brutality with
which the empire was built and had helped to form the British India Society in
1839. Thomas Davis had anathemised Britain's 'tottering and cruel Empire' in the
1840s.[9] In the 1870s and 1880s, as Britain launched itself on the expansionary
track of the New Imperialism, the radical wing of the Irish Parliamentary Party
was the most active group in the House in debating imperial affairs, F.H.
O'Donnell, J.J. O'Kelly and J.C. McCoan playing particularly prominent roles.
This attitude was far from universal among the Irish representatives and, as Alan
O'Day and others have pointed out, some Irish members held a more positive
view, their criticism of the empire mingled with admiration and recognition of
the part the Irish had played in building it.[10] H.V. Brasted has identified three

7 Ibid., fol. 38, *Jottings*, pp. 29–30. **8** Michael Davitt, *The Castle Government of Ireland* (1882);
reprinted in Carla King (ed.) *Michael Davitt: Collected Writings, 1868–1906* (8 vols, Bristol,
2001). He makes the same arguments in *Leaves from a Prison Diary* (2 vols, London, 1885), vol.
2, 170–210. **9** John Neylon Molony, *A Soul Came into Ireland: Thomas Davis, 1814–1845. A
Biography* (Dublin, 1995), p. 165. **10** O'Day, *English Face,* pp. 162–4; T.G. Fraser, 'Ireland and

broad strands in Irish nationalist thinking about the empire. In an approach first mooted by Isaac Butt, one current of opinion held that the empire should move toward a form of federalism, in which the constituent parts would be partners. At the other extreme were republicans who sought the destruction of the empire through violent means. Between these two positions came the Parnellite programme, critical of the empire but seeking reform from within.[11]

The most consistent and informed critic of the British empire in the late 1870s and early 1880s was Frank Hugh O'Donnell (1848–1916), for many years foreign editor of the *Morning Post*, and whose brother was an Indian civil servant. In words with which Davitt would have concurred, he told the House in 1884 that 'English tyranny in Ireland was only a part of that general system of the exploitation of suffering humanity which has made the British empire a veritable slave empire', and he urged that 'Parliamentary agitation would not be very effective until the Irish people, crushed down under their present tyranny, effected a coalition with the oppressed natives of India and other British dependencies, and all regarded England as the common enemy'.[12] According to Brasted, it was O'Donnell who formulated three basic principles on which Irish representatives should play an enhanced role in attacking the empire:

> One, that Irishmen were specially qualified to postulate cures for imperial disorders;
> Two, that Home Rulers were the natural representatives in Parliament of the unenfranchised empire;
> Three, that nationalists in Ireland should form an alliance with nationalists in Asia and Africa to achieve the mutual goal of self-government.[13]

Unfortunately, O'Donnell seems to have had a rather difficult temperament, and was bitterly opposed to Parnell, who refused to allow his nomination in the election of 1885. Although this put an end to his parliamentary career, he continued to exert an influence though his journalism.

It is difficult to identify the precise source of Davitt's thought concerning the British empire. The Fenians were broadly opposed to it but their approach tended to be limited to seeing 'England's difficulty as Ireland's opportunity' and they did not generally seek a broad coalition of nations within the empire. One exception to this, and a likely source of influence on Davitt's thinking, was Patrick Ford, editor and proprietor of the *Irish World*. Ford had provided indispensable support to the radical wing of the Land League during the Land War and was an adherent of the land nationalisation programme of Henry George

India', in Keith Jeffery (ed.), *'An Irish Empire'? Aspects of Ireland and the British Empire* (Manchester, 1996), pp. 77–93. **11** H.V. Brasted, 'Irish nationalism and the British empire in the late nineteenth century', in Oliver MacDonagh, M.F. Mandle and Pauric Travers (eds), *Irish Culture and Nationalism, 1750–1950* (Canberra, 1983), pp. 83–103. **12** *Hansard's Parliamentary Debates*, 3rd series, vol. 285, col. 1766. **13** Brasted, 'Irish nationalism', pp. 91–2.

(whom he employed as the *Irish World*'s Irish correspondent in 1881–2). He had served his journalistic apprenticeship in Lloyd Garrison's abolitionist newspaper, *The Liberator*, and denounced the empire in almost messianic tones as not only oppressive but also contrary to the laws of God. In April 1881 he began a series of open letters to W.E. Gladstone,[14] in which he declared: 'I hold the Genius of the British Empire is an emanation from the mouth of the Evil One,' and that 'the spirit of conquest … is sinful'.[15] He referred to the empire as 'a system of diabolism' and 'a modern Babylon',[16] later calling on the subject peoples of the empire, 'the victims of this infernal system' to combine with the Irish 'in a holy crusade' to destroy it.[17] Ford further, like Davitt, identified the crimes of the British empire with a class: 'I have said that the British oligarchy are, in fact, the British empire. They own the army, the navy, the law, established church, the judiciary and all the foreign offices.'[18] Davitt's denunciations of the empire, if lacking Ford's biblical tone, shared his strong element of moral indignation.

The closing decades of the nineteenth century saw the British empire at the peak of its strength; between 1870 and 1900 around 66 million people and 4.5 million square miles were added to its overseas possessions.[19] This expansionist policy was very popular at home and while some historians have suggested that the rising levels of imperialist fervour served in Britain to cheer up the public in the face of the economic difficulties of the late 1870s and 1880s,[20] others have pointed to the influence of British business interests in pursing the considerable profits to be made from some of the colonies.[21] Support for imperial expansion was never unanimous, however. In the 1870s the Liberals had been less than enthusiastic about the prospect of heavy expenditure on an expanding empire and preferred to see an extension of free trade. But the incoming Liberal leadership of 1880 was forced, initially by the Egyptian crisis, into a role of defending imperial interests, and in the process they developed their own interpretation of the 'white man's burden'. Some on the radical side of the Liberal party, such as John Bright, John Morley and Henry Labouchère,[22] and writers such as Herbert Spencer and J.A. Hobson,[23] continued to oppose imperialist policies. Spencer's ideas certainly influenced Davitt, who admired him greatly and made frequent references to his work. In political terms these represented

---

14 The letters were published in book form after Ford's death, as *The Criminal History of the British Empire* (London, 1915). See also Brasted, 'Irish nationalism', pp. 83–103.   **15** *Irish World*, 31 March 1881; Ford, *Criminal History*, pp. 7–8.   **16** Ford, *Criminal History*, pp. 8–9.   **17** *Irish World*, 21 April 1881, quoted in Brasted, 'Irish nationalism', p. 89.   **18** *Irish World*, 14 May 1881; Ford, *Criminal History*, pp. 51–2.   **19** L.C.B. Seaman, *Victorian England. Aspects of English and Imperial History, 1837–1901* (London, 1973), p. 332.   **20** A. P. Thornton, *The Imperial Idea and Its Enemies* ([1959] London, 1985), p. 67.   **21** See, for example, A. Redford, *Manchester Merchants and Foreign Trade* (Manchester, 1956).   **22** R.J. Hind, *Henry Labouchère and the Empire, 1880–1905* (London, 1972).   **23** J.A. Hobson (1858–1940) did not publish his famous study, *Imperialism*, until 1902, but Davitt would almost certainly have been acquainted with his ideas as he was a prominent economist interested in tackling the problems of inequality through taxation, a topic close to Davitt's heart.

the strand in British political opinion to which Davitt was closest, although he was later to transfer his allegiance to the newly-emergent British Labour Party. His dislike of the empire was perhaps more visceral than theirs, representing a fundamental part of his nationalism.

As some Irish MPs took on the mantle of critic of imperial affairs, there was a move on the part of British leaders, both Liberal and Conservative, to view the Irish question as a challenge to the integrity of the empire as a whole. Any grant of Irish demands for Home Rule would, they argued, set off a chain reaction leading to the disintegration of the British empire. Lord Salisbury initiated this version of a 'domino theory' in 1883,[24] and it was later evident among some administrators such as Lord Dufferin in India, who took to referring to the Indian National Congress as the 'Indian Home Rule movement'.[25]

Gladstone's attitude to imperial expansion had begun to shift during the Egyptian crisis in 1881–2. Until then, Egypt, while formally constituting part of the Ottoman empire, had in fact enjoyed considerable autonomy. Its strategic importance to the European powers had been notably enhanced with the opening of the Suez Canal in 1869. Ten years later, Egypt's ruler, the Khedive Ismael, who had run up considerable debts to western bankers, was deposed in favour of his son, Tewfik. This sparked off a revolt by Egyptian reformers opposed to Western involvement in their country, led by Urabi (or Arabi) Bey, who threatened to repudiate Egypt's debts to European bondholders. The Liberal government sent in battleships and a military force, bombarding Alexandria on 11 July 1882, and eventually defeating the insurgents at Tel-el-Kebir on 13 September 1882. In August, while the fighting continued, Ford published a portrait of Urabi, with the comment that he was gallantly upholding the no-rent banner in Egypt, and expressed the hope that 'the accursed British Empire and its armies and navies may melt before Arabi and the miasma of Egypt as snow before the noonday sun.'[26] Urabi Bey and some of his followers, first sentenced to death, were exiled to Ceylon, from where they petitioned to be either allowed to return home, or failing that, to be moved to Cyprus, on the basis that the climate in Ceylon did not suit them. The Irish Party had been active in denouncing the British government's actions in the early 1880s, and five years later Wilfred Scawen Blunt, the most prominent English opponent of British policy in Egypt, drew comparisons between the situations in Egypt and Ireland in the course of the Plan of Campaign, during which he was imprisoned in Ireland. He met and visited Davitt during his time in Ireland, and discussed world events in general and the possibility of achieving a broad front aimed at attacking the British empire from within.[27] Later, as an MP, Davitt questioned in 1897, 1898 and 1899

24 He outlined this view in 'Disintegration', *Quarterly Review*, 156 (October 1883), 559–95, and in a speech at Newport on 7 October 1885, see Brasted, 'Irish nationalism', p. 84. **25** Fraser, 'Ireland and India', p. 87; Howard Brasted, 'Indian nationalist development and the influence of Irish Home Rule, 1870–1886', *Modern Asian Studies*, 14:1 (1980), 37–63. **26** *Irish World*, 11 August 1882; quoted in *Freeman's Journal*, 12 August 1882, p. 5. **27** Wilfred Scawen Blunt, *The*

the refusal to grant the request of the revolt's leaders to return home; government spokesmen replied variously that it was up to the Egyptian government, and that the exiles were too dangerous to permit their return.[28]

Late nineteenth-century British opinion saw India, in the cliché of the day, as 'the jewel in the imperial crown', a vast market for British goods, a source of raw materials and the essential basis for British world power and prestige. The Irish had contributed significantly to sustaining the Raj as soldiers and administrators, and even as viceroys. Parallels had frequently been drawn between India and Ireland and a measure of solidarity was to emerge between Irish and Indian nationalists. But despite India's economic and strategic importance to Britain, unlike Ireland it had no political representation. In 1879, following an approach from the executive committee of the British Indian Association, O'Donnell put to Isaac Butt the proposal that the Irish Party might run Indian candidates in order to provide them with seats at Westminster.[29] This attempt failed, but in 1883 Davitt, possibly on the prompting of O'Donnell, suggested to Parnell that the party find a seat for Dadabhai Naoroji, whom he later described as 'a thoroughly representative Indian gentleman residing in London, and well known to Mr Parnell and others of us. Ireland would thus have the honor of giving a direct voice in the House of Commons to countless millions of British subjects who were ruled despotically and taxed without votes.'[30] Parnell, while apparently initially 'very much taken' by the proposal, eventually informed Davitt that 'he liked the plan very much, but he feared it would not be clearly understood in Ireland and might lead to trouble within the party.'[31] Naoroji himself rejected the idea on the grounds that if Ireland gained Home Rule, as appeared possible in 1886, there would be little point in the Indian movement having representation in an Irish parliament.[32] He was returned for Finsbury in 1892, but when he lost this seat in 1895, he appealed again to Davitt, whose reply was that there was 'no hope'.[33] Davitt, however, was still keen on the idea of the Irish Party providing seats for Indian candidates in 1887, when he discussed the idea with Blunt.[34]

In October 1894 Naoroji conveyed to Davitt the invitation to preside at the Tenth Indian National Congress in Madras, but Davitt refused on the grounds that it would be too risky for Congress to invite him, commenting in his diary:

Land War in Ireland: Being a Personal Narrative of Events in Continuation of 'A Secret History of the English Occupation of Egypt' (London, 1912), pp. 50–1, 76–7. **28** *Hansard*, 4th ser., vol. 45, cols 94, 95 (1897); vol. 60, col. 793 (1898); vol. 73, cols 1140, 1141 (1899); vol. 76, col. 14 (1899). Blunt wrote to express his appreciation of Davitt's effort, Davitt Papers, MS 9433/2688, Blunt to Davitt, 4 July 1898. **29** F.H. O'Donnell, *The Irish Parliamentary Party* (2 vols, London, 1910), vol. 2, 428; Brasted, 'Indian nationalist development, pp. 37–63. **30** Michael Davitt, *The Fall of Feudalism in Ireland* (London, 1904), p. 447. **31** Ibid. **32** R.P. Masani, *Dadabhai Naoroji: the Grand Old Man of India* (London, 1939), p. 227, quoted in Mary Cumpston, 'Some early Indian nationalists and their allies in the British Parliament, 1851–1906,' *English Historical Review*, 76 (1961), 279–97. **33** Naoroji to Davitt, 15 January 1896, quoted in Brasted, 'Indian nationalist development' p. 49. **34** Blunt, *Land War in Ireland*, p. 318. Blunt felt the scheme to be premature, and better pursued once Home Rule had been achieved.

Think it would be a big risk for the Congress movement for *me* to accept this invitation. The Anglo-Indian press would howl with frantic madness at such an event, while the Times and Co would scarcely be able to write from indignation. This, however, would not affect me much. The question is would my presiding at this Congress help the cause of the Indian people?[35]

His friend and fellow-nationalist MP, Alfred Webb, presided at the Congress instead.[36] The opportunity to assist by providing Irish seats for unrepresented nations within the empire was lost but in his parliamentary interventions Davitt repeatedly raised Indian issues.

In 1885, in his first book, *Leaves from a Prison Diary,* Davitt had expressed his conviction that 'the overthrow of British rule in India is only a question of time.'[37] Independence was delayed by the difficulties of organising a united movement in such a large and diverse nation and by the poverty to which it had been reduced, but, he argued, the British were deceiving themselves if they thought that India was content. He linked the abuses of British rule in Ireland and India to the class system in Britain.[38]

Imperial policies toward Canada and Australia were considerably more liberal than those pursued elsewhere. In the second half of the nineteenth century both colonies moved toward self-government and Davitt took a close interest in this process. In late 1891 he paid a visit to the north west of Canada, publishing his impressions in an article in the *Nineteenth Century.*[39] Canada had been granted dominion status as a federal state with its own national government in 1867. In certain respects it challenged his views. Normally an opponent of emigration, he could see the extent to which any future development of north-western Canada would depend on a continued influx of immigrants. He also appreciated the opportunities it offered to impoverished emigrants from the old world anxious to make a new start. Furthermore, although a lifelong proponent of national independence, he was forced to admit that this was not what the Canadians he spoke to were seeking, as it would leave their country vulnerable to absorption by the United States. They preferred the broad measure of autonomy they enjoyed by remaining part of the British empire, a fact that he recognized.

Davitt had been anxious to visit Australia for over a decade when in 1895 he undertook a seven-month lecture tour through Australia, Tasmania and New Zealand, addressing some seventy-two public meetings and gathering material

---

35 Davitt Papers, MS 9556, Diary, 3 October 1894. See Brasted, 'Indian nationalist development', pp. 57–63, on the alarm caused in India by parallels being drawn with the Irish movement.   **36** Webb described the Congress in detail in his autobiography, see Marie-Louise Legg (ed.) *Alfred Webb: The Autobiography of a Quaker Nationalist* (Cork, 1999), pp. 67–71. He had been a member of the parliamentary committee on India since its formation in 1893.   **37** *Leaves from a Prison Diary,* vol. 2, 156.   **38** Ibid., pp. 153–6.   **39** Michael Davitt, 'Impressions of the Canadian North West', *Nineteenth Century,* 31 (April 1892), 631–47.

for the book he wrote on his return.[40] As in Canada, he relished the more democratic and egalitarian atmosphere of this other new world. At the time of his visit Australia was about to be transformed from six separate colonies into the self-governing federal structure embodied in the new constitutional arrangement established in 1900. He paid close attention to the rise of the Australian labour movement, the granting of women's suffrage in some of the colonies, and the workings of the various parliaments. He could not help remarking on the discrepancy between the granting of home rule in 1890 to Western Australia, a community of only 45,000 people ('a population about equal to that of Limerick'), 'after denying in 1886 a cribb'd, cabined, and confined self-governing constitution to five millions of people in Ireland'.[41]

For some political thinkers of the day, the developments in Canada and Australia pointed the way for an evolution of the empire toward a looser federation of self-governing states, each enjoying 'home rule'. While Davitt might have accepted this as an improvement on the existing empire, he was ultimately a republican nationalist whose aim, for Ireland and elsewhere, was the establishment of sovereign national republics.

By the mid-1890s he was one of the leaders of the anti-Parnellite faction of the Irish Parliamentary Party. He evinced an intense dislike of the House of Commons, once telling it that he saw membership as a punishment, and that he 'sighed while sitting helpless on these Benches, for the days when, instead of vainly trying to make laws, I might have built up a lasting reputation in Dartmoor as a stonebreaker'.[42] Most of his activity in the House was directed to exposing abuses in the government's policy or activity, both imperial and domestic. His questions were generally brief and he once described himself as 'a rather silent member,'[43] although there were some longer interventions. Although he was first returned to Westminster in July 1892, his most active participation came in the years 1896–9.

In February 1897 he drew the attention of the House of Commons to a famine that had broken out in the Central Provinces of India in 1895.[44] The following week he was a prominent speaker at a public meeting organised by the Social Democratic Federation in London to protest at the famine, moving a resolution:

> That this meeting of the citizens of London calls upon the Government to stop now and henceforth the drain of produce from India officially certified at a value of more than £20,000,000 sterling a year, used to pay home charges, pensions, interest, etc., this drain having caused and now hideously intensifying the famine which is devastating British India.[45]

40 Michael Davitt, *Life and Progress in Australasia* (London, 1898). 41 Ibid., p. 27. 42 *Hansard*, 4th ser., vol. 53, col. 1094 (1898). This was a reference to the seven and a half years Davitt spent serving a sentence to hard labour in Dartmoor and other prisons for treason-felony. 43 Ibid., vol. 52, cols 443–4 (1897). 44 Ibid., vol. 45, col. 1555 (8 February 1897). 45 *Justice*, 13 February 1897, Davitt Papers, MS 9620, f. 20.

The famine was accompanied by a cholera epidemic and the authorities had taken sweeping powers to enforce the plague regulations, which Swift MacNeill (MP for South Donegal) claimed were enforced insensitively.[46] Shortly afterwards two British officials were murdered in Poona. Two suspects, the Natu brothers, were held under the Bombay Act that allowed arrest on the warrant of the viceroy if he considered them 'dangerous persons' and imprisonment for an indefinite period. This detention without trial was denounced by both Davitt and MacNeill, and compared to the *lettres de cachet* used by the Bourbon government against their enemies before the French Revolution. Davitt claimed that the outcry in the British press occasioned by the murders had been unfair to India and urged that the standards of justice provided under the British constitution should extend to its rule of India. He went on to question Britain's right to rule in India in general. The only justification, he argued, for 'holding India by the sword would be in making it a prosperous and contented country'. He contended that British governments had failed to do this, citing continuing high levels of illiteracy, the waste of money on twenty border expeditions and failure to carry out irrigation works.[47] While condemning what he termed 'these cowardly acts of assassination', he argued that they were very rare in India and that 'foreign domination and foreign officialism' were likely occasionally to drive men to commit them. He praised the Indian population for its patience and caused some amusement in the House by asking what would be the difficulties facing them if instead of having to deal with 250 million Indians they had to deal with 250 million Irishmen. He concluded by saying:

> He felt very strongly in sympathy with the Indian people. He felt the deepest sympathy with every people who were subject to another nation. He was one of those who believed that England had no right whatever to rule in any country outside her own borders and he sincerely hoped and trusted that, unless the British Government would extend to British subjects in India the full right of protection of the British Constitution, the Indian people would undertake by means fair and honourable, to win their own independence.[48]

Davitt's interest in the British empire was wide-ranging. He denounced the mistreatment of the Ashanti king Prempeh by the British army in 1896, 1897 and 1898;[49] questioned the Royal Niger Company's behaviour in Benin;[50] in 1897 he queried the need for British involvement in Sudan;[51] in 1898 he

---

46 *Hansard*, 4th ser., vol. 52, col. 441 (5 August, 1897). **47** Ibid., cols 447–8. **48** Ibid., cols 437–448. **49** Ibid., vol. 51, cols 1440, 1441 (19 June 1897); vol. 45, col. 678 (28 January 1897); vol. 53, cols 1632, 1633 (24 February 1898). For a succinct account of British involvement in West Africa in the late nineteenth century, see M.E. Chamberlain, *The Scramble for Africa* (London, 1999), pp. 42–57. **50** *Hansard,* 4th ser., vol. 45, col. 188 (21 January 1897). **51** Ibid., col. 1499 (5 February 1897).

demanded to know why the Chinese leader, Sun Yat Sen, had been excluded from Hong Kong two years earlier;[52] and he condemned the use of 'dum-dum' or exploding bullets in India and South Africa.[53]

The most significant challenge to the British empire of the nineteenth century came at its close with the Second Boer War. As in the case of India, developments in Ireland and South Africa were intertwined. It was in opposition to the British annexation of the Transvaal in the summer of 1877 that Parnell had first come to prominence in a forty-five-hour obstruction of the debate on the South African Confederation Bill. This opposition had been compromised somewhat by the acceptance by Parnell of a £11,000 subsidy from Cecil Rhodes in 1888.[54] Davitt had denounced the Jameson Raid in an interview in the *New York Evening Sun* on 2 January 1896, attributing its countermanding by the British government to fear of American reaction and claiming that the raid had been planned by Englishmen in the Transvaal in revenge for the Boer victory at Majuba Hill and in pursuit of 'the rich mines of Johannesburg'.[55] When in June 1899 he asked the first lord of the treasury, Arthur Balfour, whether the government claimed 'suzerain rights over the South African Republic,' he received no reply.[56] By the time war broke out on 11 October 1899 there had been a considerable build up of public opinion in Ireland in favour of the Boers. On 1 October Dublin had seen a mass meeting of over 20,000 people in Beresford Place to protest against 'the attack of England upon the liberties of Transvaal'. It was chaired by John O'Leary and Davitt proposed the motion 'That this great meeting of the citizens of Dublin sends its sympathy to the Boers, and hopes, should war result from the present crisis, that Providence will give them a victory over the tyrannous armaments of England.[57]

Three weeks later, in the most famous speech of his parliamentary career, Davitt resigned, denouncing the action against the Boers as 'the meanest war this country has ever waged against a civilised race'.[58] As a journalist, he was particularly incensed by the jingoistic press campaign against the Boers, which he saw as occasioned purely by the wish to annex the Transvaal and Orange Free State. He denounced what he saw as a 'stockbrokers' war' and argued that there was no basis to the claims that the Uitlanders were discriminated against,

52 Ibid., vol. 56, cols 219, 220 (5 April 1898); vol. 62, cols 76, 77 (18 July 1898). Sun Yat Sen wrote to Davitt to thank him for his efforts, Davitt Papers, MSS 9488/4918, 4919. **53** *Hansard*, 4th ser., vol. 56, col. 803 (22 April, 1898); vol. 74, col. 302 (10 July 1899); col. 468 (11 July 1899); cols 687, 688 (13 July 1899). **54** £10,000 was donated by Rhodes and a further £1,000 by John Morrogh, under an agreement that Parnell and his party would press for the retention of Irish representatives in Westminster in the next Home Rule bill, and arrangement which would further Rhodes' scheme of imperial federation, see Donal P. McCracken, *The Irish Pro-Boers, 1877–1902* (Johannesburg and Cape Town, 1989), pp. 23–34. **55** *New York Evening Sun*, 2 January 1896, Davitt Papers, MS 9620, fol. 43. **56** *Hansard*, 4th ser., vol. 73, col. 1155 (30 June 1899). **57** *Freeman's Journal*, 2 October 1899, p. 6. **58** *Hansard*, 4th ser., vol. 73, col. 618 (25 October 1899).

that the Boer governments were corrupt, or that they were unjust towards the Africans. He added that although Irish opposition to the war might damage the prospect for Home Rule, liberty for Ireland should never be purchased at the price of voting against liberty in South Africa.[59] His resignation made a deep impression inside and outside the House. The news was taken up and reported on the continent as well as in Britain and Ireland, and messages, both friendly and hostile, were received (including one threatening letter).[60]

Various motives were attributed to Davitt's resignation, from Tim Healy's malicious suggestion that he was piqued by his failure to win a nomination for Mayo County Council,[61] to the suggestion that he had decided to move to a warmer climate for the sake of his health. The most likely explanation, however, is simply that after the demoralising experience of backbiting and petty in-fighting of the 1890s, Davitt felt that at last he had been presented with a great struggle into which he could throw himself. He took an active part in the Irish pro-Boer movement, serving as a member of the Irish Transvaal Committee,[62] and toured Ireland addressing pro-Boer meetings. When it was announced that Trinity College had invited the colonial secretary, Joseph Chamberlain, to Dublin in December, to confer on him an honorary doctorate, he suggested another demonstration, exclaiming in a letter to Dillon,

> What a horrible sink of anti-Irish feeling Trinity College is; I am inclined to think that there should be a pro-Boer demonstration in Dublin on Saturday the 17th – the day before Joe comes. Oh, for a Corporation that would vote the Freedom of Dublin to Joubert on the 18th![63]

Whether on Davitt's prompting or independently, the Transvaal Committee organised a demonstration at Beresford Place for 17 December. On the eve of the event Dublin Castle banned the meeting and rioting followed attempts to hold the demonstration and police efforts to prevent it. Eventually it was held outside the Transvaal Committee's offices on Abbey Street; William Redmond and Davitt addressed the crowds, denouncing both the war and Chamberlain's part in it.[64]

Four months after his resignation Davitt travelled to South Africa as a war correspondent. Once he had decided to make the journey he set about trying to

59 Ibid., col. 622. His point was that there was a strong likelihood that Irish support for the Boers would alienate Liberal leaders who might otherwise have supported the cause of Irish Home Rule.　**60** Davitt Papers, MS 9419, has press cuttings from eleven French newspapers, including *La Patrie, Le Figaro* and *La Libre Parole,* two Belgian, one German and one Swiss paper. The threatening letter is MS 9419/2094.　**61** *Dublin Evening Telegraph,* 25 October 1899. **62** McCracken, *Irish Pro-Boers,* p. 48, lists him among regular attenders, along with F.B.B. Burke, A. Griff, P.T. Hoctor, George Lyons, K.J.W. O'Beirne, William Redmond, William Rooney, T. O'Neill Russell, T.D. Sullivan, Peter White and W.B. Yeats. The chief activists were Maud Gonne, Arthur Griffith and John O'Leary.　**63** Davitt Papers, MS 9410/1797, Davitt to Dillon, n.d. Piet Joubert was commander-general of the Boer army.　**64** *Freeman's Journal,* 18 December 1899; see also McCracken, *Irish Pro-Boers,* pp. 63–7.

find newspaper commissions to finance it. He had to borrow £250 to pay his travel costs and to meet family expenses while he was away. The *Freeman's Journal* agreed to take his articles and after he had started on his journey he received a cable at Marseilles informing him that Hearst's *New York Journal* would do so as well but his offer to cover the war for the *Irish World* was not accepted.[65]

Davitt spent from late March to June 1900 in South Africa, travelling through the Transvaal and Orange Free State on trains and horse-drawn cars, meeting and interviewing Boer leaders and observing the people. He attended the last meeting of the Transvaal parliament, the Volksraad, on 7 May, describing the atmosphere as funereal, despite an impassioned valedictory address by President Kruger.[66] He remained in South Africa until after the fall of Pretoria on 5 June. The Boer leaders were clearly glad of his support and gave him valuable assistance, so that the dispatches he sent back to Europe were very detailed. He had taken some risks to travel to South Africa – and not only financial ones. With Britain and the Boers at war and his open espousal of the latter in his columns, he was always likely to have attracted a certain amount of public hostility in Britain.[67] He wrote to John Dillon from Pretoria before departing to send word to Paris to let him know 'how feeling is in my regard in the London press and otherwise owing to my visit out here'. He had heard threats in South Africa that there would be an attempt to arrest him on his return and was anxious to be forewarned so that if necessary he would take his family to America until the dust settled.[68] In the event this proved unnecessary, although there were sporadic attacks in the press, such as the letter in the Unionist *Daily Express* in October 1900 asking 'can any of your readers explain how it is that Michael Davitt, after joining the enemy in the Transvaal, is still at large and at liberty to deliver electioneering harangues'.[69]

Davitt had written to Dillon from Naples of his anxiety to return home and begin work on a book about his visit to South Africa. Two years later he published *The Boer Fight for Freedom*, an analysis of the war from a strongly pro-Boer point of view. Beginning with an analysis of the background to the war, the book examines Boer society and the political constitution of the Transvaal and Orange Free State, and provides detailed accounts of the military campaigns, interspersed

---

65 Davitt Papers, MS 9572, Diary, 24 February 1900; ibid., 9411/1801, Davitt to Dillon, n.d. (early January 1900). Ford later told Davitt that his war letters, which he had read in the Dublin edition of the *Freeman's Journal*, were 'decidedly the best war letters I have seen published during the entire war', ibid., 9483/4746, Ford to Davitt, 20 July 1900. **66** Michael Davitt, *The Boer Fight for Freedom* (New York and London, 1902), pp. 421–30. **67** His diaries tell of his suspicions of being followed by detectives in Marseilles before he boarded the *Oxus* for South Africa, Davitt Papers, MS 9572, fol. 17, Diary, 25 February 1900, of a rumoured attempt to kidnap him, ibid., 9573, fols. 3–4, Diary, 9 May 1900, and a fabricated interview with him was published in the *St James's Gazette* in June 1900. **68** Davitt Papers, MS 9411/1803, Davitt to Dillon, 25 April 1900; he wrote again expressing similar fears from Naples on 23 June, MS 9411/1811. **69** *Daily Express*, 16 October 1900, press cutting pasted onto the inside front cover of Davitt's diary, Davitt Papers, MS 9573.

with his own experiences and impressions of places and leaders and is accompanied by his and other photographs. It was, as Howe puts it, 'the most substantial Irish nationalist consideration of the conflict',[70] but it was also, as Howe points out, a flawed account. Davitt's sympathy for the Boers and their struggle at times clouded his judgement and led him into inconsistencies and oversimplification. He greatly admired the courage of the small republics in their resistance to the might of the British empire. He extolled the 'manliness' and stoicism of the people, which he compared to the dissolute behaviour of the fortune-seeking Uitlanders. His denunciation of the role of the mine owners in the origins of the war was apposite, although unfortunately in both his parliamentary speeches and in his book, it led him into a measure of antisemitism. On 17 October 1899, in an address in answer to the queen's speech, he had asked 'Who are the head and front of the Uitlander agitation? Here are the names of some of the "fine old English gentlemen" for whom the British Empire is going to war. They are nearly all millionaires and leading Uitlanders – Beit, Wernher, Eckstein, Rouilot, Bernato, Adler, Lowe, Wolff, Goldmann, Neumann, and Goertz.'[71] Davitt's tone here is curious because in an age when overt antisemitism was common, in Ireland as elsewhere, he defended Jews on more than one occasion in his career. He took part in a mass demonstration against the persecution of Russian Jews held in London in 1890, and acted as investigator for the *New York American* into the Kishinev pogrom of 1903, writing his fifth book, *Within the Pale*, as a study of the situation of Jews in Russia.[72] The following year he denounced as a national disgrace antisemitic sermons by a Redemptorist priest that stirred up attacks on Jews in Limerick. As Donal Lowry has pointed out, antisemitic attitudes were widespread among opponents of the Boer War, including J.A. Hobson, the socialist Edward Carpenter and the trade union leader John Burns.[73] But in Davitt's case it appears incongruous: he clearly made a sharp distinction between privileged Jews and their downtrodden co-religionists.[74]

Even more striking is Davitt's inconsistency in his treatment of Africans. In 1898 he had defended the rights of West Africans to govern their own country,[75] a rather radical position to take in a prevailing atmosphere in which even

---

70 Howe, *Ireland and Empire*, p. 46. **71** *Hansard,* 4th ser., vol. 73, col. 125 (17 October 1899). **72** Michael Davitt, *Within the Pale: the True Story of Anti-Semitic Persecutions in Russia* (New York, 1903); see also Carla King, 'Michael Davitt and the Kishinev pogrom, 1903,' *Irish Slavonic Studies*, 17 (1996), 19–43. **73** Donal Lowry, '"The Boers were the beginning of the end"?: the wider impact of the South African War,' in Donal Lowry (ed.), *The South African War Reappraised* (Manchester, 2000), pp. 203–46. **74** This led him to the peculiar statement in the introduction to *Within the Pale*: 'Where anti-Semitism stands, in fair political combat, in opposition to the foes of nationality, or against the engineers of a sordid war in South Africa … I am resolutely in line with its spirit and programme', although he goes on to attack it in relation to the Kishinev pogrom as 'a thing deserving of no more toleration from right-minded men than do the germs of some malady laden with the poison of a malignant disease' (p. ix). **75** *Hansard,* 4th ser., vol. 53, col. 1633 (24 February 1898).

many reformers who would have granted a measure of self-government to the Indians might have denied it to Africans.[76] However, in his accounts of the situation in South Africa he adopted the same racist tone towards the African population as the Boers, describing them on several occasions as 'savages' and refusing to see in British criticism of Boer treatment of the Africans anything more than a smokescreen for their own ambitions.

Davitt considered the Boer War to be a turning point in Britain's imperial prestige, because it had alienated the other western nations by its aggressive actions towards a small and relatively defenceless country. On witnessing the arrival of some 400 English prisoners on a train after the British defeat at Sannaspos, he confided his mixed feelings to his diary: 'A personal sympathy towards them as prisoners; a political feeling that the enemy of Ireland and of nationality was humiliated before me and that I stood in one of the few places in the world in which the power of England was weak, helpless and despised.'[77]

In his day, through his books and journalism, Davitt's impact on public opinion, both in Ireland and among the Irish abroad, was considerable. In his view nationalism and imperialism were incompatible. While the imperialist assumed that, in Thornton's words, 'good government was better than self-government',[78] Davitt held that only self-government would bring good government because it alone would express the democratic will of the people governed. His internationalist approach, always a minority view among the Irish Party, was to be drowned out in the rise of Irish-Irelandism, with which he explicitly disagreed.[79] In part this was attributable to a generation difference: he was already in his fifties when he served as an MP. Throughout Europe – and Ireland was no exception here – nationalism was taking on a more chauvinistic, even racist tinge. With a few exceptions, such as Roger Casement, E.D. Morel and a handful more, Irish nationalism for the next half-century at least, was to become relatively inward-looking, dominated by the relationship with Britain. While Davitt would have identified himself first as an Irish nationalist, he also sympathised with the downtrodden everywhere, from Australian Aborigines, to Indian workers in South Africa, to Jews in Russia and others.[80] His approach may be summed up in the epitaph he once claimed for himself: 'Here lies a man who from his cradle to his grave was considered by his foes to be a traitor to alien rule and oppression in Ireland and in every land outside her shores.'

---

76 Indeed, Lord Salisbury, in a speech on Irish Catholics and Home Rule, had declared as axiomatic that: 'You you would not confide free representative institutions to the Hottentots, for instance', *The Times*, 17 May 1886. 77 Davitt Papers, MS 9572, f. 121, Diary, 4 April 1900. 78 Thornton, *The Imperial Idea*, p. 70. 79 *The Nationist*, 1 February 1906. 80 David Krause identifies him as 'the conscience of Ireland' (or its representative) in his article, 'The conscience of Ireland: Lalor, Davitt, and Sheehy-Skeffington,' *Éire-Ireland*, 38:1 (Spring 1993), 7–31, but his emphasis is firmly on Davitt's influence in Ireland. Davitt might also be seen as a pioneer of the idea of an ethical foreign policy.

'Something so utterly unprecedented in the annals of human life': William Carleton and the Famine

MELISSA FEGAN

The Ulsterman William Carleton was perhaps best placed to describe Victoria's Ireland, because he interacted with all of its elements, and in a sense created it – certainly for those who outlived his 'transition time'. In spite of the fact that he was derided by many nationalists for his conversion to Protestantism, the memorial attached to his application for a state pension in 1847 bears eloquent witness to the admiration he nevertheless inspired in all sections of the community. As Norman Vance writes:

> Carleton in a sense united his country: the list of eminent persons who petitioned the government to grant him a pension in 1847 represents all the different ways of being Irish. Nothing else could have brought together the President of the Catholic College at Maynooth and Colonel Blacker, the Orange leader, in the presence of Maria Edgeworth, Dan O'Connell's son, Oscar Wilde's father and Rev. Dr. Henry Cooke from Belfast.[1]

Or, as Thomas Flanagan placed it more sensationally in the context of the forth-coming Young Ireland insurrection, Carleton was supported by 'men who were soon to be accused of treason, some of the witnesses against them, the lawyers who prosecuted, and the judges who sentenced them to death.'[2] But perhaps the greatest proof of his role as the historian and prophet of nineteenth-century Ireland is his representation of Victoria's Ireland as Famine Ireland. The prevalence of famine in Carleton's writing suggests the immediacy of experience; he writes not with the detached guilt and horror of the outsider, like Anthony Trollope or Sidney Godolphin Osborne, or indeed with the bewildered outrage of Irish metropolitan observers such as Charles Gavan Duffy and John Mitchel, but as one who has witnessed famine at first hand, if not suffered himself. The lavish spreads in Carleton's stories, such as 'Shane Fadh's Wedding', 'The Station' and 'Going to Maynooth', have a fetishistic feel to them, and Carleton's earliest memory was of being carried by his mother to a wedding or feast, where there

---

1 Norman Vance, *Irish Literature: A Social History: Tradition, Identity and Difference* (Oxford, 1990), p. 137. 2 Thomas Flanagan, *The Irish Novelists, 1800–1850* (New York, 1959), p. 323.

were tables groaning with food; he adds, poignantly: 'I suppose the depth of the impression was occasioned by the novelty of what I saw.'[3]

Famine is pervasive in Carleton's fiction: the decision not to become a priest in the semi-autobiographical 'The Lough Derg Pilgrim' is sparked by repugnance at the demands of money for confession by priests during the 1817 famine; 'Tubber Derg' and 'The Poor Scholar' are unconcealed attacks on Irish landlords, whom Carleton blamed for the severity of the famine of 1817; and *Valentine M'Clutchy*, published in 1845 but set in 1804, scourges agents, landlords and evangelical clergymen who exploit famine for their own ends. While Carleton's primary aim is to show Irish character under duress, he is also touching upon the consequences of colonialism – absenteeism, exploitation, deprivation, starvation.

It is unsurprising that Carleton should be among the first Irish writers to reflect the Great Famine in his literature, as his work is grounded in the major events of early nineteenth-century Ireland – the tithe campaign, agrarian unrest, the temperance crusade, Orangeism, Ribbonism, emigration, land and famine. He presented himself as an historian, recording a society in transition and a dying race. He introduced his collection of stories, *Tales and Sketches*, as:

> probably, something unparalleled in the annals of literature; for the author has reason to think that several of the originals, who sat for their portraits here presented, were the last of their class which the country will ever again produce[.][4]

Written on 16 June 1845, on the very eve of the Great Famine, this prediction was to prove true more quickly than Carleton could have known. Although Carleton is now valued for his depictions of a lost pre-Famine world, his work is more representative of Famine Ireland – the Ireland of those who were vulnerable to almost annual crop failures. His chief interest (at least until after the Famine decimated them) was in the Irish peasantry – not the Big House or the Anglo-Irish or the Gaelic chieftains of famous contemporaries such as Maria Edgeworth and Sydney Owenson, but the precarious peasant world of bare subsistence. As Carleton stressed in *The Black Prophet: A Tale of Irish Famine*, famine was ever-present in so-called pre-Famine Ireland:

> Much for instance is said, and has been said, concerning what are termed 'Years of Famine,' but it is not generally known, that since the introduction of the potato into this country, no year has ever passed which, in some remote locality or other, has not been such to the unfortunate inhabitants.[5]

3 D.J. O'Donoghue, *The Life and Writings of William Carleton* (2 vols, London, 1896), vol. 1, 4.
4 William Carleton, *Tales and Sketches Illustrating the Character, Usages, Traditions, Sports and Pastimes of the Irish Peasantry* (Dublin, 1845), p. viii. 5 William Carleton, *The Black Prophet: A*

Indeed, there had been fourteen partial potato failures in Ireland between 1816 and 1842.[6] Famine was so integral to Irish malaise in the nineteenth century that it transcends the literal for Carleton, becoming a metaphor for cultural dearth and personal impoverishment. For example, in the 'General Introduction' to *Traits and Stories,* in 1842, Carleton compares the state of Irish literary production and publishing to a famine:

> During some of the years of Irish famine, such were the unhappy cir-
> cumstances of the country, that she was exporting provisions of every
> description in the most prodigal abundance, which the generosity of
> England was sending back again for our support. So was it with litera-
> ture. Our men and women of genius uniformly carried their talents to
> the English market, whilst we laboured at home under all the dark pri-
> vations of a literary famine.[7]

Metaphors of literary famine and absenteeism constitute a powerful vindication of Carleton's much-vaunted resolve to revive his country's industry by staying in Ireland and publishing there (though to an extent he had little choice in the matter). But there is a serious subversive point here also: it is fascinating to real-ize that three years before the onset of the Great Famine, Carleton is employ-ing one of the key arguments of the nationalist mythos surrounding the Famine, and the mainstay of John Mitchel's argument about England's genoci-dal agenda: that England drained Ireland of provisions while Ireland starved. Astonishingly, the criticism occurs even earlier in Carleton's work. 'Phil Purcel, the Pig-Driver', which first appeared in *Traits and Stories* in 1833, sardonically attacks the practice of exporting to Britain while the Irish starve in a barely veiled threat:

> But it is very condescending in John to eat our beef and mutton; and as
> he happens to want both, it is particularly disinterested in him to encour-
> age us in the practice of self-denial. It is possible, however, that we may
> ultimately refuse to banquet by proxy on our own provisions; and that
> John may not be much longer troubled to eat for us in that capacity.[8]

'The Poor Scholar', also published in 1833, describes the immense amount of food leaving Ireland in exports: 'the very country thus groaning under such a terrible sweep of famine is actually pouring from all her ports a profusion of food, day after day; flinging it from her fertile bosom, with the wanton excess

Tale of Irish Famine (London and Belfast, 1847), p. 175. **6** R.F. Foster, *Modern Ireland, 1600–1972* (London, 1988), p. 320. **7** William Carleton, 'General Introduction', in *Traits and Stories of the Irish Peasantry* (3 vols, Dublin and London, 1841), vol. 1, v. **8** 'Phil Purcel', in *Traits and Stories*, vol. 1, 410.

of a prodigal oppressed by abundance.'⁹ Carleton's revolutionary language long predates the militant language of Mitchel in a post-Famine and supposedly alien world.

Carleton has been criticized for not creating in *The Black Prophet* or other works a plot commensurate to the atrocity of the Great Famine. Malcolm Brown, like many others underestimating Carleton's intellect and overestimating his peasant status, believes that he was simply incapable of understanding its enormity: 'beyond communicating the raw feel of human pain, Carleton's peasant brain had trouble seizing the meaning of the catastrophe.'¹⁰ In fact, *The Black Prophet* was one of those curious prophetic quirks of Carleton's fiction, arising from the depth of social knowledge submerged in his works. The novel was first published in the *Dublin University Magazine* between May and December 1846; when it first began to appear, there had only been the partial blight of 1845, and no sign that the destruction would recur. Even when Carleton wrote his polemical 'Preface' to *The Black Prophet* in February 1847, he could foresee that there would be great hardship due to the unexpected second failure in 1846, and he knew from his own experience that disease would follow, but he could not have predicted the low yield of 1847, or the failure of 1848. It is for this reason – the fact that the Great Famine did not exist as a concept when Carleton began to write *The Black Prophet* – and not for any inability to comprehend the tragedy, that Carleton chose to use the Famine as a background to a murder mystery. Despite the well-intentioned but misguided defence of *The Black Prophet* by critics such as Sophia Hillan King, that one 'need not go to this novel for plot, but rather for its evocation of the realities of famine', this is not at all what Carleton intended.¹¹ The principal interest of the novel, he stresses in the same 'Introduction' in which he criticizes the government for failing to protect Ireland from famine, should not be 'so gloomy a topic as famine', but 'the workings of those passions and feelings which usually agitate human life, and constitute the character of those who act in it.'¹² *The Black Prophet* was in fact nothing less than a pre-emptive strike on the market.¹³ For Carleton, this was simply the latest in a long line of failures – a fact made clear by the non-specific subtitle, *A Tale of Irish Famine*. As far as he was concerned, this famine would soon be forgotten, and it would be a shame to let it pass without making some literary, political and financial capital from it: 'National inflictions of this kind pass away, and are soon forgotten by every one but those with whom they have left their melancholy memorials.'¹⁴ One hundred and fifty years later, Cormac Ó Gráda

---

9 'The Poor Scholar', in *Traits and Stories*, vol. 2, 307.   10 Malcolm Brown, *The Politics of Irish Literature from Thomas Davis to W. B. Yeats* (London, 1972), p. 92.   11 Sophia Hillan King, '"Pictures drawn from memory": William Carleton's experience of famine', *Irish Review*, 17/18 (Winter 1995), 80–9, p. 82.   12 Carleton, *Black Prophet*, p. iv.   13 *Howitt's Journal*, 1:17 (24 April 1847), 236–7, p. 236; Barbara Hayley, *A Bibliography of the Writings of William Carleton* (Gerrards Cross, 1983), p. 149.   14 Carleton, *Black Prophet*, p. iv.

concurs: 'Ironically, had the potato famine of 1845 lasted just one year, it would have merited no more than a few paragraphs in the history books.'[15]

But this famine did not pass away. In 1842, on the basis of his own exertions in periodicals and books, Carleton announced a new age of Irish literature. By 1848 that dream – and one million people – were dead. Carleton's first publisher, William Curry Jr., and seventy-two other Irish publishers, were declared bankrupt between 1844 and 1848, reflecting a wide-spread economic destruction brought on by the Famine.[16] On a visit to London in 1850, Carleton found that *The Black Prophet* had achieved a wide and appreciative English audience. However, Carleton, like Trollope, was to discover that English readers had tired of gloomy Irish subjects. The London publisher Maxwell declined to publish a Carleton novel in 1850, telling him that 'the Irish are not able to buy it, and the English will not', and making the bizarre suggestion that the Irish national novelist should 'go to Lancashire, reside there, and devote his gifts to English subjects'.[17] James Duffy, the notable survivor among Irish publishers, warned Carleton in 1855: 'The people seldom think of buying books, because they are luxuries, which they can do without.'[18] Carleton's disillusionment with both Irish literature and Ireland itself can be traced in *The Squanders of Castle Squander*, published – significantly, given Carleton's criticism of literary exportation, in London – in 1852.

Based on 'a knowledge of more than fifty years of my people and the country', *Castle Squander* also charts the destruction of fifty years of Irish literature, beginning with an Edgeworthian comic framework, and ending with a literary nervous breakdown.[19] The novel begins with the first-person narrative of Randy O'Rollick, the bailiff's son, one of the new breed of wily social climbers thriving in the ruins of feudal Ireland; Randy even mentions casually that bailiffs often make their sons attorneys in order to swindle their masters of their land – as Thady Quirk's son Jason had done in *Castle Rackrent*.[20] But as the narrative grows progressively darker, O'Rollick's narrative is usurped by authorial intrusions and extracts from the *Dublin University Magazine*, Charles Trevelyan's *The Irish Crisis*, letters by W.N. Hancock and J.S. Mill, references to Dante's *Inferno*, Mary Shelley's *Frankenstein*, Defoe's *The Great Plague*, and Carleton's own novel *Valentine M'Clutchy*. *The Black Prophet* had been mined from his own experience of the 1817 famine, but now, realising in hindsight that the Great Famine was utterly unprecedented in its horror and impact, and that he, as a member of the Dublin intelligentsia, had been spared its ravages, the Irish national novelist finds himself forced to rely on textual evidence.

15 Cormac Ó Gráda, *Ireland before and after the Famine: Explorations in Economic History, 1800–1925* (Manchester, 1988), p. 5. **16** Charles Benson, 'Printers and booksellers in Dublin 1800–1850', in Robin Myers and Michael Harris (eds), *Spreading the Word: the Distribution Networks of Print 1550–1850* (Winchester, 1990), pp. 47–59, p. 57. **17** O'Donoghue, *Life*, vol. 2, 176–7. **18** Ibid., vol. 2, 215. **19** William Carleton, *The Squanders of Castle Squander* (2 vols, London, 1852), vol. 1, iii–iv. **20** Ibid., vol. 1, 3–4.

Though bewildered by the Famine, Carleton was not confused about its cause and consequences. Like Anthony Trollope, he toys with the idea of the Famine as providential retribution. The starving in *The Black Prophet* are described as 'like creatures changed from their very humanity by some judicial plague that had been sent down from heaven to punish and desolate the land'.[21] Carleton allows us to believe, along with the people of Glen Dhu, that the Daltons' decline and fall into poverty and then starvation and sickness is punishment for a murder committed by the head of the family twenty years before: 'it became too certain to be doubted, that the slow but sure finger of God's justice was laid upon them as an additional proof that crime, however it may escape the laws of men, cannot veil itself from the all-seeing eye of the Almighty.'[22] In fact, old Dalton is innocent, and his decline is due to economic, social and political imperatives rather than supernatural agencies: the ruthless grasping of the middleman, who wants to evict the Daltons so as to profit by the £500 improvements they have made on their farm; their absentee landlord, who draws £32,000 a year from his estate, yet who contributed only £100 to the relief of his famine-stricken tenants;[23] and by implication the government, whom Carleton had criticized in the 'Dedication' for not legislating to prevent such disasters. Moreover, Providence is exposed as false currency in its use by the miser Darby Skinadre, who justifies his exploitation of his clients with providential theory: 'the thruth is, we have brought all these scourges on us by our sins and our thransgressions; thim that sins, Jemmy, must suffer.'[24] Such a doctrine in such a mouth must be discredited. As in Carleton's previous examinations of famine, fault lies not with a sinful people, but with a social chaos. However, things are different in *Castle Squander*; the enormity of the catastrophe disrupted not only his link to the authentic peasantry, but his hold on common sense. Carleton had begun *The Black Prophet* with an appeal to Lord John Russell to ameliorate the Famine and prevent it ever happening again; he ends *Castle Squander* with the assertion that the Famine 'came upon us, not from Lord John Russell, but directly from the hand of God'.[25]

Castle Squander opens in a year of famine, and Randy witnesses the excesses of the Squanders' entertainments while their tenants starve. Masses of food lie about in the dust of the kitchen floor, the dogs are treated to bins of oatmeal and potatoes, and we are reminded:

> Now it so happened, that the year in question was one of severe famine, and I could not help reflecting, even then, that the sum of five pounds, subscribed to the relief fund by Mr. Squander, took a very inhuman shape, when associated with the profuse abundance thus lavished in his kennel, whilst so many of his fellow creatures, nay, of his own tenants, were literally perishing for want of food.[26]

21 Carleton, *Black Prophet*, pp. 176–7. 22 Ibid., p. 99. 23 Ibid., p. 198. 24 Ibid., p. 53. 25 Carleton, *Castle Squander*, vol. 2, 391. 26 Ibid., vol. 1, 44.

However, whereas in his previous works famine would have provided a catalyst exposing the Irish peasant character, here it simply highlights the immoral excesses of Irish landlords; but again there is a subversive undercurrent, as Squander's £5 donation is doubtless a sly reference to the (untrue) story that Queen Victoria had given only £5 to famine relief. There is an impassable gulf established between the Big House and the cabin, which Carleton does not attempt to breach. Once Randy is established at Castle Squander, his peasant family virtually disappears from view. This is of course partly dictated by the novel's overt parody of *Castle Rackrent*, but it is also Carleton's way of distancing himself from individual famine victims. In *Castle Squander*, the process of dehumanization begun in *The Black Prophet* intensifies. Carleton was an experienced writer of the macabre – one only has to read 'Wildgoose Lodge' to see that. He often refers to the Irish peasantry as 'Frankensteins',[27] and almost forty years before J.S. Le Fanu's 'Carmilla', and sixty-four years before Bram Stoker's *Dracula*, Carleton was describing ruthless agents as 'vampyres';[28] for example, in *The Black Prophet*, Sarah is described as a 'beautiful vampire that was ravening for the blood of its awakened victim'.[29] But nothing prepares us for the amount and intensity of horror in *Castle Squander*. On a visit to Squander's tomb, Mrs Squander, Emily and Tom seem to enter an Inferno, where rotting cholera victims are tossed into trenches, only to be dragged out by ravenous dogs:

> Legs and arms stripped of the flesh and bearing about them the unnatural marks left by the bloody fangs of some hungry mastiff, were scattered about. Some had been dragged into the neighbouring fields, as might be learned by the eager and interrupted howl of the half-gratified animal, as he feasted upon the revolting meat. In a different field might be seen another wolfish hound, with a human head between his paws, on the features of which he was making his meal.
> *Now, all these frightful pictures were facts of that day, and were witnessed by thousands!*[30]

In *Red Hall, or The Baronet's Daughter*, published the same year, and with a similar Big House setting, the animals who eat putrid flesh are human beings, and with the final taboo, cannibalism, falls the myth of family solidarity in the face of famine:

> all the impulses of nature and affection were not merely banished from the heart, but superseded by the most frightful peals of insane mirth, cru-

---

27 For example, *Castle Squander*, vol. 2, 88. Carleton makes the common mistake of believing 'Frankenstein' was the monster, not its creator. **28** 'Poor Scholar', in *Traits and Stories*, vol. 2, 332; William Carleton, *Valentine M'Clutchy, the Irish Agent; or, Chronicles of the Castle Cumber Property* (2 vols, Dublin, 1845), vol. 2, 175. **29** Carleton, *Black Prophet*, p. 10. **30** Carleton, *Castle Squander*, vol. 2, 139.

elty, and the horrible appetite of the ghoul and vampire. Some were found tearing the flesh from the bodies of the carcasses that were stretched beside them… fathers have been known to make a wolfish meal upon the dead bodies of their own offspring. We might, therefore, have carried on our description up to the very highest point of imaginable horror, without going beyond the truth.[31]

While famine offers the ultimate in artistic license for Gothic and realist authors, this is Carleton's nightmare, a vision he strove desperately to escape. The narrator of *Castle Squander* in a post-Famine Ireland recalls that the Famine was:

> something so utterly unprecedented in the annals of human life, as the mingled mass of agony was borne past us upon the wild and pitiless blast, that we find ourselves absolutely incompetent even to describe it. We feel, however, as if that loud and multitudinous wail was still ringing in our ears, against which and the terrible recollections associated with it, we wish we could close them and the memory that brings them into fresh existence.[32]

This author, who had traded for so long on his authenticity and shared experiences with the Irish peasantry, could no longer claim the status either of victim or historian: he had not starved, or emigrated, he was no longer representative, in either sense of the word. He responds by deliberately distancing himself from famine victims: first by dehumanising them, making them carrion for dogs or worse, for each other; then, by isolating the Famine in the south and west of the country.

In a comic scene near the start of *Castle Squander*, Randy, applying for the post of tutor to the Squander boys, avoids exposing his ignorance of mathematics to Dr M'Claret, the Protestant rector, by answering his questions in Irish. M'Claret, who, like Carleton, had begun life as a northern Catholic, does not understand Irish, and asks Randy to explain:

> 'It is the vernacular, sir, of a certain country, with whose history you are evidently unacquainted. Of a country, sir, whose inhabitants live upon a meal a month; keep very little – for sound reasons – between themselves and the elements, and where abstinence from food is the national diversion.'
>
> 'God bless me!' exclaimed the parson, 'that's very odd, very odd indeed, I shall take a note of that; how very like Ireland!'[33]

---

31 William Carleton, *Red Hall or, The Baronet's Daughter* (3 vols, London, 1852), vol. 2, 34–5.
32 Carleton, *Castle Squander*, vol. 2, 105.

Irish is thus established as the vernacular of a famine-stricken people, isolating it among the peasantry from whom Carleton had escaped. But the north of Ireland, Carleton's homeland, is spared in *Castle Squander*, despite contemporary reports in the *Banner of Ulster* and the *Belfast Vindicator*, and historical evidence that Ulster certainly partook of the Famine. Tom Squander's property luckily lies in an industrious northern county, and even during the Famine his income is maintained. Henry Squander, also from the north, is in the end able to buy up his ancestral residence in the Encumbered Estates Court. On a visit to Henry's home in Ulster, Randy is amazed at the contrast: 'The trim hedges, the neat and clean culture, the superior dress, the sober and thoughtful demeanour, and the calm air of self-respect and independence which marked the inhabitants of the north, were such as could not for a moment be mistaken.'[34] While Carleton is scoring a didactic point about the virtues of his adopted religion, he is also denying that his people, the people of Ulster, were affected by famine. He had suppressed their accent in *Traits and Stories* to achieve cohesive nationality, but now he resurrects it as a barrier against the vernacular of a famine-stricken people. He had revisited his native Clogher Valley in 1847 and found it depopulated by eviction and emigration, but in *Castle Squander* it is repeopled, newly prosperous, untouched. Like Lord Dunroe of *Red Hall*, Carleton has come to associate Irishness with starvation, brutality and cannibalism: 'call me profligate – spendthrift – debauchée – anything you will but an Irishman.'[35] His response was a retreat to history in later novels such as *Willy Reilly* and *Redmond O'Hanlon*.

Carleton's friend, Charles Gavan Duffy, travelling in the west of Ireland in 1849, despaired at what the Famine had done to his countrymen:

> Connaught has reached that lowest depth in which there is no lower deep. I declare before Heaven that looking upon the peasantry of the West I have over and again been tempted to pray that GOD by some sudden merciful plague would cut them off the earth and save the land from another generation lower than men, and more unmercifully tasked and driven than the beasts of burden ... The entire peasant children of Mayo seem to be reared up to whine with their first speech, 'give us a hep-ney.'[36]

Carleton was similarly devastated by this Famine which had divorced him from his people and destroyed his hopes for Irish literature. In *Castle Squander*, he recants his belief in Irish civilisation:

---

33 Ibid., vol. 1, 31. **34** Ibid., vol. 2, 185. **35** Carleton, *Red Hall*, vol. 2, 50. **36** *Nation*, 8 September 1849, p. 24.

> Is there any great poem that the country can claim as particularly her own? … Away then with the cant of ancient civilisation. We Celts were never civilised, and are not civilised, nor will be properly so for at least another half century, if even at that period.[37]

The Famine had proved that, and had destroyed not only Carleton's hopes for Irish literature, but the people who had formed the raw material of his work.

---

37 Carleton, *Castle Squander*, vol. 2, 207.

Anthony Trollope's representation of the Great Famine

YVONNE SIDDLE

In a talk which he gave to the Royal Society of Literature, Terry Eagleton recalled a theatre-bar eavesdropping which, in its own incidental way, has something to say about the complexity of the relationship between Ireland and England and the blurring of Irish and English identities in particular. During the interval of a London performance of his play about Oscar Wilde, *Saint Oscar*, he overheard a woman ask her companion, 'Was Wilde really Irish, or is Eagleton just making that up?'[1] I am not sure whether this question tells us more about an English audience's ignorance of Wilde's nationality, the convincing nature of the playwright's representation of the English, or Terry Eagleton's reputation for inventive interpretation. Be that as it may, Eagleton went on to report that it was asked 'with mild indignation, as one might I suppose, if someone presented Shakespeare as a Zulu or Wordsworth as Bulgarian'.[2]

Since a similarly surprised, if not always indignant, response has occasionally greeted me on announcing that I am researching Anthony Trollope's Irish fiction, I should perhaps make it clear from the outset that I am not claiming that Anthony Trollope was Irish. Equally, however, I have no need to invent or exaggerate a strong Irish connection for this writer who is usually perceived as quintessentially English. Trollope was resident in Ireland for eighteen years, and his first and last novels were set there. Moreover, Ireland was the location and, to some extent, the means of transformation of his personal, social and professional life. He arrived there in 1841 at the age of 26, by his own estimation a failure in all of these areas.[3]

Trollope's childhood had been blighted by his father's disastrous financial investments. In his autobiography, he records the depths of despair experienced when he found himself socially excluded as a relatively impoverished, scruffy child among the wealthy and well-born at Harrow and Winchester.[4] The

---

1 *Independent,* 10 November 2000. **2** Ibid. **3** Anthony Trollope, *An Autobiography* ([1883] London, 1996), pp. 27–44. For accounts of Trollope's time in Ireland, see also N. John Hall, *Trollope: A Biography* (Oxford, 1991), pp. 81–110, 501–6, and Victoria Glendinning, *Trollope* (London, 1992), pp. 110–40, 149–67, 494–6. Roy Foster, in *Paddy and Mr Punch: Connections in Irish and English History* (London, 1993), deals with Trollope's Irish fiction and his relationship with that country, and devotes a chapter of *The Irish Story: Telling Tales and Making It Up in Ireland* (London, 2001) to Trollope's response to Ireland, and particularly the Famine, and its enduring effect on him. **4** Trollope, *Autobiography,* pp. 7–18.

Anthony Trollope who became a clerk in the General Post Office in London in 1834 was, by his own account, 'an idle, desolate hanger on, that most hopeless of human beings, a hobbledehoy of nineteen without any idea of a career, or a profession, or a trade'.[5] Nor did his position at the Post Office prove to be the making of him. For seven years, he insisted, he had been a card-playing wastrel and a difficult and tardy employee.[6] Even allowing for the hyperbole he employs in his autobiography to enhance its effectiveness as an exemplary narrative, his superiors in London do seem to have had reason to celebrate when, in 1841, he volunteered for the post of surveyor's clerk in the Central District in Ireland.[7]

Whilst Trollope might have harboured some hopes that a new start in Ireland would improve his lot, his relocation seems to have been born more of reckless desperation than acquisitive ambition. Again in his autobiography, he explains:

> In truth I was wretched, – sometimes almost unto death, and have often cursed the hour in which I was born. There had clung to me a feeling that I had been looked upon always as an evil, an encumbrance, a useless thing, – as a creature of whom those connected with him had to be ashamed.[8]

The rehabilitation made possible by his move to Ireland, he offers as almost magical in its suddenness and completeness, simply declaring, 'from the day on which I set foot in Ireland all these evils went away from me. Since that time who has had a happier life than mine?'[9]

In Ireland Trollope was transformed. He shook off his profligate ways, embraced the work ethic and became a conscientious and valued official sent on troubleshooting and fact-finding missions to England, Wales, Scotland, the Channel Islands, Egypt and the West Indies.[10] Moreover, he married, had two sons and began his writing career.[11] He thrived in a job which freed him from his desk and allowed him to gallop around the Irish countryside. Importantly, the spirits and confidence of the young Trollope can only have been boosted by his elevation from social pariah to the elite position enjoyed by British officials in Ireland. The extent of his social acceptance is suggested by the offended reaction of what he calls his 'Irish circle' to his choice of an English, rather than an Irish, bride. There had evidently been some expectation in Banagher society that the young surveyor's clerk, if he was to marry at all, should return their hospitality by marrying one of their daughters.[12]

Whilst his literary ambitions pre-date his time in Ireland, his new stability and happiness seem to have created the ideal conditions for these to flourish, and Ireland provided the inspiration and material for his first two novels *The*

5 Ibid., p. 23.   6 Ibid., pp. 27–42.   7 Ibid., p. 42.   8 Ibid., p. 43.   9 Ibid.   10 Ibid., pp. 44–5, 78–83, 85–7.   11 Ibid., pp. 50, 66.   12 Ibid., p. 50.

Macdermots of Ballycloran (1847) and *The Kellys and the O'Kellys* (1848). More typically Trollopian and English novels followed – *The Warden* (1855), *Barchester Towers* (1857), *The Three Clerks* (1858), *Dr Thorne* (1858) and *The Bertrams* (1859) – and by the time of his transfer back to England in 1859, although his career was yet to reach its peak, his standing was such that he was contracted to write a serialised novel for the first edition of the new *Cornhill Magazine* which Thackeray was editing.[13]

Despite a noted resistance among the reading public to Irish tales and Trollope's undoubted concern for commercial success, he returned to the subject of Ireland in his fiction throughout his life. *Castle Richmond,* published in 1860, is a valedictory novel which he was determined to write in open opposition to a prevailing hostility to all things Irish.[14] In the 1860s he wrote two short stories set in Ireland, 'The O'Connors of Castle Connor' and 'Father Giles of Ballymoy'. His novel *An Eye for an Eye,* written in 1870, is predominantly an Irish story, and Phineas Finn, the eponymous protagonist of two of Trollope's Palliser novels, is Irish. In the final months of his life he twice visited Ireland to gather material for *The Landleaguers* (1882) which even, perhaps especially, in its bitterest pronouncements, announces Trollope's lifelong entanglement with Ireland.

Trollope's arrival in Ireland in 1841 in one sense placed him ideally to enter the discourse on the causes, progress and consequences of the Great Famine. He had the opportunity to acquaint himself with the country and its people before the appearance of the potato blight and to track its course. Certainly, in his own mind, his objective of educating what he perceived to be an English public largely ignorant or misinformed about Ireland,[15] combined perfectly with his extensive knowledge to make him an expert witness. In the first of a series of letters he wrote to the *Examiner* about the Famine in 1849 and 1850, he affirmed:

> I have this advantage on my side in the observations I am about to make: – I have been eight years in the country, and have passed those years in continual journeys through its southern, western, and midland portions. During this time I have been thrown much among Irishmen of every class.[16]

Contemporary reviews and some more recent literary criticism applaud his knowledge of the complexities of Irish society, idiom, topography and politics.[17]

Furthermore, the humorous short story 'Father Giles of Ballymoy', based on Trollope's early experiences in Ireland, suggests a man prepared to be informed

13 Hall, *Trollope*, pp. 190–1. **14** Anthony Trollope, *Castle Richmond* ([1860] Oxford, 1989), p. 1. **15** Anthony Trollope, letter to the *Examiner*, 30 March 1850, in Helen Garlinghouse King (ed.), 'Trollope's Letters to the *Examiner*', *Princeton University Library Chronicle* (Winter 1965), p. 77. All subsequent references are to this edition. **16** Letter to the *Examiner*, 25 August 1849. **17** Unsigned notice, *John Bull*, 22 May 1847; R. Tracy, introduction to Anthony Trollope, *The Macdermots of Ballycloran* ([1847] Oxford, 1989), pp. xiii–xxvi.

and to lay aside preconceptions. His narrator Archibald Green, a rather brusque, nervous young Englishman, arrives in Ireland with no factual information about the country, but with a ready set of stereotypical notions. Not least among these is an image of conniving and coercive Catholic priests prepared to stoop to any extreme of torture – perhaps, he speculates, even depriving an Englishman of his trousers – in order to force mass on Protestant travellers. Panicked by his own prejudices, Green fails to appreciate that the local priest has kindly agreed to let him share his hotel room. Therefore when the eponymous Father Giles inno- cently tries to retire for the night to the bed next to Green's, the Englishman pushes him down the stairs and has to be protected from an avenging local pop- ulace. Significantly, in the end all is well and Green and the priest become firm friends. The folly of preconceptions has been revealed and underlined.[18]

However, the course of Trollope's life in Ireland before and during the Famine also indicates belief in a level of normality, even progress, which, what- ever his opportunities to intelligently observe the spectrum of Irish experience, was not available to 'Irishmen of every class'. Having lived first in Banagher, Kings' County (County Offaly), he moved to Clonmel, County Tipperary, in June 1845. He had regularised his finances sufficiently to marry Rose Heseltine in the previous year. The acceptance for publication of his first novel *The Macdermots of Ballycloran* coincided with the first reports of the potato blight. As the Famine developed, Trollope's two sons were born, Henry Merivale on 13 March 1846, and Frederick James Anthony on 27 September 1847. He began writing his second novel, *The Kellys and the O'Kellys*, in 1846 and continued it as the Famine took its heaviest toll. It is a more comedic piece than his first, and very precisely set in 1844 and therefore before the blight. It was published in 1848, the year in which the Trollopes moved to Mallow, County Cork, and the Young Irelanders staged their rising – an event which Trollope claimed did not unduly worry him. Thus, while he was travelling in some of the most severely famine-stricken areas of Ireland, he was becoming a husband, a father, a respected official and a published author.[19]

The main body of Trollope's representation of the Irish Famine is contained in a series of letters he wrote to the *Examiner*, and in his novel *Castle Richmond*. The first *Examiner* letter appeared in August 1849, the remaining six between March and June 1850. They were ostensibly written to refute complaints which had been made about government relief measures in several letters to *The Times* by Sidney Godolphin Osborne. Yet while he does directly counter some points raised by Osborne, the *Times* letters become a convenient peg on which to hang a thesis which had been preoccupying Trollope for some time. The explanation of the Famine which emerges is of a blight visited by God on a

---

18 Trollope, 'Father Giles of Ballymoy' (1866), in John Hampden (ed.), *Novels and Stories by Anthony Trollope* (London, 1946), pp. 397–414. **19** Trollope, *Autobiography*, pp. 42–113; Hall, *Trollope*, pp. 81–184; Glendinning, *Trollope*, pp. 114–17.

financially and morally impoverished land. The impoverishment has been brought about by extravagant landowners borrowing money they cannot repay and by middle-class tenants with genteel aspirations subdividing the land they rent and living an idle life on the proceeds. The availability of these subdivisions has in turn encouraged the peasantry to rely on 'the easy root'.[20] God has sent the Famine, therefore, to correct this state of affairs which the Irish have created, while a conscientious English government battles against unprecedented and overwhelming odds to provide effective relief.[21] He admits that the sufferings of the poor are 'awful', and that relief measures were not always without drawbacks, but his emphasis is not on this but on the efficacy of the measures taken, the wisdom of a reticence to intervene and on signs of recovery.[22] He encourages his English readers to place their faith in the amended Poor Law and the Encumbered Estates Acts, urging those who can to become Irish landowners.[23]

There is evidence in these letters of the detailed knowledge Trollope had acquired of the country, and of his capacity to reach beyond his position as a privileged Englishman. Yet a strong sense also emerges of a man battling conflicting emotions and motivations, measuring his own state against the suffering around him, or rather trying to avoid doing just this. Perhaps understandably he retreats behind the party line to the comforting territory governed by political economy and providentialism.

If his insistently optimistic tone can be explained by his mission to counteract excessively negative images and encourage investment in Ireland, the lengths to which he goes to achieve this by minimising the catastrophic consequences visited on the Irish poor are confusing and unconvincing. In his third letter, for example, he refutes the ubiquity of untended dead bodies reported by so many other eyewitnesses:

> During the whole period of the famine I never saw a dead body lying exposed in the open air, either in a town or in the country. I moreover never saw a dead body within a cabin which had not been laid out in some sort of rough manner. Now it may be said that if I did not enter cabins, I could not see the horrid sights which were to be met within: but such a remark cannot apply to that which is said to have been of such frequent occurrence out under the open sky.[24]

Does he intend the reader to believe that he never saw a dead body lying in the open air, or that he specifically never saw an exposed, that is, uncovered, body? Is he stating the latter but hoping the reader will infer the former? Is he even

---

20 Letter to the *Examiner*, 30 March 1850. **21** Letter to the *Examiner*, 25 August 1849. **22** Letters to the *Examiner*, 30 March 1850, 28 August 1849, 15 June 1850. **23** Letter to the *Examiner*, 15 June 1850. **24** Letter to the *Examiner*, 6 April 1850

confessing that he did not enter any cabins and is therefore unqualified as a witness to the 'horrid sights' within?

This fumbling logic is matched by semantic awkwardness later in the letter when Trollope seeks to further minimise Famine deaths by separating deaths attributable to starvation and therefore to famine, from those caused by disease. Not wanting to confirm a connection by using the word 'famine', he writes of 'deaths from disease consequent on the sudden alteration in the nature and bulk of food'. Since he calculates such deaths as probably four times those caused by starvation, he is then able to make the astounding claim that 'deaths from absolute famine were comparatively speaking, few'. Moreover, Trollope even discourages his reader from contemplating the possibility that more lives could have been saved. 'The question is', he insists, with due regard for the tenets of political economy, 'could an equal amount of life have been saved at less expense, and fewer ill consequences?'

It was 1859 before Trollope produced a fictional representation of the Famine. Although *Castle Richmond* is retrospective and therefore obviously able to benefit from the omniscience of hindsight, Trollope's basic contentions about the Famine, at least as they appear in direct pronouncements in the novel, are the same as those offered in the *Examiner* letters – that God sent the blight to correct an intolerable situation largely of Ireland's own making, and that the government did its best in overwhelming circumstances. He is now able to support these claims with what he regards as evidence of Ireland's economic recovery, and to celebrate the disappearance of the landlords whose idleness and extravagance necessitated divine intervention. He allows himself to focus not on this reprehensible group, but on the Fitzgerald family, who exemplify those worthy landowners who rose to meet their responsibilities during the crisis.

He also offers a more thorough and prominent consideration of his providentialist stance. Where the intervening years seem to have left Trollope more prepared to question the practical difficulties, if not the moral correctness, of adhering to the principles of political economy, his conviction that the Famine was divinely ordained seems to have grown stronger and he carefully delineates the precise strain of providentialism to which he subscribes. His is not a vengeful but a merciful God doing for Ireland what she could not do for herself. In his scheme there can only be a limited role for state intervention to stay the Famine since 'no human power could suffice to put it down'.[25] Although there is a more extensive exploration in the narrative of the weaknesses of government relief measures, the dominant authorial voice is one of conscience-salving reassurance.

As Trollope is careful to emphasise in its last chapter, *Castle Richmond* does not purport to be a tale of the Famine but a 'Tale of the Famine Year'.[26] The Famine does not take centre stage but provides a backdrop for a conventional

25 Trollope, *Castle Richmond,* p. 83. **26** Ibid., p. 488.

'Big House' plot of love thwarted and an inheritance threatened. Trollope does intervene to make a number of direct authorial statements which bring the Famine into the foreground, but it mainly functions in the narrative as a means of dramatising the Fitzgerald family's strong sense of duty and responsibility, their social and economic value as landlords and conduits of the government's relief policy.

Though twenty-first century sensibilities tend to balk at this marginalisation of such a catastrophic event and automatically discern sinister intentions, given Trollope's belief in the possibility of treating serious issues in a romantic novel his motives are not necessarily base. It is not impossible to envisage a novel which marries the fates of the Irish of elevated and humble origins in such a way as to tell a convincing Famine tale. Trollope, however, fails to achieve this. In a way he neither fully intends nor appreciates, his fiction offers a message which undermines the sustainability of both his main plot and his explanation of the Famine.

This is best exemplified in a pivotal chapter in the novel entitled 'The Last Stage'.[27] Both Trollope the novelist and Trollope the government apologist have a great deal invested in this chapter. Given the importance he attached to sympathetic characterisation and his need to validate his concentration on the 'Big House' plot, it is vital to the success of the novel that the reader identifies favourably in this episode with Herbert Fitzgerald, Trollope's main protagonist. Moreover, Trollope creates the scene to dramatise the providential nature of the Famine – the last stage in which human agency, no matter how well intentioned, is powerless. In this sense both his novel and his explanation of the Famine are being tested.

The episode occurs as Herbert is about to leave for London, believing himself to have been disinherited by his parents' bigamous marriage. He is on his way to bid farewell to his fiancée, Clara Desmond, when a rainstorm forces him to take shelter. He dismounts and enters a roadside cabin, leading his horse in after him. Inside he is confronted by desperate scene. It is a scene which, as Christopher Morash has noted, provides 'a shock of ethical awareness'.[28] A near-naked woman sits on the wet earth clutching a child who is almost dead, while another lies dead in the corner.[29]

Aspects of the scene are recreated with genuine poignancy. Herbert is convincingly horror-stricken and the woman and her family are individualised, not left as part of an undifferentiated crowd. However, other aspects of the encounter emphasise an unresolved imbalance in the novel, give rise to what Margaret Kelleher has identified as an 'anxiety' in the reader, and sabotage Trollope's novelistic and ideological intentions for the chapter.[30]

---

27 Ibid., pp. 366–75. **28** Christopher Morash, *Writing the Irish Famine* (Oxford, 1995), p. 50. **29** Trollope, *Castle Richmond*, pp. 369–73. **30** Margaret Kelleher, 'Irish Famine in literature', in Cathal Póirtéir (ed.), *The Great Irish Famine* (Dublin, 1995), p. 235.

An uneasiness is created from the moment Herbert, as an upper-class man, enters the cabin with his horse. The woman's near-nakedness does seem to be an attempt to represent the actual state of Famine victims, rather than an instance of insensitive voyeurism, but in emphasising the contrast between her inferior and vulnerable state and Herbert's superior and powerful one, it raises both questions about his right to be there and expectations that he has a responsibility to act. Trollope, however, in keeping with his reading of the Famine, puts it beyond Herbert's powers to do so. He places the woman and her younger child in an irretrievable state of starvation. The actions left to Herbert, whose worth has been partly predicated on his responsible and effective relief work, are either inadequate or doomed to failure. He gives the woman some money which she seems to have no means of spending and arranges for someone to take her to the union workhouse. This transport arrives after she and her baby have died.[31]

Significantly, the action by which Trollope seems to intend to indicate Herbert's compassion and respect serves more effectively to highlight the divisions of wealth, class, experience and, in Trollope's case, nationality, which separate Herbert and his author from the starving Irish poor. Herbert folds his silk handkerchief around the body of Kitty, the four-year-old lying dead in the corner. The anxiety excited by his presence at the scene is, however, heightened and not diminished by this act. The silk handkerchief alerts the reader to resources at Herbert's disposal which were not employed to avert the death and Trollope's claims that these could have done no good seem insulting. What is intended as an act of engagement and respect becomes one of concealment and offence. As Melissa Fegan has pointed out, 'Herbert is mimicking his author, covering the corpse of the dead child with his silk handkerchief, as Trollope in the Six Letters shrouded the starving with words.'[32] The scene he has created demands a more active response than Trollope's reassurances that nothing could have been done, and his passive stance is exposed as ethically inadequate by his own fiction.

Similarly, Trollope's own novel provides an eloquent opposition at the point in the chapter at which Herbert is forced to recognize the insignificance of his own misfortunes when measured against the death of this family. When he concedes this, Trollope admits the impossibility of expecting the reader to continue to view Herbert's fate as the dominant issue. However, Trollope's closing comment on the scene, far from acknowledging a disruption, reiterates that the prevention of the woman's death was beyond the power of human agency and the reader is expected to follow the remainder of Herbert's story with undiminished interest.[33]

31 Trollope, *Castle Richmond*, p. 374. 32 Melissa Fegan, 'The Impact of the Great Famine on Literature, 1845–1919' (unpublished DPhil, University of Oxford, 1999), pp. 176–7. Melissa Fegan's *Literature and the Irish Famine, 1845–1919* (Oxford, 2002), includes a chapter devoted to Anthony Trollope's writings about the Famine. 33 Trollope, *Castle Richmond*, p. 374.

Recent commentators have been struck by the incongruity of Trollope's representation of the Great Famine. Roy Foster, while recognizing Trollope's perceptiveness in other aspects of his representation of Ireland, has described his view of the administration during the Famine as 'deliberately myopic'.[34] Trollope's biographer Victoria Glendinning has remarked upon the 'pathological insensitivity of some of his perceptions and attitudes among much that was sensible and accurate'.[35]

Why then did Anthony Trollope, a writer capable of perceptive and unorthodox representations of Ireland, adopt and cling so tenaciously to a pro-government, providentialist explanation of the Great Famine even in the face of challenges from his own fiction? An important key is his problematic relationship with Ireland. While Trollope's residence in Ireland at the time of the Famine placed him ideally to observe and comment on it, he was neither a native nor a neutral observer. He was genuinely fond of the country, and he was a British official. The opportunity afforded by Ireland for him to transform himself left him with a duty of friendship which he endeavoured to fulfil, but the events of the Famine brought him up against extreme distress – which some blamed on British misrule. This was an accusation that, as an Englishman, he felt it his duty to refute. Moreover, for Trollope to question the Union would be to question not only the basis of his official position but also the basis on which he had built his longed-for social acceptance, personal happiness and professional success. An energetic defence of the government when combined with a providentialist explanation of the Famine provided a soothing balm for battling affections and loyalties.

An interesting and illuminating echo of Trollope's struggle to resolve the emotional, moral, and ideological conflict created by his residence in Ireland, exists in a twentieth-century representation of the Famine – William Trevor's short story 'The News from Ireland'.[36] In his first letter to the *Examiner* Trollope debates the precise term which accurately conveys his relationship with Ireland. That he is English is incontestable, but is he an 'alien', a 'foreigner' or a 'stranger'? In the end he settles for 'stranger' perhaps as conveying distance but without hostility.[37] The central figure in Trevor's 'The News from Ireland', Anna Maria Heddoe, is an English woman 'of principle and sensibility' who arrives in Ireland during the Famine to work as a governess.[38] The letters and diary she writes chronicle the distress she feels at the catastrophe unfolding around her, her religious and moral struggle to make sense of it all. In the end, however, lured by an advantageous marriage to the estate manager, she makes an accommodation and stays in Ireland. The story ends:

34 R.F. Foster, *Paddy and Mr Punch* (London, 1995), p. 145. **35** Glendinning, *Trollope*, p. 185.
36 William Trevor, 'The News from Ireland' (1986), in *Ireland: Selected Stories* (London, 1995), pp. 141–66. **37** Letter to the *Examiner*, 25 August 1849. **38** Trevor, 'News', p. 166.

It is she ... who is the scholar and humanitarian. It is she ...who came from England and was distressed. She has wept into her pillow, she has been sick at heart. Stranger and visitor, she has written in her diary the news from Ireland. Stranger and visitor, she has learnt to live with things.[39]

39 Ibid.

The making of mid-Victorian Ireland? Political economy and the memory of the Great Famine

PETER GRAY

The Ireland of the 1850s and 1860s has been periodised variously by historians as 'post-Famine' or 'mid-Victorian'.[1] The distinction is one loaded with historiographical controversy. While one chronological tag stresses the lasting significance of the catastrophic prelude and implies that it continued to cast a profound shadow over the following decades, the other tends to normalise Irish experience in these years as a regional variant of British mid-Victorianism.[2] Lying behind the latter is a tendency to read the Famine as a phenomenon that was essentially restricted and transitory in its impact. Negatively affecting the poorer rural classes (especially in the west) through destitution, excess mortality and mass emigration, it is taken to have strengthened the position of the remaining 'strong' farmers, consolidating them into a rural bourgeoisie competing vigorously with the landowners for the profits of the land. Simultaneous with this social rationalisation, the mid-Victorian economic boom is argued to have lifted all classes in rural Ireland (especially the working farmers) to unprecedented levels of prosperity. It took a 'revolution of rising expectations' consequent on the sudden collapse of the boom in the later 1870s to again plunge the Irish countryside into turmoil. The Famine's legacy, it follows, played a relatively small role in the lives of the majority of survivors, once having creating the preconditions for their physical betterment.[3] This thesis has, of course, its critics, who stress regional and class variations of post-Famine experience, and question whether the bulk of Irish farmers made more than marginal and unstable gains in the 1850s–60s.[4]

It is not the intention of this essay to examine the economic-historical debates underlying this controversy. Rather, it considers the contestations of

---

1 See, for example, James O'Shea, *Priest, Politics and Society in Post-Famine Ireland* (Dublin, 1983); W.E. Vaughan, *Landlords and Tenants in Mid-Victorian Ireland* (Oxford, 1994). 2 For the argument that 'post-famine Ireland is also mid-Victorian Ireland', and a period characterised more by continuity and anglicisation than disruption and antagonism, see R.V. Comerford, 'Ireland 1850–70: post-famine and mid-Victorian', in W.E. Vaughan (ed.), *An New History of Ireland. V: Ireland under the Union, i, 1801–70* (Oxford, 1989), pp. 372–95. 3 A summary of this interpretation can be found in W.E. Vaughan, *Landlords and Tenants in Ireland, 1848–1904* (Dublin, 1984). 4 See Cormac Ó Gráda, *Ireland Before and After the Famine: Explorations in Economic History, 1800–1925* (Manchester, 1988), pp. 128–52; K. Theodore Hoppen, *Ireland since 1800: Conflict and Conformity* (London, 1989), pp. 83–94.

meaning ascribed to the Famine in the two to three decades following its ravages – contestations which in some ways prefigure those of economic historians
writing more recently. The concern here is not with the nationalist tradition of
Famine exegesis, well known through the narratives and polemics of John
Mitchel, Charles Gavan Duffy, John O'Rourke and others, and anatomised by
historians such as Patrick O'Farrell and James Donnelly.[5] Rather, the focus here
is on their rivals for influence and authority in post-Famine Ireland, particularly
those Irish non-nationalists employing the discourse of political economy.

Political economy in Ireland was, as Tom Boylan and Tadgh Foley have demonstrated, conceived of by its promoters as a programmatic and didactic activity.
Richard Whately, Anglican archbishop of Dublin from 1831, believed the introduction and dissemination of such a universal, 'scientific' and non-sectarian discourse a fundamental precondition for Irish social and moral advancement. The
institutions established or promoted under his patronage – the Whately chair of
political economy at Trinity College and later those at the Queen's Colleges, the
elementary lessons in political economy embedded in the National Education
Board's curriculum, the Barrington public lectures, and the Dublin Statistical
Society – were all directed towards the public advancement of this new science in
conscious competition with other popular discourses.[6] Irish political economists
were never unanimous on all matters, but by the later 1840s it is possible to discern
a distinct 'Dublin school' of economic thought, acknowledging Whately as its
founding father, but developing an increasingly self-conscious Irish voice in dia-
logue with the dominant British (and continental) forms of political economy, and
in strong opposition to the twin heresies of demagogic nationalism and landed
protectionism. Fitting the troubled economic and discursive context in which it
emerged, Irish political economy tended to be 'applied' or problem-oriented in
form, inductivist in method and didactic in style.[7] In a perhaps unconscious echo
of the divine trinity, Sir Robert Kane described the new science as 'one yet tripar-
tite', appealing in due measure to 'the thinker, the observer and the man of action'.[8]

Interpreting the Famine, rationalising its consequences, and seeking to shape
how the event should be remembered by the educated classes of both Ireland
and Britain, was a pressing consideration in these decades. A remarkably unified

5 Patrick Farrell, 'Whose reality? The Irish Famine in history and literature', *Historical Studies*,
20:78 (1982), 1–13; James S. Donnelly, Jr., 'The construction of the memory of the Famine in
Ireland and the Irish diaspora, 1850–1900', *Éire-Ireland*, 31:1&2 (1996), 26–61.   **6** Thomas A.
Boylan and Timothy P. Foley, *Political Economy and Colonial Ireland: the Propagation and
Ideological Function of Economic Discourse in the Nineteenth Century* (London, 1992).   **7** R.D.C.
Black has identified a 'Dublin school' of economists associated with the Whately chair tend-
ing towards dissent from Ricardian orthodoxy. The term is used here more loosely to denote
those Irish economists for whom the Dublin Statistical Society and its successor became the
main intellectual forum from 1847. See R.D.C. Black, 'Trinity College, Dublin, and the
theory of value', *Economica*, ns, 12 (1945), 140.   **8** Sir Robert Kane, *The Address on the Opening
of the Fifth Session of the Dublin Statistical Society* (Dublin, 1851), p. 4.

and concerted interpretation was articulated by the Dublin school in the late 1840s and achieved some public success in the 1850s. This trajectory was interrupted from the early 1860s both by renewed economic problems and novel intellectual conceptions, undermining the optimistic certainties of the previous decade. The outcome of the controversies of the 1860s were more pessimistic and polarised readings of the Famine, pointing some towards a harsh neo-Malthusian re-interpretation, and others towards the legitimation of state intervention in Irish society that underlay both the Gladstonian Liberal and moderate nationalist social agendas of the final third of the nineteenth century.

The political-economic 'memory' of the Famine was shaped by the policy debates and interpretative polemics produced during the catastrophe itself. The later 1840s witnessed a rage of controversy, a struggle to assert and impose meaning, played out in speeches, lectures and sermons, the press and pamphlets, and in popular literature. With the collapse of mass popular politics from 1846, and the suppression of both revolutionary insurrectionism and agrarian conspiracies in 1848, the voices of famine victims and their (self-appointed) advocates were largely stifled. Other voices continued, however, to contest the purport of events and the optimal outcome of the catastrophe.

For Irish political economists, the late 1840s was a moment of acute importance. Irish society had, most believed, been dissolved through an unexpected but certainly not arbitrary act of nature or divine providence. The social reconstruction of the country was imperative, but if attempted upon erroneous economic principles would merely replicate the social and economic evils that had, painfully, been exposed and swept away in the wake of the potato blight. Their shared belief that the principles of Smithian political economy, combined with rigorous statistical investigation, offered a scientific blueprint for Irish regeneration, gave the Dublin school an intense sense of self-conscious mission. Optimism flowed from a combination of providentialist theodicy (a confidence that the potato blight had been divinely willed for ultimate human good), and an assurance, in the wake of the repeal of the corn laws, that the hegemony of free-trade liberalism was imminent, if not yet fully assured. Heresies of various kinds – nationalist, protectionist, statist, radical – still needed to be identified and refuted, but there was a confidence that the implementation of sound policy would rapidly produce universal benefits which would soon silence any remaining critics.

The profound optimism of these Irish political economists – an optimism dependent on the conscious suppression of consideration of the human devastation involved – is evident at the very nadir of the Famine itself. In contrast to their English mentors Richard Whately and Nassau Senior, who denounced the Whig government's poor-law policy as disastrous for Irish recovery,[9] the Dublin economists were generally more positive about the likely outcome of the crisis.

9 Peter Gray, 'Nassau Senior, the *Edinburgh Review*, and Ireland 1843–49', in Tadgh Foley and Sean Ryder (eds), *Ideology and Ireland in the Nineteenth Century* (Dublin, 1998), pp. 130–42.

As professor of political economy at Trinity College in 1846-51, William Neilson Hancock was one of the foremost defenders of rigid adherence to 'sound' economic doctrine during the crisis. While critical of some aspects of policy (mainly for departing too far from strict laissez-faire), Hancock was less concerned about the consequences of a well-regulated poor law. Ireland was, he argued in 1847, suffering from the legacy of protectionism and the unnatural social system it had promoted; but the crisis was simply an 'instance of the operation of the law of Divine economy in the moral government of the world', which, if acknowledged and acted upon, would lead to national deliverance.[10] Hancock felt the necessity of publicly refuting Charles Trevelyan's dictum that 'there is no hope for a nation which lives on potatoes', contending that potatoes were merely the symbol and not the cause of Irish poverty, and that fetishising them as the root of Irish social evil merely distracted attention from the true causes. Despite this, it is evident that the two men shared much ideological ground in the late 1840s, as Hancock publicly praised both Trevelyan's actions and the 'most enlightened philanthropy' informing his apologia, *The Irish Crisis*.[11] Both men were fundamentally anti-Malthusian, holding, in Hancock's words, that it was 'unscientific and erroneous to describe the population of Ireland as excessive'. Insufficient demand for the labour available to exploit Ireland's abundant resources was the real problem; but the stimuli to productive employment, both agreed, must come from private enterprise rather than the state, as 'every interference with the natural course of industry will retard' the future 'happy era' of full employment and prosperity.[12]

Hancock's solution to the problem of providing a non-interventionist stimulus to labour demand took the classic free-trade liberal form of the removal of obstacles to development – in this case taking the shape of 'feudal' land laws. Damned both by scientific economics and providential example, outdated legal restrictions on the sale and transfer of land, and on leasing and tenancy arrangements, were, he argued, the major blockages in the path of Irish recovery.[13] Free trade in land would unlock the potential of Irish agriculture (and industry) by removing incapable proprietors, and by promoting capital investment in improved production. All classes, he concluded, would benefit through the increase of farming profits, and the demand for and remuneration of labour. No small part of the optimism of the Irish economists in the early 1850s was due to the endorsement of this reconstructivist vision provided by the government's Encumbered Estates Act. With this legislative intervention, it appeared the preconditions for progress

10 W. Neilson Hancock, *Three Lectures on the Questions, Should the Principles of Political Economy be Disregarded at the Present Crisis? And If Not, How Can They Be Applied towards the Discovery of Measures of Relief?* (Dublin, 1847), p. 56. 11 W. Neilson Hancock, *Two Papers Read before the Dublin Statistical Society ... II. A Notice of the Theory 'That there is No Hope for a Nation Which Lives on Potatoes'* (Dublin, 1848), pp. 7–10. 12 W. Neilson Hancock, *On the Condition of the Irish Labourer, being a Paper Read before the Dublin Statistical Society* (Dublin, 1848). 13 W. Neilson Hancock, *The Economic Causes of the Present State of Agriculture in Ireland, Parts I and II* (Dublin, 1848).

had at last been laid; 1849 was thus, for many economic commentators, what we might now term the 'year zero' of Ireland's regeneration.

Although by some degree the most prolific writer in the genre, Hancock was not alone in his campaign. The Dublin Statistical Society, founded in late 1847 as a debating and proselytising society under Whately's aegis, rapidly became a focus for like minds.[14] Active members in its early years included Mountifort Longfield, a sophisticated economist and a former holder of the Whately chair, but also, as an Encumbered Estates Commissioner from 1849, a leading advocate of 'free trade in land'. Other prominent members were Jonathan Pim, the Quaker philanthropist who had also campaigned for such legislation since 1847, Sir Robert Kane, whose 1844 *The Industrial Resources of Ireland* had made the case that Ireland possessed vastly under-exploited natural resources, and similarly minded figures such as James A. Lawson and W.E. Hearn. The heterodox figure of Isaac Butt, a former Whately chair but deeply suspect because of his overt protectionism (and strident opposition to government famine policies), was kept firmly on the margins and was the target of a number of polemical attacks emanating from the Society.

In the early 1850s the Dublin economists saw their primary role as three-fold: to defend and further advance the principles of 'free trade in land' against landed obscurantism, to face down calls for state assistance to economic development or interference in landlord-tenant relations, and at the same time to promote Irish self-reliance in the face of British condescension. Their simultaneous critique of 'feudal' landownership patterns and 'communistic' calls for state regulation of landlord-tenant relations echoed the Cobdenite attack on landed power in Great Britain, but the Dublin school lacked both the political radicalism and the biting class antagonism of its counterpart. Their objective was a revivified landlordism based upon strictly contractual relationships with capitalist tenant farmers and landless wage-labourers. For them, the overriding importance of Famine remembrance was thus to demonstrate the appalling consequences of adhering to traditional practices or false panaceas.

Hancock's 1850 essay on 'the causes of distress at Skull and Skibbereen' (two of the most notorious famine 'hot spots') was targeted at both. While John Stuart Mill's *Principles of Political Economy* was regarded by Irish economists as authoritative on many matters, his comments on Irish land were seen as highly suspect. In place of Mill's opinion that free competition for land by cottier peasants had promoted the rack-renting and immiseration on which famine preyed, Hancock insisted it was the land law which had impeded sale of indebted estates to the capitalist proprietors who would have employed more, raised wages and hence widened peasant diet, that had created acute vulnerability here and elsewhere in Ireland.[15] Famine suffering was thus instrumentalised to sup-

---

14 For a recent history of this Society and its successor, see Mary E. Daly, *The Spirit of Earnest Inquiry: the Statistical and Social Inquiry Society of Ireland, 1847–1997* (Dublin, 1997). **15** W. Neilson

port Smithian economic doctrines; if its horror was recalled, it was to be rationalised within an abstracted utilitarian calculus – as a measure of pain necessary
to shock Ireland into reform and self-assistance.

W.E. Hearn, writing in an 1851 prize essay on the condition of Ireland,
agreed: the Famine had been 'the most dreadful ... known to the history of
modern times', but there were grounds for optimism now that 'the system of
cruel and abominable restraint [that] counteracted the kindness of Providence
and superseded the industry and enterprise of man' had been abandoned and
the land 'set free'.[16] The 1851 census report (largely the work of Dublin
Statistical Society members Thomas Larcom and William Wilde) had revealed a
huge loss of population, but this could be rationalised as a necessary, if painful,
part of Ireland's reawakening – not because the country had been overpopu-
lated, but because it had stagnated. In Hearn's opinion:

> this tempest of calamity has served to scourge before it the lazy elements,
> which, in our case at least, had stagnated into so fatal a pestilence. The
> indications exist of, it may be a slow, but still a steady, recovery ... The
> fearful decrease in our population ... could never have occurred except
> from a total disregard of all the laws which regulate social progress[.] ...
> Had the calamity befallen us under a sound social system, we could only
> bow with resigned submission to the stroke which we could not avert.
> But now we can distinctly trace the operation of human agencies, and
> we have to deal with results which man has caused, and which man can
> cure ... we must conquer nature by obeying her.[17]

Precisely which human agents were best suited to taming Irish nature was disputed. In the later 1840s the idea of a 'new plantation' of Ireland by entrepre-
neurial British landowners and farmers had acquired some popularity, particularly through the advocacy of Robert Peel. Some of the Encumbered Estates
Act's promoters regarded such a development as essential, and Queen Victoria's
first visit to Ireland, in August 1849, was partly predicated on the conviction that
the visit would both symbolise the start of a new era in Ireland and render both
tourism and investment in Irish land fashionable for the British propertied
classes. *The Times*, for example, enthused that the queen had discovered the
'secret of regenerating Ireland'; the visit was no 'vain, fantastic or unmeaning
pomp' – but the outward show of a national unity which would be underpinned by economic integration. The 'host of tourists and travellers' who would
follow in the queen's train, would soon take advantage of the Encumbered

Hancock, *On the Causes of Distress at Skull and Skibbereen, during the Famine in Ireland, a Paper read
before the Statistical Section of the British Association, at Edinburgh, August 2nd 1850* (Dublin, 1850).
16 William Edward Hearn, *The Cassell Prize Essay on the Condition of Ireland* (London, 1851), pp.
2, 14. **17** Ibid., pp. 122–3. Hearn was at this time professor of Greek at Queen's College,
Galway.

Estates Act to invest in Ireland's future progress.[18] The Irish government simultaneously commissioned the agriculturalist James Caird to prepare a survey of the suitability of Ireland for such a new British 'colonisation'. Indeed, throughout the 1850s a steady stream of literature appeared lauding the achievements and profits of (especially Scottish) purchasers and large tenant farmers, and urging more to follow the beneficial example of the pioneers who had helped Ireland escape from the horrors of famine.[19]

Hancock and his associates were, however, adamant that Ireland did not require such external assistance in its regeneration. Combining patriotic pride with a critique of erroneous conceptions of capital, Hancock argued that even in the depths of the disaster Ireland had never lacked reserves of capital, but simply the opportunity to employ these reproductively. Figures for holdings of government stock in Ireland appeared to indicate substantial surpluses throughout the 1840s, until the opportunities for land purchase siphoned much of this away after 1849. It was with some glee that he reported that only a small minority (around five percent) of purchasers under the Act were from outside the island. Ireland needed neither English capital nor Scots farmers, but merely the same laws that had unleashed dynamic entrepreneurship in Britain.[20] This was potentially an explosive argument, implying that large amounts of hoarded wealth had existed in Ireland in a time of mass mortality – something Irish landowners and their political allies had always denied – but for Hancock, immersed in a benign providentialism, this demonstrated not the illegitimacy of inequitable property rights but the folly of pre-scientific legislation.

Dublin school writers were confident that the apparent national prosperity of the mid to late-1850s demonstrated the accuracy of their analysis and soundness of their policy prescriptions. There had been some ambiguity in their attitudes towards mass emigration – while rejecting Malthusian claims of over-population, economists had welcomed voluntary migration as a necessary corrective to previous social dislocation, and as likely to create a beneficial equilibrium of wages and conditions for the emigrant and those who remained.[21] Nevertheless, there was much satisfaction at the falling emigration rate by the mid-1850s, which was taken as evidence that 'reparative agencies' of emigration were working themselves

18 *The Times*, 3, 9, 11 August 1849. **19** James Caird, *The Plantation Scheme; or, the West of Ireland as a Field for Investment* (Edinburgh, 1850); William Bullock Webster, *Ireland Considered as a Field for Investment or Residence* (Dublin, 1852); Thomas Scott, *Ireland Estimated as a Field for Investment* (London, 1854); Thomas Miller, *The Agricultural and Social State of Ireland in 1858, being the Experience of Englishmen and Scotchmen who have Settled in Ireland* (Dublin, 1858). **20** W. Neilson Hancock, *Is There Really a Want of Capital in Ireland? A Paper read before the Statistical Section of the British Association at Ipswich, July 3rd 1851* (Dublin, 1851); W. Neilson Hancock, *What are the Causes of the Prosperous Agriculture in the Lothians of Scotland?* (Belfast, 1852). **21** See, for example, D. Caulfield Heron, *Celtic Migrations; a Paper read before the Dublin Statistical Society* (Dublin, 1853); James A. Lawson, *On the Agricultural Statistics of Ireland. A Paper Read before the Dublin Statistical Society* (Dublin, 1854).

through. The process had been, Jonathan Pim assured the Dublin Statistical Society at its first meeting of the 1854–5 session, self-correcting. Famine destitution had now been swept away, the principles of political economy were everywhere gaining ground, and every economic indicator showed signs of unprecedented prosperity.[22] Ireland was thus becoming what we might term 'mid-Victorian',[23] but, crucially for the Irish economists, it was doing so under its own steam, transforming itself from a diseased to a healthy limb of the British body politic.

This tone of liberal triumphalism dominated the proceedings of the Dublin Society in the following years. Ireland's recovery, claimed Longfield in late 1855, had been rapid and uniformly beneficial. Agricultural wages were up by over 50 per cent, more land was cultivated than ever, prices were high, and profits evenly distributed. Political economists should now, he advised, address themselves to the evils of prosperity (such as public drunkenness) rather than those of poverty. So persuaded were the people of the truths of political economy, Lawson added, several years later, that 'there is hardly a child in the national schools that could not establish the fallacy of … [socialist] doctrines'.[24]

This claim may have been somewhat exaggerated, but these hubristic conclusions were echoed by the intellectual organs of both the Whig-Liberal and Conservative parties in 1857. The *Edinburgh Review* and *Quarterly Review* both took advantage of the publication of George Nicholls' history of the Irish poor law and the tenth anniversary of 'Black '47' to draw attention to the 'strange regeneration' of Ireland, due equally, they claimed, to Providence and wise legislation. W.O. Morris's article in the Liberal *Edinburgh* was enthusiastically positive: famine had 'hastened to maturity' both the 'Repeal of the Corn Laws and the Social Revolution in Ireland – the two economic changes of our times which have been the best securities against national scarcity'. Trevelyan's 'steadfast faith in the wise purposes of Providence' had been vindicated by events, for the last ten years had seen Ireland's 'deliverance from the bondage which had fastened a legal sterility on her fertile soil, and the apathy of pauperism on her intelligent people.'[25] It was in this intellectual climate that Trollope's notorious excursus in the closing pages of *Castle Richmond* was composed. While the novelist had been acutely defensive of Trevelyanite policy in his *Examiner* letters of 1849, by 1860 he could be sure that a well-informed English readership would recognise that famine, pestilence and exodus 'these three wonderful events, fol-

22 Jonathan Pim, 'Address at the opening of the eighth session of the Society', *Journal of the Dublin Statistical Society* [hereafter *JDSS*], 1 (January 1855), 6–25. **23** James H. Murphy prefers the term 'Albertine' to describe the 'improving' vision of many (including royal) observers of post–Famine Ireland, see *Abject Loyalty: Nationalism and Monarchy in Ireland during the Reign of Queen Victoria* (Cork, 2001), pp. 109–45. **24** Mountifort Longfield, 'Address at the opening of the ninth session of the Society', *JDSS*, 1 (January 1856), 153–64; James Anthony Lawson, 'Address delivered at the opening of the eleventh session of the Society', ibid., 2 (March 1858), 142–60. **25** [W. O'C. Morris], 'Social progress of Ireland', *Edinburgh Review*, 106 (July 1857), 98–123; [Anon.], 'Ireland past and present', *Quarterly Review*, 102 (July 1857), 59–88.

lowing each other, were the blessings coming from Omniscience and Omnipotence by which the black clouds were driven from the Irish firmament', and that 'Ireland in her prosperity' was the foreordained consequence.[26]

Nor was such optimism restricted to British observers. The celebrated French economist Léonce de Lavergne, reviewing the recent agrarian history of Ireland in 1855, was similarly impressed. Ireland's improvement had begun in the 1820s when English statesmen had renounced oppression for 'the more correct ideas of political economy', but it had taken the Famine to undo the results of misrule: 'the question remained to be solved by God; and that proved a terrible solution. All the long arrear of crime and error was to be atoned for only by an unexampled catastrophe.'[27] Emigration, consolidation and the Encumbered Estates Acts were now, he concluded, rapidly restoring Ireland to the pastoral agriculture which nature had intended for the country.

Irish economists continued to argue that additional measures were yet required to create a full contractualisation of land law in Ireland, but with Hancock now acting increasingly as a semi-official economic advisor to the Irish government, it was only a matter of time before these were implemented. The Cardwell-Deasy land acts of 1860, forming the pinnacle of 'free trade in land' in Ireland, were largely based on blueprints prepared by him for Dublin Castle. The powers of limited owners to grant leases and charge their estates for improvements were extended, tenants given a right to compensation for specified improvements made with the landowner's consent, and the landlord-tenant relationship was henceforth to be determined by 'the express or implied contract of the parties and not upon tenure or service.'[28]

Yet simultaneously with this triumph of doctrinaire liberalism, doubts began to emerge. Between 1859 and 1864 Ireland was hit by a run of very poor harvests, a depression of agricultural prices, and by outbreaks of sheep-rot and foot-and-mouth disease that devastated the pastoral economy. While the threat of a return to famine conditions was exaggerated by some for political reasons, the west of Ireland did suffer acutely. If, as James Donnelly has suggested, the proliferation of the small retail shops and massive imports of maize now helped stave off the risk of starvation, it was at the cost of a credit nexus that left both smallholders and small shopkeepers mired in debt.[29] The indicators of prosperity so lauded in the 1850s now pointed in a wholly different direction, and were readily grasped by both Conservative and nationalist critics; falling output and living standards and rising emigration seemed to give the lie to the idea that the

---

26 Anthony Trollope, *Castle Richmond* ([1860] Oxford, 1989), p. 489. See also Yvonne Siddle's chapter, above, pp. 141–50. **27** Léonce de Lavergne, *The Rural Economy of England, Scotland and Ireland* (Edinburgh, 1855), p. 375. **28** W. Neilson Hancock, *Report on the Landlord and Tenant Question in Ireland, 1860–6: With an Appendix containing a Report on the Question, 1835–59* (Dublin, 1866); R.D. Collison Black, *Economic Thought and the Irish Question, 1817–70* (Cambridge, 1960), pp. 45–6. **29** James S. Donnelly, Jr., 'The Irish agricultural depression of 1859–64', *Irish Economic and Social History*, 3 (1976), 33–54.

1845–50 Famine had permanently ushered in a new era of prosperity.[30] More ominous for the Dublin school was evidence of dissension within its own previously cohesive ranks. In January 1862 Denis Caulfield Heron, formerly professor of jurisprudence and political economy at Queen's College, Galway, questioned the narrative of progress in a paper read to the Dublin Statistical Society. Putting the economic history of Ireland into longer historical perspective, Heron identified the collapse of population since 1841 as a national disaster 'perfectly unparalleled in ancient or modern history', and one uncompensated for subsequently by any real socio-economic improvement. Ireland, he concluded, was 'beaten in the struggle for existence'. Heron repeated his charges, further supported by statistical evidence, in the 1864 session.[31]

Worryingly for the advocates of orthodoxy, Heron's papers were taken up and commented upon in other public arenas. One Protestant pamphleteer cited Heron's authority in his attack on Ireland's transformation into a 'cattle farm of England', to the benefit of a narrow class of 'dealers in corn, exporters of butter, provisions and cattle, … the proprietors of the "monster" shops, [and] grocers', and at the expense of the agricultural poor. The horrors of the Famine, the author continued, had been aggravated by Russell's imposition of laws of political economy unsuited to Irish conditions; subsequent policy had sought to impose these same laws on Irish land at the cost of continuing depopulation and real economic stagnation.[32] Other non-nationalists shared this sense of unease. One scientific pamphleteer warned that cattle plague might produce a crisis similar to the potato blight, and denounced 'the Red Indian or savage system of economic policy [which] will die, plague-stricken, like that system itself'.[33]

While Heron's comments received some support from within the Dublin Society – one commentator agreed the evidence showed Ireland was now 'going to the dogs'[34] – the majority response was at first resoundingly negative. Randall MacDonnell and Hancock took pains to demonstrate that conditions were still substantially better than in 1845 and argued that a run of poor seasons should not be mistaken for a return to the status quo ante.[35] Hancock's semi-

30 See, for example, Joseph Fisher, *How Ireland May be Saved; the Injurious Effects of the Present System of Agriculture on the Prosperity of Ireland and the Social Position of the Irish People* (London, 1862); Earl of Clancarty, *Ireland: Her Present Condition and What it Might Be* (Dublin, 1864). **31** D. Caulfield Heron, 'Historical statistics of Ireland', *JDSS*, 3 (June 1862), 235–55; 'Ireland in 1864', in ibid., 4 (October 1864), 105–9. **32** [Anon.], *The Present and Future of Ireland as the Cattle Farm of England, and her Probable Population. With Legislative Remedies. By an Irish Merchant* (Dublin, 1865). **33** [Anon.], *Cannabiculture in Ireland, its Profit and Possibility. By a Fellow of the Linnaean Society* (Dublin, 1866), p. 32. This writer urged instead agricultural diversification into cannabis cultivation, for which he alleged Ireland was ideally suited. Profit could be extracted from the production of hemp for rope and sacking, although the varied properties of its resin, 'first introduced into Europe as a medicinal agent by our countryman Dr O'Shaughnessy of Calcutta', were not to be overlooked. **34** Michael Morris, in *JDSS*, 4 (October 1864), 111. **35** Hancock, in ibid., pp. 109–10; Randal W. MacDonnell, 'Statistics of Irish prosperity', in ibid., 3 (December 1862), 268–78.

official report on the agricultural depression in 1863 urged its readers to recall the sufferings of the later 1840s and contrast these with the limited destitution of the early 1860s. Real improvement since the Famine, he reiterated, had reduced the country's vulnerability to such shocks.[36]

Despite the seeming certainty of this rebuttal, there is evidence of ground starting to shift. Hancock's report lacked the providential assurance of his writings a decade previously, and his tone had become defensive rather than crusading. Emigration rather than entrepreneurship had now assumed the role of the primary agent of change; indeed Hancock tended now to rationalise Famine population decline as overwhelmingly a function of emigration rather than mortality, and thus as an unavoidable necessity rather than as the lamentable product of bad laws. This indicated something of a loss of confidence in the resolute anti-Malthusianism with which Hancock and associates had been previously associated.[37] Perhaps as significant was a growing sense that the 'defeudalising' project in land legislation was failing to deliver its anticipated returns. The 1860 legislation did not produce the idealised contractual relations its advocates had foretold, not least because the depression tended to antagonise economic competition in the countryside coinciding with a renewal of nationalist agitation. In his 1862 offensive Heron revived the call for state guarantees of tenant security and drew attention to the model of continental peasant proprietories. This was one of the heresies of the 1840s which the Dublin Statistical Society had sought to combat, but which it now increasingly lacked the confidence to resist. Hancock was particularly exposed; he had long argued that the customary tenant right of his native Ulster would be best protected by voluntary contracts, but post-1860 experience threw this into doubt. Others also showed signs of wavering; John Kells Ingram in a November 1863 address stressed the economic benefits of mass emigration, and echoed the call to remember the Famine as a lesson in the costs of backwardness, yet also drew attention to the need for improved tenant security and raised the possibility that Ireland might follow the continental rather than English path of agrarian development.[38] In the following decades, Ingram and others would shift decisively to the former proposition, embracing a historicist and particularist reading of the Irish situation.

The ambiguities evident in the early 1860s were further developed as the decade proceeded. The economy may have recovered somewhat from the trough of 1859–63, but the political challenge posed by Fenianism perpetuated the sense of crisis in Ireland. Isaac Butt also now returned to the forefront of economic and political controversy, denouncing the perennial 'transition stage' of Irish development that seemed to offer no end to mass emigration, and seek-

36 W. Neilson Hancock, *Report on the Supposed Progressive Decline of Irish Prosperity* (Dublin, 1863), pp. 67–8. **37** Ibid., pp. 9–15. For criticism of Hancock's earlier stance, see Frederick G. Evelyn, 'Malthus', *JDSS*, 1 (July 1855), 125–36. **38** J.K. Ingram, 'Considerations on the state of Ireland, an address delivered at the opening of the seventeenth session', *JDSS*, 4 (January 1864), 13–26.

ing to tie moderate nationalism to land reform.[39] Butt was frank in citing his emotional repulsion to obligatory emigration scenes as the prime motivation for his initiative, but the Famine also played a significant part. The catastrophe had been no new departure, he asserted, but the awful outcome of what should have been a 'golden period' for Irish agriculture, marred by political and economic oppression. 'Is it too late' he concluded rhetorically, in an 1867 treatise on Irish land, 'to lay the lessons [of the Famine] to our hearts?'[40]

The 'turn' in more mainstream economic thought was most noticeable in the case of that cornerstone of Dublin economics, Mountifort Longfield. His expert evidence to the parliamentary committee on the Landed Estates Court in 1865 publicised doubts concerning the consequences of what had been lauded in 1849 as Ireland's panacea: 'speculators', he now recognised, had purchased a considerable proportion of estates with the express intention of subdivision and exploitative rent-extraction. Increased tenant insecurity and under-investment had been the inevitable result.[41] His presidential address at the opening of the 1865 session of the Statistical and Social Inquiry Society of Ireland (as the Dublin Statistical Society had become in 1862) indicated the need for practical remedies. 'Wise legislation' was now required to control the 'oppressive landlord', to guarantee tenant compensation for improvements and check unjustified rent increases.[42] Longfield's suggestions remained cautious and in line, he believed, with the general opinion of the Society, but the departure of principle from the 1850s could not have been greater and was widely reported.

Longfield's ideas were worked out at greater length in his Cobden Club essay on Irish land tenure published in 1870. While he did not renounce his opinion that the condition of Irish farmers had steadily improved since the Famine, with land values rising more rapidly than rents, and that the Encumbered Estates Act had introduced more improving landlords, he acknowledged that rural discontent had a real basis (albeit exaggerated by interested agitators):

> The reason for [it] is partly that they fear their present prosperity is insecure, and partly that they hope to seize upon something more. Their wealth is as safe as that of any other class, so far as it depends upon their capital, or their skill and industry; but it depends upon the will of the landlords, so far as it is a consequence of their holding land at less than the competition value. They are too dependent upon their landlords. It is not convenient that the prosperity of one class of men should depend upon the liberality of another class.[43]

39 Isaac Butt, *The Irish People and the Irish Land: A Letter to Lord Lifford* (Dublin, 1867). **40** Ibid., pp. 294–5. **41** *Select Committee on Tenure and Improvement of Land (Ireland) Act … Minutes of Evidence*, Parliamentary Papers, 1865 [402], XI, 2. **42** Mountifort Longfield, 'Address at the opening of the eighteenth session', *Journal of the Statistical and Social Inquiry Society of Ireland*, 4 (January 1865), 129–37. **43** Mountifort Longfield, 'The tenure of land in Ireland', in J.W. Probyn (ed.), *Systems of Land Tenure in Various Countries: A Series of Essays Published under the*

This was not a wholesale repudiation of his previous pronouncements, rather an implicit admission of their limitations. Longfield's scheme – which would grant of fixity of tenure while retaining a role for the market in rent adjustment – came to nothing in 1870, but his intervention marked an abandonment of the rigid laissez-faire principles of the 1850s.

If Longfield's conversion was cautious and piecemeal, the most important Irish economist to emerge in the decade, T.E. Cliffe Leslie, was scathing of the assumptions he had himself shared as a member of the Dublin Statistical Society in the 1850s.[44] Claims for Irish regeneration, Leslie wrote in 1867, had been repeatedly made in various historical moments, but invariably falsified by experience. The period since Famine was no exception. Ireland had in fact gained relatively little from the international economic boom of the 1850s due to non-interventionist policies and the slavish imitation of the flawed English system of rural development. What economists had lauded as proofs of unprecedented growth turned out on further inspection to indicate a profound failure to exploit the unprecedentedly favourable economic climate.[45] This seeming blindness to reality led Leslie to assault the deductivist principles of the discipline; what had previously passed for the 'science' of political economy had in practice been, he argued in 1868 in a turn of phrase oddly prescient of postmodern critiques, merely language employed in the service of powerful interests. This applied most clearly with respect to emigration – the causes and consequences of which Leslie held to be widely and wilfully misconstrued. Famine emigration, as well as that which followed, amounted merely to a 'wasteful depopulation', which had produced much misery but few if any net gains.[46] It followed for Leslie that radical land reform was the chief solution (albeit accompanied by public works and improved agricultural education); in a series of articles in the late 1860s he advocated legislative interference to grant security to small occupiers, and state assistance to land purchase. He would reiterate this position in an article published at the height of the Land War in 1880.[47]

Leslie became widely known in the 1870s as the foremost advocate of historicist economics and a leading player in the so-called 'English *Methodenstreit*', but his 'almost pathological' rejection in the 1860s of the form of classical economics he associated with Nassau Senior appears to have been provoked primarily by moral anger at the perceived state of Ireland. Sir Henry Maine's stadial historicism was available as an alternative model (Leslie had attended Maine's lectures in 1857), but Leslie transcended the rather quietist conclusions of his mentor. As one commentator has recently stated, 'the order of Leslie's consideration … was not so much from methodology to theory to policy, as traditionally perceived, but more from policy to theory to methodology'.[48]

Sanction of the Cobden Club ([1870], new edn, London, n.d. [1881]), p. 6. **44** Leslie had been a Barrington lecturer in 1852–3. **45** T.E. Cliffe Leslie, 'The state of Ireland, 1867', in *Land Systems and Industrial Economy of Ireland, England and Continental Countries* (London, 1870), pp. 5–33. **46** T.E. Cliffe Leslie, 'Political economy and emigration', in ibid., pp. 85–116 **47** T.E. Cliffe Leslie, 'The Irish land question', *Fraser's Magazine*, 22 (1880), 828–42. **48** Gregory

In the later 1860s Irish (and British) political economy fractured. Leslie's advocacy of an Irish solution suited to specifically Irish historical development (although drawing on European and Indian parallels) attracted the attention of British Liberals and other Dublin school figures like Ingram and H.D. Hutton. J.S. Mill's radical instincts on Irish land, dormant since the appearance of the first edition of his *Principles of Political Economy* in 1848, were revivified in the wake of Longfield's declaration and further inspired by Cliffe Leslie. Other historicising voices – most notably the Indian administrator Sir George Campbell (also a disciple of Maine) – joined the tumult that would bear first fruit in Gladstone's 1870 Land Act and the interventionist principle this embodied. Leslie's critique (building on Heron's) rejected the assertion that Famine and post-famine 'defeudalisation' had brought Ireland into the mainstream of Victorian British life. Even Hancock arrived at a similar position through a different route, converting to a historicist perspective whilst serving as editor of the Brehon Law tracts in the mid-1860s, and subsequently endorsing Gladstone's 1870 and 1881 land acts.[49] His collaborator on the Brehon tracts, Alexander Richey, later summed up the historicist view in an 1880 book: no law dealing with contracts in land was in itself objectively good or bad, all depended on the context of the social conditions in which it was applied. The political economists of the 1850s had profoundly misunderstood the developmental stage of Irish society, and their policies had therefore failed.[50]

Adherents to economic orthodoxy in turn shifted away from optimism to pessimism in the 1860s. One anonymous member of the Statistical Society warned in 1865 that lower rents were necessary for social peace, but saw no way of achieving this except by appeals to landlord conscience. A more direct way to relieve misery, the author continued, would be to promote further emigration, but only in the context of a strict Malthusian re-education of the lower orders. Ireland's (and implicitly Irish political economy's) neglect of such truths had been the cause of recent suffering:

> Had our instructors in bygone years invariably given due prominence to this self-evident principle, and we had taken the instructions to heart, our country would never have been visited with the awful calamities of 1846 and 1847. Our numbers would have steadily increased with the expansion of our national wealth, but not more rapidly; the demand for land would not have outgrown the supply; rents would have continued moderate, and would have left our farmers the means of a comfortable

C.G. Moore, 'T.E. Cliffe Leslie and the English *Methodenstreit*', *Journal of the History of Economic Thought*, 17 (1995), 57–77; see also Gerard M. Koot, 'T.E. Cliffe Leslie, Irish social reform, and the origins of the English historical school of economics', *History of Political Economy*, 7 (1975), 312–36. **49** Clive Dewey, 'Celtic agrarian legislation and the Celtic revival: historicist implications of Gladstone's Irish and Scottish land acts 1870–1886', *Past & Present*, 64 (1974), 43–9. **50** Alexander G. Richey, *The Irish Land Laws* (London, 1880), pp. 3, 47–61.

subsistence; labour would have received an adequate compensation, and even our poorest class of workmen would have been able to make some provision for the incidence of a year of scarcity.[51]

The responses of Lords Dufferin and Rosse, previously patrons of the Dublin Statistical Society, to the turn in economic debate was also resoundingly negative. Rosse wrote in response to those 'original thinkers' who now denied the universalism of economic laws and the assimilationism this had endorsed; the Famine, he lectured the deluded Millites, had been foreseen by enlightened political economists like Malthus, Ricardo and Senior as the consequence of excessive population. Then as now, only mass emigration and consolidation offered any hope for the future.[52] Dufferin agreed, arguing that mass emigration was no calamity but the most beneficial mode of responding to the Malthusian imperative. In an extraordinary *volte-face* from his own youthful opinions during the Famine, Dufferin now recalled that event as a stern test of the resolve of Ireland's landlords in doing their economic duty:

> [the landlord's] position was every whit as bad … his lands lay around him a poisonous waste of vegetable decay, while 25s. in the pound of poor-rate was daily eating up the fee-simple of his estate. Self-interest, duty, common sense, all dictated the same course – the enlargement of the boundaries, the redistribution of farms, and the introduction of a scientific agriculture, at whatever cost of sentiment or of individual suffering. Even so, the struggle too frequently proved unsuccessful, and the subsequent obliteration of nearly an entire third of the landlords of Ireland, while it associates them so conspicuously with the misfortunes of their tenants, may be accepted in atonement of whatever share they may have had in conniving at those remoter causes which aggravated the general calamity.[53]

Even the Statistical Society stalwart William Wilde concluded that the Famine had been essential to begin the thinning of Ireland's population, and that the 'manifest destiny of the Celt' now lay in emigration. The 'stern policeman of progress' should not be impeded in moving on those who were incapable of prospering in the land of their birth.[54] Such 'pessimistic' views found their supporters, in England as well as Ireland,[55] but were now decidedly defensive in tone; political economy no longer spoke with a single tongue on the legacy of the Great Famine.

51 [Anon.], *The Real Wants of the Irish People. By a Member of the Statistical and Social Inquiry Society of Ireland* (Dublin, 1865), pp. 38–9. **52** Earl of Rosse, *A Few Words on the Relation of Landlord and Tenant in Ireland, and in Other Parts of the United Kingdom* (London, 1867), pp. 49–50. **53** Lord Dufferin, *Irish Emigration and the Tenure of Land in Ireland* (London, 1867), p. 54. **54** William R. Wills Wilde, 'Ireland: past and present: the land and the people', in *Lectures Delivered Before the Dublin Young Men's Christian Association in Connexion with the United Church of England and Ireland, during the Year 1864* (Dublin, 1865), pp. 220–6. **55** By the 1880s a Malthusian interpretation of the Famine was common in British commentary, see for example *The Times*, 21

In conclusion, what can be termed the 'Dublin school' of political economists united in the 1850s in devoting considerable attention to the meaning and significance of the Famine.[56] The dominant reading of the Famine was through the prism of a formula at once utilitarian and providentialist. The mass suffering and social upheavals of the 1840s had been a horrific yet necessary measure of pain, essential to force the removal of obstacles to the future happiness of all. The intensity of the catastrophe had in fact been merciful, Jonathan Pim declared in 1854, as 'the excess of suffering was the very reason why that suffering should be of short duration'.[57] Yet this interpretation proved vulnerable to economic fluctuations, intellectual innovation, and the more unsettled political climate of the 1860s, all promoting something of a paradigm shift in Irish economics. Neither the agricultural crisis of the early 1860s nor the Fenian alarms that followed could easily be accommodated by the liberal political-economy narrative so strongly and confidently articulated in the post-Famine decade.

Furthermore, Dublin school economics had difficulty accommodating itself to the decline of providentialist modes of thought from the 1850s. In the wake of the *Origin of Species* and *Essays and Reviews* wholehearted assurance in the benign divine governance of human affairs was more problematic for public intellectuals, and the developing incarnationist turn in Protestant theology offered little to Christian political economy.[58] What replaced it was something more secular – either a neo-classical turn to a Malthusianism shorn of its originator's concern for theodicy, or a new historicist economics that stressed the particularity of national developments but left little place for universal 'laws of God and nature'. Both tended to perceive the Famine and its legacy more negatively, to deprive it of the emancipatory role it had once held. The catastrophe now served increasingly as a symbol of Irish difference, and no longer as the dawn of a new Victorian age of integration and prosperity.

June 1887. **56** This interpretation contradicts that of Nien-he Hsieh, 'The conspicuous absence of examination questions concerning the Great Irish Famine: political economy as science and ideology', *European Journal of the History of Economic Thought*, 6:2 (1999), 169–99. Hsieh argues that the absence of questions relating to the Famine in examinations for the Whately chair between 1846 and 1882 demonstrates the Famine's marginality to Irish political economy. Such a 'silence' may, however, be more apparent than real; if there were no specific references to a fully conceptualised 'Great Famine' in the questions, it is evident that candidates were invited to address topics closely associated with political-economic interpretations of the crisis, including questions of population, free trade, the poor law and land tenure. In the absence of the candidates' answers it is impossible to analyse the extent to which they were prepared to respond to such questions with reference to the Irish experience of the later 1840s, and this lack of evidence must render Hsieh's thesis 'not proven'. It might, however, be safely inferred from the writings, lectures and debates of examiners and candidates such as Whately, Hancock, Longfield and Leslie – public discourse which Hsieh appears unduly ready to dismiss – that the Famine did continue to preoccupy Irish political economists in the post-Famine decades. **57** Pim, 'Address', *JDSS*, 1 (January 1855), 10. **58** See Boyd Hilton, *The Age of Atonement: the Influence of Evangelicalism on Social and Economic Thought, 1785–1865* (Cambridge, 1988), pp. 298–349.

'With the experience of 1846 and 1847 before them': the politics of emergency relief, 1879–84

VIRGINIA CROSSMAN

The Great Famine cast a long shadow over Irish politics. Public memory of the Famine permeated political discourse in Ireland in the second half of the nineteenth century, influencing perceptions of the past, the present and the future. Irish and British politicians agreed that the lessons of the Famine should not be forgotten. Where they differed was in their view of what those lessons were. Within nationalist ideology the Famine was presented as a damning indictment of British rule, and became a symbol of the suffering of the Irish people at the hands of the British. For the British also the Famine symbolised deeper ills, being associated with Irish improvidence, ingratitude and economic backwardness. These divergent interpretations coloured attitudes to subsequent economic crises and food shortages. This article re-examines the economic and political upheaval of 1879-81 and explores how the experience and memory of the Great Famine shaped responses to the crisis and its aftermath.

Eighteen seventy-nine brought a third consecutive bad harvest. A combination of bad weather, the poor harvest, and depressed livestock prices precipitated a major subsistence crisis. The small farmers of Connacht and Donegal were particularly hard hit since agriculture in the west had remained heavily dependent on the potato. Supplies of food and fuel were virtually exhausted by the end of 1879 and it was clear that the winter months were likely to see serious and widespread distress among the poorer classes. People had no money and were unable to get credit. Tenant farmers, many of whom were in arrears with their rent, were unable to meet demands for payment from their landlords and thus faced the very real prospect of eviction. The number of ejectment decrees applied for by landlords in Mayo, for example, almost doubled between 1877 and 1879.[1] It was against this background that a protest meeting was organised at Irishtown in County Mayo in April 1879 to publicise the problems facing tenant farmers and to demand a reduction in rents. The agitation spread to other parts of the country and led to the establishment, first of the Land League of Mayo, and then, in October 1879, of the Irish National Land League. The Land League brought together tenant activists, Fenians and Home Rulers to

---

1 Donald E. Jordan Jnr., *Land and Popular Politics in Ireland: County Mayo from the Plantation to the Land War* (Cambridge, 1994), p. 217.

fight for reform of the land system and self-government. These were the long-
term goals. In the short term the leaders urged members of the agricultural
community to unite in their own defence since it was only by doing so that
they would be able to prevent a repetition of the events of the Great Famine.
As Michael Davitt explained in his history of the Land League, arable land in
Ireland had earned no rent in 1879:

> and we were resolved as far as possible to prevent any being screwed out
> of the impoverished people. One thing was determined upon: there
> should be no slavish moral cant like that of 1846–47 – that the tenants
> should starve rather than 'defraud' the landlord of his rent ... No matter
> from what quarter, religious, social or political, this was to be met and
> stamped upon remorselessly by the power of our organisation.[2]

Davitt's political outlook owed much to his own experience of the Great
Famine and its effects. His parents had been evicted from their holding in
County Mayo in 1852 and had been forced to emigrate. 'That eviction and the
privations of the preceding famine years, the story of the starving peasantry of
Mayo, of the deaths from hunger and the coffinless graves on the roadside', provided, he was later to recall, 'the political food ... which had fed my mind in
another land'. As he saw it, the sufferings of the Irish people during the Famine
were the responsibility primarily of Irish landlords. But he did not absolve the
Irish people themselves from blame. He was fiercely critical of the 'epidemic of
national cowardice which was common to all Ireland at the period of the great
famine',[3] and had been determined to prevent a similar outbreak in 1879. Davitt
was not the only one to draw direct comparisons between the situation facing
tenant farmers in 1846–7 and 1879. In his speech to a meeting at Westport in
June 1879, C.S. Parnell declared that tenants must be guaranteed security of
tenure so long as they paid a fair rent. His definition of a fair rent was a rent that:

> the tenant can reasonably pay according to the times, but in bad times a
> tenant cannot be expected to pay as much as he did in good times three
> or four years ago. If such rents are insisted upon a repetition of the scenes
> of 1847 and 1848 will be witnessed. Now what must we do in order to
> induce the landlords to see the position? You must show the landlords that
> you intend to keep a firm grip of your homesteads and lands. You must
> not allow yourselves to be dispossessed as you were dispossessed in 1847.[4]

By linking economic and political grievances, the leaders of the Land League
were able to build a mass-based, popular organisation capable of promoting sub-

---

2 Michael Davitt, *The Fall of Feudalism in Ireland* (London, 1904), pp. 187–8.   **3** Ibid., p. 45,
53.   **4** *Freeman's Journal*, 9 June 1879, cited in T.W. Moody, *Davitt and Irish Revolution, 1846–82*
(Oxford, 1982), p. 305.

stantial levels of agitation across the country. But that linkage was in one sense counter-productive, for it encouraged the government to dismiss reports of famine conditions following the harvest failure of 1879 as political propaganda. The initial reaction within both government and the British press had been to downplay the crisis, claiming that its seriousness and extent were being exaggerated. Reports of famine conditions, one official recalled, were regarded as 'a move in the political agitation rather than a well-founded cry of distress'.[5] For Irish MPs this was the Great Famine repeating itself. In May 1879, A.M. Sullivan, MP for County Louth, attempted to alert the government to the extent of the agricultural depression in Ireland. Contrasting the situation in England, where landlords helped their tenants in hard times, with that in Ireland, where the tradition was 'that distress was all pretended', he recalled that 'the cry of famine in 1847 was said to be the pretence of agitators'.[6]

Conservative ministers were doubtful of the veracity of newspaper reports detailing the spread of famine,[7] and were reluctant to act precipitously on the warnings of either nationalist representatives or Catholic priests. In order to obtain reliable information on which appropriate action could be taken, a number of temporary local government inspectors were appointed in November 1879 to investigate the state of the country. One of these was H.A. Robinson, the 23-year-old son of the vice-president of the Local Government Board. In his memoirs, Robinson admitted that, like many others, he had initially assumed that reports of famine and starvation were 'grossly exaggerated'. A visit to a remote village in the Galway mountains in the autumn of 1879 had, however, brought him face to face with people who 'were living skeletons, their faces like parchment. They were scarcely able to crawl … It was appalling'.[8] This description is startlingly reminiscent of eyewitness accounts of the Great Famine itself. Shocked by what he had seen, Robinson wrote to the under secretary at Dublin Castle, Thomas Burke, alerting him to the severity of the situation. Robinson's letter brought him to the attention of the Irish government and led to his appointment as a temporary inspector.[9]

The temporary inspectors' reports convinced ministers of the necessity for government action. They also reveal the extent to which officials viewed Irish distress through the prism of the poor law. The operation of the poor law rested on a distinction being made between independent labourers and paupers, a distinction that was policed by requiring applicants for relief to demonstrate their eligibility by entering the workhouse. Even though the experience of the Great Famine had clearly demonstrated the deficiency of the workhouse test during a

5 Sir Henry Robinson, *Memories: Wise and Otherwise* (London, 1923), p. 22. **6** *Hansard's Parliamentary Debates,* 3rd series, vol. 246, col. 1395 (27 May 1879). **7** See, for example, the series of reports in the *Freeman's Journal* on the land crisis in Ireland, August–September 1879, and a further series on famine in the west, February–August 1880. **8** Robinson, *Memories,* p. 10. **9** Ibid., pp. 10–11.

period of exceptional distress, officials found it very difficult not to apply it as a
test of eligibility in 1879–80. In January 1880, temporary inspector, Algernon
Bourke, concluded that the people of County Clare could not be 'absolutely in
starvation', since they were not entering the workhouse. He refused to believe
that a man who saw 'his family starving about him, and he himself feeling the
sharp pangs of hunger, with its warning of death', would not 'sink his pride and
seek safety and life in the workhouse'. In the same report, Bourke described
seeing 'a father standing idle at his door, a woman with her children crouching
round the dying embers of a meagre fire [and] poor hunger-stricken children
wandering with aimless purpose on the road'. These were scenes, he acknowledged, that 'would force themselves upon us, and which spoke to those who will
observe with an eloquence which carries with it the convictions of the truth'.[10]

The difficulty Bourke experienced in assimilating and interpreting what he
had seen is typical of famine witnesses.[11] Although he was able to describe the
scenes themselves simply and clearly, he could not articulate their meaning. He
also expressed an ambivalent attitude common to famine writing, empathising
with the plight of the victims but at the same time denying the extent of their
suffering. The discomfiture felt by both Robinson and Bourke on being forced
to confront their own preconceptions and prejudices is evident from their
responses to what they had witnessed. Both men were clearly sympathetic to
the plight of the western peasantry. They were also deeply imbued with the ideology of the poor law believing that it was morally wrong to give public aid to
people unless they were truly desperate.

Drawing a distinction between eligible and ineligible applicants for relief
encouraged fears of ineligible applicants abusing the system. Local government
inspectors were on constant guard against this danger. In January 1880,
Robinson visited Ballinrobe Union in County Mayo where he found a considerable amount of distress. He observed, however, that there was

> a wide difference … between 'distress' and 'famine' and while a pressure
> for relief from the poorest classes may without much foresight be prog-
> nosticated, it will not be so general this year, or so alarming as the visions
> which are being conjured up by local agitators would lead me to
> believe.[12]

In March, he noted that a personal inspection of places where distress was said
to exist had revealed 'comfortable farms with a large complement of potato pits,

10 Report of the Hon. A. Bourke, 13 January 1880, *Annual Report of the Local Government
Board for Ireland*, Parliamentary Papers [hereafter PP], 1880 [c 2603], xxviii, 155. **11** Scott
Brewster and Virginia Crossman, 'Re-writing the Famine: witnessing in crisis', in Scott
Brewster et al. (eds), *Ireland in Proximity: History, Gender, Space* (London, 1999), pp. 52–3. **12**
Report of H.A. Robinson, 2 January 1880, National Archives, Dublin (hereafter NA), Chief
Secretary's Office Registered Papers (hereafter CSORP), 1880/7070.

oat-stacks, pigs and cattle'. Furthermore, money was by no means as scarce as it was represented to be. He had encountered very few people after the market was over 'who were not more or less intoxicated'. His observations led him to conclude that,

> the question as to whether there really is distress depends entirely on the definition which is put on the word. If a worthless supply of seed, a low price for stock, a complete withdrawal of credit and heavy incumbrances (*sic*) are signs of distress, then I have to report that distress there is, throughout the entire Union. But here the terms distress and starvation are often used in precisely the same sense although they are by no means synonymous. Starvation, however, should only be applied in the gravest sense of the term, and although there is something akin to it over the Cappaghduff mountains, I am happy to say that generally the union is far removed from it.[13]

Robinson believed that a distinction between starvation and distress was central to a responsible relief policy. If mere distress was to be relieved the labour market and the economy would be weakened, and the poor law undermined. It was only by limiting emergency relief to the prevention of starvation that the government could protect the wider interests of the country. He did not blame local people for seeking government help:

> Who, indeed, could be surprised at it? Conceive what weekly payments of wages must have meant to a people living on credit … Small wonder, then, when relief works were hinted at, that the people were almost beside themselves in their efforts to persuade the Government that the distress was acute and overwhelming near their homes[.][14]

He was nevertheless convinced that ministers were morally obliged to reject such demands, however unpopular that rejection might make them.

Memories of the Great Famine reinforced the belief within government that relief measures should not be introduced lightly. It was only in exceptional cases, the chancellor of the exchequer, Sir Stafford Northcote, reminded the House of Commons in February 1880, that the government 'would be justified in departing from the principles of the poor law'. Ministers, he explained,

> remembered the years 1846 and 1847, and we know at that time a very large amount of money was unfortunately wasted upon works undertaken without due consideration and carried on in a manner which nec-

---

13 Report of H.A. Robinson, 12 March 1880, ibid.   **14** Sir Henry A. Robinson, *Further Memories of Irish Life* (London, 1924), pp. 78–9.

essarily involved considerable waste ... [T]he fact was that a very great evil was done, the people were demoralised.[15]

Ministers and officials played down comparisons with the Famine as regards the nature of the crisis and the extent of distress. In its annual report for 1879–80, the Local Government Board acknowledged that there had been

> much suffering and exceptional distress in many parts of Ireland ... but we are glad to be able to state that privation did not reach starvation in any union, and having caused careful inquiry to be made by our Inspectors into every case in which it was alleged that death had been occasioned by want, we usually found that it had resulted from other causes which were clearly ascertained.[16]

The following year it was noted that the outbreak of fever in some southern and western unions was not the relapsing fever associated with the Famine but either typhus or typhoid, or a fever of 'a mild continuous character'.[17]

Ministers insisted that they were only acting responsibly in obtaining accurate information before introducing any relief measures. Nationalist MPs interpreted the government's failure to act promptly in 1879–80 as wilful negligence. Those who had warned the government of the impending disaster, A.M. Sullivan complained, had been 'charged with exaggeration' and 'told that they were panic-mongers'. Requests for assistance had been treated with 'contemptuous indifference'. People had died in 1846 and 1847, he reminded the Commons,

> because they had a Government almost as inactive as that now presided over by the Chief Secretary for Ireland. In 1846 there was much circumlocution, but nothing was accomplished. They who saw the fearful slaughter then were alarmed now, as they recollected those memories, and compared what they saw then with that which was happening now before their eyes.[18]

Irish MPs had no hesitation in using highly emotive language in their attacks on government inaction. Sullivan, for example, accused the government of 'wilful murder ... because, though forewarned and forearmed, they were again allowing the people to perish, and were not averting the spread of famine'.[19] John Redmond rejected the government's claim that everything necessary had been done, asserting that 'men and women had already died for want of food

---

15 *Hansard*, 3rd series, vol. 250, col. 170 (6 February 1880). **16** *Annual Report of the Local Government Board for Ireland*, PP 1880 [c 2603], xxviii, 13. **17** *Annual Report of the Local Government Board for Ireland*, PP 1881 [c 2926], xlviii, 275. **18** *Hansard*, 3rd series, vol. 250, col. 140 (5 February 1880). **19** Ibid., col. 232, (6 February 1880).

... but for the great charity of private individuals thousands of people would have starved'.[20]

Liberal and radical MPs were equally critical of the government for ignoring the warnings of impending famine, but they accepted ministers' assurances that nobody had actually died of starvation. Joseph Chamberlain charged the government not with allowing deaths by starvation, but

> with not taking steps to prevent the deaths which would have taken place but for private charity; they are charged with having allowed a number of the Irish people to be so reduced by starvation that if an epidemic were now to occur the people would be swept away by tens of thousands.[21]

English MPs were also notably more reluctant than their Irish colleagues to make comparisons with the Great Famine. W.E. Forster, who had visited Ireland during the Famine, was being typically cautious when he observed that while he had no doubt there was great distress in Ireland, the present state of things was different to what had occurred in 1846 and 1847 and could not be described as famine.[22]

The Irish poor law system had proved an inadequate mechanism for the distribution of famine relief in the 1840s, and was to do so again in 1879–80. It was widely acknowledged that Irish people were extremely reluctant to enter the workhouse, due partly to the association in the popular mind between workhouses and Famine deaths. There was disagreement, however, over the full extent of this reluctance. Government officials such as Bourke and Robinson insisted that if people were really starving they would choose entry over death. Others, such as Joseph Chamberlain, maintained that the Irish people had such 'a rooted terror of the workhouse, it is not surprising that many of them would even prefer death by starvation rather than go to the workhouse'.[23] This disagreement reflected the gulf between the resolutely prosaic approach that characterised the attitude of most Irish officials, and the more fanciful notions of some British politicians who invested the Irish people with exceptional sensitivity. The reality probably lay somewhere in between. The genuine reluctance of people to enter the workhouse in many western unions in 1879–80 seems to have been as much due to practical problems such as the distances involved, and the difficulty of travel, as to any emotional or cultural proscription. Aid from charitable sources enabled many people to avoid having to choose between starvation and the workhouse. Visiting two remote and inaccessible villages in the Cappaghduff mountains in March 1880, Robinson had found that there was sickness due to malnourishment in nearly every cabin. Yet few people had

20 Ibid., cols 154–5 (6 February 1880). **21** Ibid., cols 390–1 (10 February 1880). **22** Ibid., col. 293 (9 February 1880). **23** Ibid., col. 391 (10 February 1880).

applied for aid to the relieving officer, 'for while they were receiving meal from the Charitable Committee at Cappaghduff, they preferred living on the half-rations which it afforded to going to the workhouse'.[24]

The popular view of outdoor relief was hardly more positive than that of the workhouse. It was generally assumed that boards of guardians would not grant outdoor relief. Although the statutory prohibition on outdoor relief had been relaxed during the Famine so that boards were able to grant outdoor relief in certain circumstances – to relieve the sick and disabled for example – it remained the case that the vast majority of applicants received indoor rather than outdoor relief. Bourke attributed the growing level of distress in Ballyvaughan Union (County Clare) in January 1880 to a continued absence of employment combined with 'the withholding of outdoor relief by the Board of Guardians from those classes to whom they possess the legal authority for affording it'. He warned that the disinclination of the board to grant outdoor relief was, 'so well understood by the poor that applications for the purpose have ceased, and on that account the limited number of people in receipt of that form of relief affords no criterion of the real condition of the poor'. The chief secretary, James Lowther, noted that it appeared from Bourke's report that 'had it not been for the voluntary relief committee, the machinery of the poor law as exercised by the Guardians would have been totally insufficient. I do not think this is satisfactory'.[25] One of the problems facing the Local Government Board, as a member of the Mansion House Committee observed, was that it could not compel guardians to grant outdoor relief where people were receiving charity.[26]

As this case indicates, in many districts the primary providers of emergency relief over the winter of 1879–80, as they had been in 1846–7, were voluntary and charitable organisations. In December 1879 the duchess of Marlborough, wife of the viceroy, had established a fund for the relief of distress. The fund amassed a total of £135,000, the money being used to supply food, fuel, clothing and seeds, and to establish relief works. The Mansion House fund, established in January 1880 under the presidency of the lord mayor of Dublin, Edward Dwyer Gray, was even more successful, collecting over £180,000. This fund appealed, R.V. Comerford has suggested, to 'all those who as catholics, catholic nationalists, or liberals were unwilling to give the duchess a free run for

24 Report of H.A. Robinson, 12 March 1880, NA, CSORP, 1880/7070. Robinson instructed the relieving officer to grant emergency outdoor relief, and the board of guardians to apply to the Local Government Board for authorisation to grant outdoor relief to the able-bodied. **25** Report by A. Bourke, 17 January 1880; note on Bourke's report by James Lowther, 31 January 1880, NA, CSORP, 1880/4115. The Local Government Board subsequently wrote to the Ballyvaughan guardians reminding them of their legal responsibilities and of their power to grant outdoor relief to some categories of destitute persons (Secretary of the Local Government Board to the Clerk of Ballyvaughan Union, 3 February 1880, ibid.). **26** J.A. Fox, *Reports on the Condition of the Peasantry of the County of Mayo in 1880* (Dublin, 1881), p. 47.

the title of chief benefactor of Ireland'.[27] Further aid was made available via the Land League and in the form of private gifts and donations from members of the Irish community in America. Ministers privately acknowledged the vital role of voluntary activity in relieving distress. Their critics were less reticent. Speaking in the Commons in June 1881, Gray declared that it was solely owing to charitable organisations such as the Mansion House Fund, 'that the people had been preserved from starvation. It certainly was not owing to anything that had been done by the … Government'.[28]

It was not until the beginning of 1880 that the government announced emergency measures to combat the crisis. In January 1880 up to £500,000 was made available for loans to landowners and local authorities to undertake improvement projects, and thus provide employment. The following month, a bill was introduced to provide a further £250,000 for such projects and to authorise poor law boards to relax the restrictions on the granting of outdoor relief to enable them to relieve the able-bodied and small land-holders outside the workhouse. In addition they were empowered to borrow money at a low rate of interest to fund the provision of such relief. Most importantly, on the suggestion of Irish MPs, the government agreed to make loans available via the Board of Works to enable poor law boards to provide distressed districts with supplies of seed potatoes and seed oats so that crops could be planted for the following year. By this means it was hoped to avoid the situation that had occurred during the Famine whereby people had eaten their seed potatoes or planted diseased seed thus exacerbating food shortages. The government's approach was intended to avoid the mistakes made during the Famine era. Landowners were seen as appropriate initiators of works schemes in 1879–80 because 'the public funds would be lent on good security and would be disbursed among the most necessitous of the people'.[29] Public money would thus be expended to good purpose and not wasted on unproductive, untargeted relief works. This did not prove a popular policy and its adoption indicates the disparity between public and official opinion. At a time when landlordism was under attack as the root of Ireland's social and economic problems, channelling large amounts of public money into the pockets of landowners was not the most politic solution to the problem of tenant distress.

Irish nationalists denounced the government's relief measures as inadequate and inappropriate. Many Liberals shared this negative judgement and following Gladstone's return to power at the general election of April 1880 a different approach to distress was adopted. The Liberal chief secretary, W.E. Forster, had held back from criticising the previous administration's handling of the crisis but had made clear his belief that if

---

27 R.V. Comerford, 'The politics of distress, 1877–82', in W.E. Vaughan (ed.), *A New History of Ireland: VI, Ireland under the Union, 1870–1921* (Oxford, 1996), p. 37. **28** *Hansard*, 3rd series, vol. 252, col. 1806 (11 June 1880). **29** Report of Relief Measures in 1880–81, 23 June 1891, NA, CSORP, 1891/17944.

the Government with the experience of 1846 and 1847 before them, had not been alive to the danger of another famine, and had not done what they could to ward it off, no words could sufficiently express the censure that ought to be conveyed.[30]

Forster believed Britain had a moral obligation to assist Ireland to recover from the effects of the Great Famine. During his tour of the west in 1846–7 he had come to the conclusion that it would take a long time, 'before, with her utmost efforts, [Ireland] can recover from this blow, or be able to support her own population. She must be a grievous burden on our resources, in return for long centuries of neglect and oppression'. Forster's perception of Ireland was clearly coloured by his experience of the Famine. It could hardly have been otherwise, as he himself acknowledged in 1847, observing that the 'impression made on me by this short tour can never be effaced'.[31] Like Davitt, Forster reserved some of his harshest criticism for evicting landlords. He had seen 'so much of evictions, starvation and disease', Robinson recalled, 'that at the very mention of evictions the iron seemed to enter his soul'.[32] In June 1880, Forster's adopted daughter, Florence, noted in her diary how much her father hated having to authorise the use of military force in order to help landlords 'to clear their estates by evicting the peasants under the present circumstances of unavoidable distress and poverty'.[33]

That Forster saw evictions and distress as closely linked is evident from his reaction to the introduction of a bill sponsored by John O'Connor Power, the Home Rule MP for County Mayo, intended to deprive landlords of the power to evict for non-payment of rent. Forster believed that the bill went too far. However, since it dealt with a real grievance, and 'a grievance, moreover, which was so intimately connected with the distress which the Government had pledged themselves to relieve',[34] he felt the government could not ignore it without appearing to side with evicting landlords. He therefore decided to include a clause in the government's Relief of Distress Bill requiring landlords to pay compensation to tenants evicted for non-payment in cases where the tenant was unable to pay due to the pressure of distress caused by the famine. Such was the outcry from Conservative MPs that Forster was obliged to abandoned the clause and introduce a separate Compensation for Disturbance Bill.[35]

The government's relief bill, minus the compensation clause, reached the statute book at the beginning of August 1880. This measure provided a further £750,000 for relief works and eased the repayment terms of loans taken out by

30 *Hansard*, 3rd series, vol. 250, col. 293 (9 February 1880). **31** *Transactions of the Central Relief Committee of the Society of Friends during the Famine in Ireland in 1846 and 1847* (Dublin, 1852), p. 159. **32** Robinson, *Memories*, pp. 29–30. **33** T.W. Moody and R.A.J. Hawkins (eds), *Florence Arnold-Forster's Irish Journal* (Oxford, 1988), p. 6. **34** Ibid., p. 5. **35** The Bill passed the Commons but was rejected by the Lords.

boards of guardians for the provision of outdoor relief.[36] During the debate on the Bill, Parnell proposed that a relief commission should be established to take responsibility for the distribution of emergency relief. It was unrealistic, he argued, to expect boards of guardians to provide outdoor relief to all those who needed it. Most Irish guardians looked on outdoor relief 'with the utmost repugnance and aversion as a plan opposed to all their most cherished convictions'.[37] Forster rejected this proposal as 'altogether without precedent', and insisted that while there was great distress in some districts the poor law had been 'found sufficient'. He did, however, accept an amendment to enable the Local Government Board to make grants rather than loans to poor law boards for the provision of outdoor relief if it was found that distress could not be relieved otherwise.[38]

The response of Conservative and Liberal governments to the Irish crisis highlighted the gulf between the parties in their approach to Ireland. While the Conservatives remained the party of property, the Liberals perceived Irish landowners as part of the problem of Irish distress, rather than part of the solution to it. In February 1880 the Conservative chief secretary, James Lowther, had declared his belief that the less governments interfered in 'the relations between man and man in connection with land the better'.[39] Liberals argued that the prevailing distress necessitated further reform of the land system. Gladstone justified the Compensation for Disturbance Bill as an exceptional measure 'produced by an extraordinary and exceptional state of things'.[40] Even though it failed to pass, the Bill was of enormous political significance, for, as Comerford notes,[41] it represented a public acknowledgement by government of the justice of tenant grievances regarding eviction.

The Liberals' policy opened them to attack from those who believed government intervention in economic affairs to be wrong, and who saw the events of the Famine as confirmation of their convictions. Sir Charles Trevelyan, who, as assistant secretary to the treasury, had been closely involved in framing relief measures during the Famine, issued a public condemnation of Forster's approach to Irish distress. The Irish government, he complained, had abandoned the policy that had proved so successful in 1845–6. The object of the relief operations during the Famine, Trevelyan asserted, had been to maintain the physical condition of the people. This object had been pursued, 'irrespective of every question of land tenure, leaving free scope to the natural process, whereby an overcrowded, pauperised population adjusts itself to the means of subsistence and rises to a higher state'. Forster had abandoned this principle and instead of con-

36 The rate of interest was reduced from 3.5 per cent to 1 per cent, and payment postponed for two years without incurring any interest. **37** *Hansard,* 3rd series, vol. 253, cols 801–2 (24 June 1880). **38** Ibid., cols 804, 1459–60 (3 July 1880). **39** *Freeman's Journal,* 23 February 1880. **40** *Hansard,* 3rd series, vol. 253, col. 1654 (5 July 1880). **41** Comerford, 'The politics of distress', p. 41.

fining himself to giving relief had 'stereotyped the system of small holdings and inflicted a deadly blow and great discouragement upon the system of responsible, improving proprietors, substantial farmers and well-paid labourers'.[42]

Even though the 1880 harvest was good, the relief effort continued. This was the result partly of the severity of the winter of 1880–1, and partly of the poor state of landlord-tenant relations. Annoyed by the participation of their tenants in the land agitation, many landlords had either refused to establish employment schemes for their tenants, or endeavoured 'to employ the tenants with whom they were on friendly terms, rather than those who were most necessitous'.[43] Forster was concerned by the manner in which the political situation was undermining the efficacy of the government's relief policy. In December 1880 he notified Gladstone of a request from poor law guardians in County Carlow to grant outdoor relief to unemployed labourers. To allow this, Forster observed, 'would be a most dangerous and mischievous precedent at the beginning of the winter and in such a county as Carlow'. Carlow was a prosperous county and labourers were out of work mainly because landlords were not receiving their rents and were therefore refusing to give employment.[44]

During 1881 the situation improved sufficiently to allow relief works to cease. The power to extend the provision of outdoor relief expired on 1 March 1881.[45] Towards the end of 1882 serious distress was reported to have returned to the west. The *Kerry Sentinel* claimed in January 1883, that 'the condition of the people in some parts of Ireland is more desperate now than it has been at any time since the great famine'.[46] Alarmed by the extent to which 'small farmers all over the country, and particularly in the western seaboard, had been utterly demoralised by the constant succession of overlapping relief measures ever since the winter of 1879',[47] the government determined not to open fresh relief works. Destitution was to be relieved by the poor law alone. In its annual report for 1883–4, the Local Government Board claimed that although the numbers receiving both indoor and outdoor relief rose significantly during the spring and summer of 1883, 'all who were really destitute had the means of obtaining needful aid and support'. It was found necessary, however, to make grants amounting to over £10,000 to five western unions to relieve ratepayers of the financial burden of the relief provided.[48] This was a tacit acknowledgement that destitu-

---

42 *The Times*, 27 July 1880. **43** Report of Relief Measures in 1880–81, 23 June 1891, NA, CSORP, 1891/17944. **44** Forster to Gladstone, 2 December 1880, British Library, Gladstone Papers, Add MS 44158, f. 1. Poor law boards in 75 unions were authorised to give outdoor relief to the able-bodied during the winter months (*Annual Report of the Local Government Board for Ireland*, PP 1881 [c 2926], xlviii, 278). **45** *Annual Report of the Local Government Board for Ireland*, PP 1882 [c 3311], xxxi, 12. **46** *Kerry Sentinel*, 9 January 1883. **47** Robinson, *Memories*, p. 43. **48** *Annual Report of the Local Government Board for Ireland*, PP 1884 [c 4051], xxxviii, 13–14. The report contradicts Robinson's claim that 'in spite of the prophecies in the press there were no authentic cases of anything approaching starvation and no increase in numbers admitted to the workhouse' (*Memories*, p. 50).

tion in the west could not in fact be relieved by the poor law alone. Its severity was such that it required the intervention of central government.

Official returns indicate that in total over £2 million was expended in government grants and loans 1879–80, with a further £600,000 being provided in the period up to 1884. The bulk of this money was used to provide loans for relief works.[49] In addition over £1.2 million of private money was distributed. The combined relief effort did achieve its objective. As Comerford has noted, while there 'were deaths in 1880 from diseases related to malnutrition … the general picture is one of successful aversion of threatened calamity through practical and sensible effort on many fronts'.[50] This achievement has been attributed to a number of factors. The crisis itself is generally agreed to have been less severe than in 1846–9. Moreover the rural economy had developed since the 1840s. Fewer people were dependent on the potato, Indian meal had become a staple element in the diet of the poor and internal communications had greatly improved. Fears of a repeat of the Great Famine were almost certainly unwarranted in 1879. Changes to the social and economic fabric of Ireland had radically reduced the likelihood of such an event recurring. Those fears did, however, help to ensure that people reacted to the crisis very differently from their forebears. The assertive popular response to the crisis of 1879–80 both locally and nationally provided a significant contrast to the 'fatality and passivity shown by the peasantry in the great famine'.[51] This contrast can be overdrawn, but it is clear that the role of voluntary relief organisations, including the Land League, was vital in the early months of the crisis. During this period, J.S. Donnelly has concluded, 'the enormous work undertaken by private relief organisations was considerably more important than government activity in relieving distress'.[52] For most historians the significance of the economic crisis of 1879–80 lies in its political consequences. 'In 1879', Moody observed, 'the distress precipitated a well-organised movement of resistance to the landlords – the "land war" – that challenged the very authority of the government.'[53] Less well appreciated are the consequences within government.

The experience of 1879–84 reinforced official concerns about the provision of emergency relief. The success of the relief effort had, officials believed, been achieved at a high cost. Not only had public money been wasted, but people had also been encouraged to look to the government for assistance instead of to their own efforts. A report drawn up by the Local Government Board in 1891 noted that 'although the intentions of the government were excellent in theory, the practical effect of the relief measures by which they sought to carry

---

49 Expenditure on Relief of Distress 1879 and 1890, 13 July 1891, NA, CSORP, 1891/17944. **50** Comerford, 'The politics of distress', p. 38.   **51** Moody, *Davitt and Irish Revolution*, p. 330. **52** J.S. Donnelly Jnr., *The Land and People of Nineteenth-Century Cork: The Rural Economy and the Land Question* (London, 1975), p. 261; see also, Moody, *Davitt and Irish Revolution*, p. 331. **53** Moody, *Davitt and Irish Revolution*, p. 332.

out their policy was entirely disappointing'. Lack of co-operation between those organising relief schemes had meant that 'the Irish peasant passed through a season which for many of them was characterised by rapidly alternating periods of scarcity and abandon'.[54] This judgement would probably have carried little weight with Liberal MPs such as the Sheffield MP, A.J. Mundella. It was 'far better that the Government should have recourse to the most lavish and open-handed relief', Mundella had declared in February 1880, 'than that it should be said the English people and Parliament allowed any number, however small, to perish of famine'.[55] Nor would it have unduly concerned Irish nationalists, for whom a more pressing issue was the fact that relief of distress monies came predominantly from the Irish Church Surplus Fund, rather than from Treasury funds. As John Daly, MP for Cork City, had argued in July 1880, since 'the distress in Ireland was national in its character', it ought to be treated nationally. 'It was most unfair that the people of Ireland were to have no claim upon the Imperial Exchequer in times of natural distress.'[56] The view of the Local Government Board did, however, prove influential amongst ministers.

Henry Robinson described English ministers in Ireland in the 1880s, as being:

> exasperated or amused, according to their several temperaments, by the determined efforts of the western peasantry, year after year, to establish the existence of famine conditions demanding the immediate institution of relief works as the only means of preventing wholesale deaths from starvation.[57]

Robinson was not a disinterested observer, but his account is corroborated by other sources. John Morley recounted in his memoirs how he had refused to grant the clamorous requests for relief works that greeted his appointment as chief secretary in 1892, after seeing police reports denying the existence of widespread distress. A chief secretary, Morley noted sanctimoniously, 'need not be a wizard to see the moral mischief that has been wrought by the timorous alms-giving of British governors'.[58] Presenting the issue of emergency relief as a problem of 'famine-mongering'[59] was one way of avoiding the contradiction at the heart of government policy. The primary aims of that policy were to relieve distress, to do so for the least possible outlay of government money, and to ensure that relief went only to those actually in need of it. The problem was that these aims were not always compatible. No government agency had over-

54 Report of Relief Measures in 1880–81, 23 June 1891, NA, CSORP, 1891/17944. **55** *Hansard*, 3rd series, vol. 250, col. 424 (10 February 1880). **56** Ibid., vol. 253, col. 1496 (3 July 1880). **57** Robinson, *Further Memories*, pp 78–9. **58** John Viscount Morley, *Recollections* (2 vols, London, 1917), vol. 1, 331. **59** This term was used by Robinson in a letter to Gerald Balfour concerning emergency relief measures in 1898: Robinson to Balfour, n.d., Scottish Record Office, Edinburgh, Balfour Papers, GD433/2/114/14.

all control of relief efforts. The Local Government Board was responsible for relief under the poor laws but had no control over the loans for relief works provided by the Board of Works. The poor law was not designed to cope with exceptional distress, and as a result the Local Government Board found it difficult to switch its priorities from poor relief to famine relief. The operation of the poor laws rested on a distinction between poverty and pauperism. The Local Government Board approached famine relief in a similar way, assuming that the situation was not as bad as was being claimed, and that all applicants should be regarded with suspicion. Poor law guardians were normally encouraged to restrict the provision of outdoor relief not to extend it. Expecting guardians to change their whole approach to relief overnight was, as Parnell argued, simply unrealistic. His proposal for a relief commission would have helped to overcome this problem, as well as that of lack of co-ordination, but it also threatened the primacy of the poor law and thus the central plank of government policy.

Many of the attitudes that hampered the effectiveness of relief during the Great Famine continued to hamper relief efforts in the post-Famine period. The fear of relief being abused led to the imposition of restrictions and limitations on relief that were so strict that many people simply did not bother to apply. Levels of mutual suspicion – government of people and people of government – clearly made the effective administration of relief more difficult. Furthermore the difficulties encountered confirmed the negative view held by government of the people, and vice versa. Provision of emergency relief had become, and remained, a highly political issue and was used on all sides for propaganda purposes. Allegations that reports of distress were exaggerated for political purposes formed part of the broader critique of Irish untrustworthiness and incapacity for self-government. Official refutation of and refusal to act on such reports were presented as evidence of the failure of the imperial government to listen to Irish people, or their representatives, or to rule in their interests. The debate over emergency relief became part of the wider debate over the most appropriate form of government for Ireland. Though evident from the time of the Great Famine, this process acquired fresh impetus and significance following the events of 1879–84.

Index